WAGNER AND THE VOLSUNGS

None of Wagner's works is more closely linked with Old Norse, and more especially Old Icelandic, culture. It would be carrying coals to Newcastle if I tried to go further into the significance of the incomparable eddic poems. I will just mention that on my first visit to Iceland I was allowed to gaze on the actual manuscript, even to leaf through it . . . It is worth noting that Richard Wagner possessed in his library the same Icelandic–German dictionary that is still used today. His copy bears clear signs of use. This also bears witness to his search for the meaning and essence of the genuinely mythical, its very foundation.

Wolfgang Wagner
Introduction to the program of the
production of the *Ring* in Reykjavik, 1994

Selma Guðmundsdóttir, president of Richard-Wagner-Félagið á Íslandi, presenting Wolfgang Wagner with a facsimile edition of the Codex Regius of the Poetic Edda on his eightieth birthday in Bayreuth, August 1999.

Árni Björnsson

Wagner and the Volsungs

Icelandic Sources of *Der Ring des Nibelungen*

Viking Society for Northern Research
University College London
2003

© Árni Björnsson

ISBN 0 903521 55 5

The cover illustration is of the eruption of Krafla, January 1981 (Photograph: Ómar Ragnarsson), and Wagner in 1871 (after an oil painting by Franz von Lenbach; cf. p. 51). Cover design by Auglýsingastofa Skaparans, Reykjavík.

Printed by Short Run Press Limited, Exeter

CONTENTS

PREFACE

This volume contains a translation, made partly by Anna Yates and partly by Anthony Faulkes, of a revised version of my Icelandic book *Wagner og Völsungar: Niflungahringurinn og íslenskar fornbókmenntir*, published in Reykjavík in 2000 by Mál og menning, who have kindly made available the digital reproductions for the illustrations. The quotations in the original German from Wagner's librettos and those from medieval sources, and many of the English translations of them, have been added by Anthony Faulkes, who has also edited the entire book and is responsible for the layout. David Ashurst has read a proof and I am greatly obliged to him for his many corrections and suggestions for improvement of both style and content.

I am grateful to the Richard Wagner Society of Iceland for first suggesting the idea of the work and commissioning it, to Dr Árni Tómas Ragnarsson for his help with the overall research project, particularly in the selection and preparation of the illustrations, and to Jóhann J. Ólafsson for various kinds of encouragement, advice and help. I would also like to thank Die Richard-Wagner-Stiftung in Bayreuth for assistance in locating books and documents, the Icelandic Ministry of Education and Deutscher Akademischer Austauschdienst for financial support for the research involved, and Jónas Kristjánsson, formerly head of Stofnun Árna Magnússonar á Íslandi, who first proposed that the Viking Society should undertake the publication of this English edition.

Á. B.
May 2003

Note: Though all the Icelandic quotations have been translated into English, it may be helpful to state that in names, when given in their Icelandic form, the symbols *Þ (þ)*, *Ð (ð)* and *ǫ* are pronounced respectively like the letters *th* in English *thin* and *then*, and like German *ö*.

I became especially attracted to the unusually rich pages of Mone's investigations of these heroic legends, even though stricter scholars have criticized them as overly audacious. This drew me irresistibly to the nordic sources of these myths, and to the extent that it was possible without fluent knowledge of the Scandinavian languages, I now tried to get to know the Eddas, as well as the prose fragments comprising the basis for large parts of these legends. Viewed in the light of Mone's comments, the *Wälsunga saga* exerted a decisive influence on the manner in which I began to form this material to my own purposes. The consciousness of the close primeval kinship of these old myths, which had been shaping within me for some time, thus gradually gained the power to create the dramatic forms which governed my subsequent works.

My Life 1983, 343.

Although the splendid type of *Siegfried* had long attracted me, it first enthralled my every thought when I had come to see it in its purest human shape, set free from every later wrappage. Now for the first time, also, did I recognise the possibility of making him the hero of a drama; a possibility that had not occurred to me while I only knew him from the medieval *Nibelungenlied*.

A Communication to my Friends, 1851.

The sources mentioned here, the Poetic and Prose Eddas and *Vǫlsunga saga*, all belong to Old Icelandic literature. It has long been known to scholars that Wagner made extensive use of the poems in the Poetic Edda along with Icelandic Heroic Sagas, and indeed he said so himself on various occasions (see p. 99 below). The name of his work as a whole — *The Ring of the Nibelung* — has, however, carried the unconscious implication that most of its material is derived from the well-known medieval German poem, *Das Nibelungenlied*. There is therefore a need to emphasise that Wagner's main sources were originally written in Iceland in the thirteenth century, and preserved in Icelandic manuscripts until they were printed in mostly Swedish and Danish editions of the seventeenth century and later.

Wagner's own claim has now been confirmed by new and precise textual comparison. The conclusion is that about 80 per cent of the derived motifs are drawn exclusively from Icelandic literature, and only about 5 per cent exclusively from German literature, while about 15 per cent are common to Icelandic and German literature. Derived

motifs in *Das Rheingold*, *Die Walküre* and *Siegfried* are almost entirely drawn from Old Icelandic literature. Many motifs from *Das Nibelungenlied* are found in the latter part of *Götterdämmerung*, but most of these also occur in *Þiðreks saga* (an Old Norse prose saga based on medieval German sources that are now lost). But neither *Das Nibelungenlied* nor *Þiðreks saga* has in it pagan gods, valkyries or norns, or any mention of the Twilight of the Gods.

About Iceland

Geologically, Iceland is one of the youngest countries on earth, created by undersea volcanic eruptions about 15 million years ago. These forces of nature are still at work, and the island is constantly evolving. Iceland still is the only volcanic country in northern Europe, and volcanic activity there is frequent. It is worth recalling that the motif of magical flames around the sleeping valkyrie on her mountain top is very reminiscent of volcanic activity, while the Sleeping Beauty motif clearly belongs in a European forest. After the end of the Ice Age, the climate of Iceland was rather mild for several thousand years, and flora and fauna flourished undisturbed. When Scandinavian seafarers reached Iceland in the second half of the ninth century, having succeeded in building ships good enough to sail the north Atlantic, this virtually untouched island must have seemed a promising place to settle, with thriving vegetation, low-growing woods and plenty of fish and birds for food. But four centuries after the settlement of Iceland a cold period began, which continued with little abatement until around 1900. The average annual temperature dropped by 1–2° C. Such cooling of the climate would not have been crucial in more southerly regions, but in these northern latitudes it had drastic implications for vegetation and livestock, and hence for all human life on the island.

The People of Iceland

The Icelandic nation is also one of the youngest in the world (the North American and Australian immigrant populations are, of course, younger). Iceland lies about 800 km from Shetland, and about 1,500 km from the coast of Norway. In the late ninth century attempts to settle Iceland began in earnest. The settlers were largely from Scandinavia, mainly south-west Norway, but there were also considerable numbers from the northern isles of Britain (Shetland, Orkney, and the Hebrides) as well as from mainland Scotland and Ireland.

The latest DNA research indicates that about 60 per cent of the settlers were of Nordic stock and about 40 per cent Celtic. The West Norse language, however, came to predominate, though the culture of the island was otherwise mixed; before long, Icelanders began to see themselves as a separate nation, regardless of where settlers had originated. The vast majority were simply farmers, wishing to live in peace, free from pirates and from taxation by kings, who in their home countries were growing ever more powerful and greedy for revenues. In the period of independence (900–1262) Icelandic society was extremely unusual. The main class of society comprised independent farmers, rich or poor, and there was no king, no government and no hereditary aristocracy. The Church was under the domination of secular leaders. The Alþingi (parliament) assembled once a year in the open air to legislate and to settle disputes. Thirty-nine *goðar* (chieftains) sat in the parliament, and individual farmers could choose which chieftain they wished to safeguard their interests. No such democratic leanings could be found anywhere else in Europe at that time, except perhaps in the city states of northern Italy. During this period Icelanders began to write their renowned medieval literature.

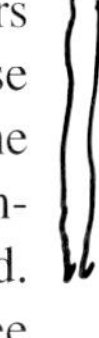

The Viking Myth

In this context it is necessary to correct the persistent Viking myth about the Icelanders. According to the myth, Icelanders are all descendants of ferocious Viking raiders who founded a Viking colony on the island. A grim-faced Viking wearing a horned helmet sometimes appears in tourist literature, to advertise Iceland. Although Iceland was settled during the period known as the Viking Age, the fact is that only a handful of Vikings (in the sense of piratical seafarers) came to Iceland, which had nothing to offer them. There were at that time no monasteries, no churches, no palaces to pillage, no gold or other treasures to make it worth while to sail for many days across the wild ocean. And Iceland was much too far away from the wealth of Europe to function as a 'military' base for raids. Icelanders, sons of farmers, naturally travelled abroad from time to time, trading and even raiding with Scandinavian Viking crews, but those few real Vikings who settled in

Iceland in their declining years appear to have seen it as a sort of retirement home.

The main connection between Iceland and the Vikings is that two or three hundred years after the end of the Viking Age, Icelandic authors composed many thrilling tales of ancient Vikings, the stories known as Heroic Sagas. These sagas gained popularity in Europe in the nineteenth century, and have led to the assumption that the Icelanders themselves were Vikings. The stories of Viking exploits are, however, just a small part of medieval Icelandic literature. The actual Sagas of Icelanders or 'family sagas' deal with a far broader spectrum of human life.

Post-Medieval Iceland

In 1262–63 Iceland lost its independence, to become a part of the Norwegian state, and in 1397, together with Norway, Iceland came under Danish rule. The old agrarian democracy was abolished, and the Catholic Church, along with a few very wealthy families, came to own almost all the property in the country. The class structure grew to resemble that of other European countries. By 1500, free farmers of small- to medium-sized estates had practically disappeared, being replaced by tenants. Cooling climate, exploitation by landowners and Danish trading monopoly all contributed to lowering living standards, so reducing resistance to disease and natural disaster. Through these hard times, Icelanders sought comfort in the memory of their ancient freedom, stored up in their old manuscripts.

After the Enlightenment and the Romantic Revival, an Icelandic independence movement finally began in the nineteenth century. The most important steps on the way to autonomy were the re-establishment of the Alþingi (parliament) as an advisory assembly in 1845, Free Trade in 1855, the granting of a separate constitution for Iceland in 1874, Home Rule in 1904, sovereignity under the Danish crown in 1918, and finally the establishment of the modern Icelandic Republic in 1944. Today, Iceland's nearly 300,000 people enjoy one of the highest living standards in the world.

Prerequisites for Literary Activity in the Middle Ages

In this context it is worth considering why so many more sagas and poems were written in Iceland than elsewhere in northern Europe in the Middle Ages. Why were Icelanders appointed as sources of information and recorders of history at the courts of foreign kings? And why did Icelanders write mainly in the vernacular, instead of in Latin? These questions have been asked for centuries, and many theories have been put forward; a few factors appear to be important.

Iceland adopted Christianity around AD 1000, and in the eleventh century, with Christianity and the Church, the art of the pen arrived in Iceland. At that time, Iceland still had many independent farmers who owned their own land (cf. pp. 9–10 above); this was unlike the situation in mainland Europe, where the vast majority of farmers had long been reduced to tenancy or serfdom on land owned by the crown, monasteries, churches, the aristocracy and other large landowners.

The Icelandic Church had limited power *vis-à-vis* temporal leaders during the first few centuries after Iceland had become a Christian nation. The first churches were built by prosperous farmers, who owned the churches and employed priests to serve in them. These priests could thus act as scribes for their employers, in the language understood by the farmers and the common people. This situation persisted well into the thirteenth century, when the bishops succeeded in exerting their authority over most churches and clergy.

The free Icelandic farmers appear to have been interested in the art of writing, both for practical purposes and entertainment, for themselves and their households. Farmers and other lay people did not understand Latin, which was the language of the learned, especially the clergy. Hence most books came to be written in the vernacular, whether lives of saints, histories of kings, scholarly writings or Sagas of Icelanders, which tell of the Icelanders' forefathers and of events in their own familiar environment.

In feudal Europe, of course, costly vellum was not squandered on writing stories for the illiterate and unfree peasantry. Works of scholarship were written in Latin, while the relatively small quantity of poetry of chivalry and romance written in the vernacular was, naturally enough, about kings and queens and brave and noble men and their fair ladies. The differences in social status between farmers in Iceland and those in Europe appear to be the main reason for Iceland's unique medieval saga tradition, with regard to content, language and style. Another reason for the writing of sagas was that, in a newly-settled country, a need was perceived to preserve the story

Medieval Icelandic manuscript books

Víðimýrarkirkja, an Icelandic church built in the ancient manner of turf and stone of how Iceland was settled, and make a history, as this was a nation without traditions. In addition, rights of inheritance were valid for up to five generations, and hence it was necessary for potential heirs to property of whatever size to keep records of the original settlers and their descendants. In continental Europe, the nobility kept records of their genealogy for the same reason, to ensure their inheritance. Such genealogical records, and tales about disputes over old boundaries and other conflicts between the first generations of settlers, might develop into family sagas, if a writer had the gift of the story-teller and literary talent. There are other contributory factors, which could be applicable to many different nations. But the crucial thing was that in Iceland free independent farmers gained the power of the pen, precisely when the art of writing arrived in Iceland (Árni Björnsson 2001).

For these reasons, various remnants of ancient Germanic oral traditions were written down only in Iceland, and preserved there, not least in the Heroic Sagas and in the heroic poems in the Poetic Edda. German scholars and writers such as Jakob Grimm and Richard Wagner thus had to seek such traditions in Icelandic literature, though they chose to call it Old Norse, Old Germanic or even *Urdeutsch*, and actually believed it to be such.

Written Icelandic and Icelandic grammar have changed relatively little since the thirteenth century, though the vocabulary has grown and the pronunciation is different. This means that any intelligent twelve-year-old child can read and understand sagas written in the thirteenth century, if they are printed in modernised spelling. Thus 'Old' Icelandic is really a misnomer.

What Does 'Icelandic' Mean?

About three and a half centuries ago, medieval Icelandic literature began to be translated into other languages, and excerpts appeared in print. This process has continued ever since, although for the past two to three centuries this literature has generally been known internationally by such terms as (Old) Norse, Scandinavian, Nordic, *norrön*, *nord*, *septentrional*, teutonic, *altnordisch*, *altgermanisch* and *urdeutsch*, but very rarely by its proper name, Icelandic.

Wagner himself used some of these terms, and this was quite natural in the mid-nineteenth century. Even well-informed people in mainland Europe were not aware of the existence of such phenomena as the

Icelandic nation, its culture or its language. All they knew was that Iceland had been settled from Norway in the Middle Ages, and was now a Danish dominion. The Icelanders' campaign for independence from Denmark was just beginning at this time, and was scarcely known to anyone outside Iceland and Denmark — not even to Richard Wagner, though he sympathised with movements for national freedom elsewhere.

The first German scholar who presented Icelandic as a literary language in its own right was Konrad Maurer (1823–1902), professor of legal history at the University of Munich. As a specialist in the history of Scandinavian and Germanic law, he favoured the Icelanders' side in their campaign for independence, and spent six months in Iceland in the summer of 1858. That same year he edited *Gull-Þóris saga*, the first German scholarly edition of one of the Sagas of Icelanders. In 1867 he published carefully-researched essays refuting the views of the Norwegian Rudolf Keyser, published the previous year, that all Old Icelandic literature was in fact Norwegian. Maurer explored the concepts *altnordisch*, *altnorwegisch* and *isländisch*, and explained the differences between them (Keyser 1866; Maurer 1867; 1869).

In nineteenth-century England, similar views to those of Maurer were upheld by George Dasent (1817–96) and William Morris (1834–96). The term 'Norse' is sometimes, of course, used for the supposed common language of the Scandinavian countries in the Middle Ages, but medieval Icelandic literature was far more strongly influenced by Roman, Greek and French literature, and the Bible, than by the rather few works of literature written in other parts of Scandinavia.

Today it should be obvious that considerable differences exist between the Scandinavian nations, that Iceland is not really a part of Scandinavia, and that Icelandic culture has, for geographical and social reasons, been quite unlike the cultures of other Scandinavian countries right from the start, though its language shares the same roots. Yet this old misunderstanding is remarkably persistent even today. Even people who otherwise maintain high standards of scholarship are sometimes guilty of inaccurately terming Old Icelandic literature 'Scandinavian', 'Old Norse' or 'Germanic'.

Truth, however, will out, and so a few obvious facts will here be stated. The Poetic Edda, the Prose Edda and *Vǫlsunga saga*, as Wagner knew them, were written down in Iceland, in Icelandic, by Icelandic

Die Walkyrien

der

skandinavisch-germanischen

Götter- und Heldensage.

Aus den nordischen Quellen dargestellt

von

Dr. Ludwig Frauer

in Tübingen.

Weimar.

Druck und Verlag des Landes-Industrie-Comptoirs.

1 8 4 6.

Ludwig Frauer, *Die Walkyrien der skandinavisch-germanischen Götter- und Heldensaga*, Weimar 1846, title page. This work has an extensive account of medieval Icelandic sagas without once mentioning Iceland.

Ueber die Ausdrücke:

altnordische,

altnorwegische & isländische Sprache

von

Konrad Maurer.

München 1867.

Verlag der k. Akademie,

Druck von F. Straub.

Konrad Maurer, *Ueber die Ausdrücke: altnordische, altnorwegische & isländische Sprache*, München 1867, title page.

authors in the thirteenth century, three centuries or more after Iceland was settled. No doubt the stories were based to some extent on much older oral traditions. Even *Þiðreks saga af Bern*, too, survived only in Norway and Iceland, though the person who recorded the saga clearly says that it consists of German narratives. The Eddas and sagas must thus be regarded as Icelandic literature. It makes no sense to call them Scandinavian, pan-Nordic, pan-Germanic or pan-European, though these terms are not exactly wrong — merely imprecise.

By the same token, one might argue that American writers such as Henry Longfellow and Mark Twain were English or European, when they were born in the New World more than two centuries after the European conquest of the continent. One might equally well ask whether Johann Wolfgang von Goethe was a German writer, or simply Germanic or European, whether Henrik Ibsen was Norwegian, Nordic or just Germanic, or whether William Shakespeare was English or West Germanic.

It is true that some of the stories tell of events far from Iceland, for example in areas of Germanic culture in southern Europe, involving for instance the Burgundians, Attila the Hun and Frankish kings. But that does not make the literature German. Or should we perhaps regard Shakespeare's plays *Hamlet* and *Romeo and Juliet* as Danish and Italian, because they are set in these countries and based on stories from Denmark and Italy? Should we regard Aventiure 6–8 of *Das Nibelungenlied* as Icelandic because they take place partly in a country called 'Islande'?

BRIEF BIOGRAPHY OF RICHARD WAGNER

Early Years

Richard Wagner was born 22 May 1813 in Leipzig. His mother was Johanna Rosine Pätz, daughter of a master baker in the town of Weißenfels, not far from Leipzig. His father was Friedrich Wagner, a clerk with the police force in Leipzig. Richard was the ninth and last child of his parents. His father died at the age of 43 from typhus in an outbreak which came about after the great battle with Napoleon's army near Leipzig, 16–19 October 1813, when Richard was less than six months old.

Friedrich Wagner had been interested in the theatre and other arts and named his daughters after characters in the plays of Goethe and Schiller. One of them, Luise, married the publisher Friedrich Brockhaus, and another, Ottilie, married his brother, the antiquarian Hermann Brockhaus. Friedrich's connections with amateur theatres led to a friendship with the versatile artist Ludwig Geyer, who for a time lodged with the Wagner household. Geyer married the widow nine months after her husband's death, and they moved to Dresden. Six months after the wedding their daughter Cäcilie was born. Geyer died in 1821 when Richard Wagner was eight. He greatly missed his stepfather, who some maintained was his real father, though later scholarly research suggests that this is very unlikely (Gregor-Dellin 1995, 34–5.).

Wagner attended a primary school in Dresden and was confirmed there, but in 1828 the family moved back to Leipzig, where he went to a grammar school. Interest in literature and exceptional quickness in learning revealed themselves in him much sooner than musical gifts. Here they were close to Richard's uncle Adolf Wagner, who was regarded as a classical scholar and had a very good library, which his young nephew, a fast reader and quick learner, devoured greedily. Already in the year he was confirmed he had begun writing a drama called *Leubald und Adelaïde*, a kind of juvenile imitation of the bloodiest of Shakespeare's plays, and he continued work on this sporadically. At the age of sixteen he saw Beethoven's opera *Fidelio* and says that then he decided to be a composer (*Mein Leben*, I 46).

Richard Wagner's birthplace in Leipzig

Minna Planer, Richard Wagner's first wife (1809–66)

Würzburg, Magdeburg, Riga

For the next few years Wagner studied music, composed a symphony in C and started work on an opera that was to be called *Die Hochzeit* (The Wedding), and was about the love of two young people from feuding families. All that remains of this opera is the first scene. About this time he got to know the composer Robert Schumann, who was editor of a musical periodical in Leipzig.

In 1833, when Wagner was just twenty, he visited his brother Albert in Würzburg. Albert worked there as an actor, singer and producer, and Richard was taken on as temporary chorus-master. Here he composed his first opera, *Die Feen* (The Fairies), which is based on a story by the Italian fairy-tale writer Carlo Gozzi and is about the tragic love of a fairy and a human. The music seems to have particular affinity with that of Weber and Beethoven, and yet some hints can be heard of what was to come later. The opera, however, did not receive a performance until 1888, five years after Wagner's death. It was conducted by Hermann Levi in Munich.

In 1834 Wagner became conductor at the opera in Bad Lauchstädt, and later in Magdeburg, where he got to know the actress Minna Planer. She was four years older than he and at the age of 16 had had an illegitimate daughter, Natalie, who throughout her life was said publicly to have been her sister. Wagner and Minna became engaged the following year and he composed the opera *Das Liebesverbot* (The Ban on Love; based on Shakespeare's *Measure for Measure*), which was first performed in Magdeburg in 1836. The music this time was more reminiscent of Donizetti, Rossini and Bellini, and also of Auber, though there are also some novel scenes that Wagner was to develop further later on (*SSD* XI 1–124).

These early operas are already characterised by the unusual procedure of the composer writing his own librettos, and Wagner regarded himself as a poet just as much as a composer. In his view the text was not accessory to the music, rather words and melody ought to form an integrated whole. The normal thing had been for professional writers to be commissioned to compile librettos for operas, and great composers were sometimes able to make good use of hastily put together productions of various hacks who moreover regarded the words as meant for nothing more than a vehicle for making vocal music sound pleasant. Wagner had far more respect for the words. He believed

they ought to have strength and integrity in their own right, even though they were always designed to be complemented by music.

In 1836 Minna ran off to Königsberg and Wagner followed her. They got married there, but Minna left him again for another man. She finally returned to him for good in 1837 when he was appointed to a post as conductor in Riga in Latvia.

In Riga Wagner began to compose his opera *Rienzi*, which is set in fourteenth-century Rome. He now began to amass debts, and this proclivity continued to plague him all his life. In the summer of 1839 the couple managed to escape their creditors and the threat of debtors' prison by crossing the Baltic on a ship bound for London, from where they travelled on to Boulogne and Paris. Wagner claimed later that the idea for the opera of *The Flying Dutchman* (based on the legend of the sea-captain under a curse, doomed to sail the seas for ever with his ghostly crew) first came to him when sailing in a violent storm off the coast of Norway (*Mein Leben*, I 190).

Paris

For the next two and a half years Minna and Richard lived in straitened circumstances in Paris. He got to know various artists, such as the composers Berlioz, Meyerbeer and Liszt, and the German poet Heine. He found it difficult to get any of his works performed, though the just-mentioned acquaintances tried to recommend him. He completed *Rienzi* in Paris and eventually, in the middle of 1841, partly on the recommendation of Meyerbeer, the Dresden Opera decided to put the work on. At this Wagner became full of optimism, and he composed *The Flying Dutchman* in two months. About the same time he began work on *Tannhäuser*. The inspiration for the plots of both came from Heine, though as usual he went his own way in the treatment of the stories (see Gregor-Dellin 1995, 128, 167).

Dresden

Wagner became ever more interested in medieval German stories and myths. At the beginning of April 1842, he and Minna moved to Dresden. On the way they drove past the Wartburg castle, and the surroundings became fixed in his mind as the setting for the second act of *Tannhäuser*, with the song contest taking place in the castle itself (*Mein Leben*, I 253–54).

Wedding-song for Richard Wagner and Minna Planer, Königsberg 1836.

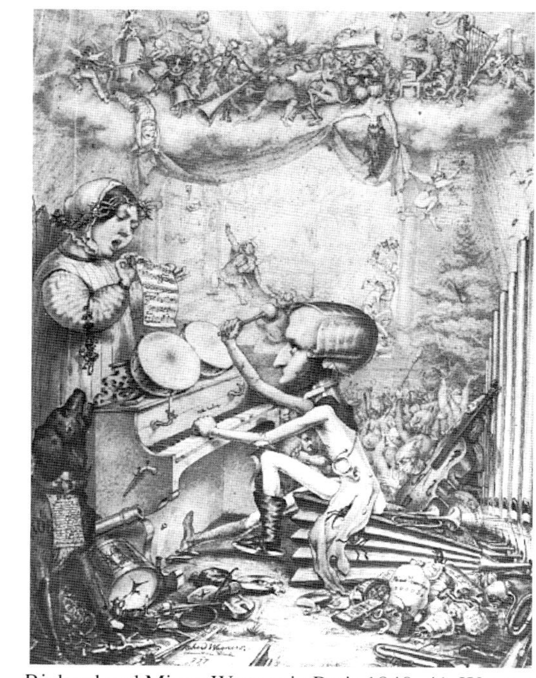

Richard and Minna Wagner in Paris 1840–41. Wagner is furiously composing Rienzi with the help of Minna and the dog. On the floor lie empty money-bags.

To begin with he and Minna lived to a large extent at the expense of his in-laws the Brockhaus family, but in the autumn *Rienzi* was given its première in Dresden and was very well received. Wagner still seems to have been rather under the influence of older composers, this time particularly Spontini and Meyerbeer. It looked as though he was all set to continue on the same lines and achieve speedy popularity; but his mind was aiming higher.

The Flying Dutchman was first performed at the beginning of January 1843, when Wagner was just thirty. This work is stamped with the genuine marks of his own individual style which was now going to develop over four decades. Soon after, he was appointed *hofkapell-meister* (director of the royal orchestra) in Dresden. His enhanced status and increased salary did nothing to prevent him plunging ever further into endless debts. About this time he managed to get *The Flying Dutchman* performed in Berlin. He met Mendelssohn, who did not care much for Wagner's music (see Gregor-Dellin 1995, 171–2, 190–92).

For the next few years Wagner continued as conductor in Dresden, getting on at the same time with his own composing. He finished *Tann-häuser*, which is about the conflict of flesh and spirit and the possibility of salvation, a type of legend which turns up in many parts of the world. The opera was given its first performance in Dresden in October 1845. In the same year Wagner began the libretto of *Lohengrin*, also on a widely occurring theme, that of one from another world who comes to the world of men as a saviour-figure but may not even tell his bride who he is.

Wagner soon started the music for *Lohengrin*. About the same time he got the first idea for *The Mastersingers*, and in the autumn of 1846 he also wrote a rough draft of a libretto for an opera about Barbarossa, but he very soon laid both of these aside.

In January 1848 his mother Johanna Rosine died. A little later the February revolution broke out in Paris and was followed by riots in Saxony and other German-speaking areas. Wagner participated in the demand for the abolition of the monarchy and from the first made particular efforts to ensure that the position of artists should be better than in the past. King Friedrich August II promised to abolish censor-ship and authorised certain other reforms of the law.

Wagner completed Lohengrin on 28 April 1848 and on 18 May the first German national assembly met in St Paul's church in Frankfurt and demanded among other things a parliamentary government.

Wagner in 1842 (after a drawing by E. B. Kietz)

Semper's Opera House in Dresden (from a lithograph of 1841)

Wagner was no longer engaged on any major work and he devoted all his energy to politics. He was seldom cautious either in speech or writing, and made an inspired speech at the assembly in the middle of June. He spoke among other things about a political redeemer in a way which could have been interpreted as a demand for the abolition of the monarchy. The speech was printed and Wagner was on the point of being dismissed from his post as conductor. So he wrote an apology to His Royal Majesty with involved explanations in which he appeared to be actually wanting to support the monarchy as a defence against the evil power of capitalism. The affair was allowed to drop for the time being.

As a continuation of his political ponderings about power, Wagner went back to the subject of Barbarossa. This led him to embark on a great flight of fancy, and the result was a 40-page poetically elevated anthropological treatise, *Die Wibelungen* (translated by W. A. Ellis in *Pilgrimage to Beethoven and other Essays by Richard Wagner*, 1994, 257–98). This dealt among other things with an imaginary primeval kingship from the time of Noah, with patriarchy and half-mythological royal lines such as the Nibelungs and Welfs, with ancient Roman kingship and with the Franks as descendants of the Trojans.

Using a primitive kind of etymological argument, Wagner manages into the bargain to make Barbarossa a descendant of Siegfried, who in turn is supposed to have had divine descent. He ends up interpreting the story of the Nibelungs' treasure and the origin of the myth about it in the spirit of the French philosopher Proudhon, who was one of the originators of anarchism and argued that private property was equivalent to theft. Thus Wagner seems to be attempting to link socialist ideas with ancient Germanic legend (*SSD* II 115–55; XI 270–72).

Wagner was now entering mythological territory again, and the otherworld became ever more prominent in his works. Myths and fairy-tales seemed to him to reveal deeper and more universal truths than secular history, novels and everyday life. This attitude had already appeared in *Die Feen*, his Dutchman was cursed with immortality, Tannhäuser lived among creatures of pagan mythology, Lohengrin is from the other world, the *Ring* takes place partly in the world of the gods, and Parsifal is on the borders of the supernatural. Wagner's preference for myth over history is derived from the Romantic view that folk-legend is truer than chronicle.

In October 1848 Wagner, now thirty-five, wrote his own myth on a theme similar to that of *Die Wibelungen* and called it *Die Nibelungensage (Mythus)*. For the first printed edition he changed the title to *Der Nibelungen-Mythus. Als Entwurf zu einem Drama* (The Nibelungen-Myth. As Sketch for a Drama). This piece is only ten pages long and was supposed to be the background to an opera which he was planning to compose and which was at first given the title *Siegfrieds Tod* (Siegfried's Death). By the end of November he had finished the first draft of the libretto of this opera. Eventually *Der Nibelungen-Mythus* itself turned out to be the basis and framework of the whole of the *Ring*.

But the composition of this opera was not continued for the time being. Wagner was still playing with the idea of a political redeemer, and early in 1849 he wrote a long draft of a play about Jesus of Nazareth in which Christ appears unequivocally in the role of revolutionary (*SSD* XI 273–324). It was not long before Wagner himself came to play such a role. Little had come of the reforms in the law that had been promised by the king the previous year. Wagner got to know quite well the Russian anarchist Mikhail Bakunin, who had just arrived in Dresden from Paris where he had associated with Proudhon, George Sand and Karl Marx. Wagner became very zealous in the revolutionary movement and took an active part in the Dresden uprising of May 1849. It was suppressed and he only just managed to escape to Switzerland.

Zürich

Wagner was in exile from his native land for thirteen years. He first settled in Zürich and applied himself to conducting and writing treatises, not least about the links between the arts and sociological questions, and spent little time on composing for the first year. Still, he went now and again to Paris to try his luck at the Opera, but success was very slow in coming. In the autumn of 1850 he wrote in a great burst of passion one of his most notorious articles, *Das Judentum in der Musik*, which was a bitter attack on the artistic influence of Jews, whom he regarded as mere intruders into European music (*SSD* V 66–85; Gregor-Dellin 1995, 310–14).

This article aroused a great deal of harsh response, to which there is still today no end in sight. Lizt, for example, who had by then become

14.

Volksblätter,

von

A. Röckel.

Dresden, Sonntag, den 8. April 1849.

Die Revolution.

Revolutionary newspaper article by Wagner from Dresden, April 1849.

Politisch gefährliche Individuen.

Richard Wagner

ehemal. Kapellmeister und politischer Flüchtling aus Dresden.

Steckbrief.

Der unten etwas näher bezeichnete Königl. Capellmeister

Richard Wagner von hier

ist wegen wesentlicher Theilnahme an der in hiesiger Stadt stattgefundenen aufrührerischen Bewegung zur Untersuchung zu ziehen, zur Zeit aber nicht zu erlangen gewesen. Es werden daher alle Polizeibehörden auf denselben aufmerksam gemacht und ersucht, Wagnern im Betretungsfalle zu verhaften und davon uns schleunigst Nachricht zu ertheilen.

Dresden, den 16. Mai 1849.

Die Stadt-Polizei-Deputation.

von Oppell.

Wagner ist 37—38 Jahre alt, mittler Statur, hat braunes Haar und trägt eine Brille.

Police notice for Wagner's arrest as a revolutionary in Dresden, May 1849.

director of the opera in Weimar and had somewhat earlier given *Lohengrin* its first performance, was horrified. The same autumn Wagner helped the young, later world-renowned, pianist and conductor Hans von Bülow take the first steps in his career. Between them developed an indissoluble lifelong respect in spite of what was later to take place in their dealings together.

Wagner compiled early in 1850 the libretto for an opera that was going to be called *Wieland der Schmied* (Wayland the Smith; *SSD* III 178–206). The main features of the concept are clearly derived from Karl Simrock's paraphrase of *Vǫlundarkviða (Wieland der Schmied*, 1843), though some details are evidently drawn from other versions of the Vǫlundr story. It shows that Wagner still sporadically had his mind on Old Norse legend, and there can here be distinguished various ideas that turn up again later in the *Ring*, such as the forging of the best sword, the ring of power, fateful questionings, release from captivity, redemption through love and a final conflagration.

Here again there are traces of revolutionary ideas about the redemption of 'the people', who need to create wings for themselves like Vǫlundr and fly free from their oppression. Wagner never, however, wrote any music for this libretto, and some people find this regrettable. On the other hand he began in the summer of 1850 to tinker with music for *Siegfrieds Tod* (*SSD* III 178–206; Gregor-Dellin 1995, 293–99; Guðrún Þórðardóttir 1998; *Dokumente*, 36).

Before going on any further with that he felt he needed to order his thoughts about the composition of operas. The first four major works that he had completed, *Rienzi*, *The Flying Dutchman*, *Tannhäuser* and *Lohengrin*, were still too conventional in his view and did not satisfy his visions of the future. With this aim he wrote during the following winter his longest treatise on artistic matters. It covers more than three hundred pages and the overall title is *Oper und Drama*. He read the greater part of this work to his friends and acquaintances over twelve evenings, and some of them found the reading rather soporific. He himself must have learned a lot from sharing his thoughts with others, and it would have strengthened his own ideology (*SSD* III 222–320; IV 1–229; Gregor-Dellin 1995, 322).

Early in 1851Wagner got his hands on the epoch-making translation by Karl Simrock of the poems of the Poetic Edda and most of the narrative parts of the Prose Edda. Much of this material he had of course come across before in extracts of various lengths, but now he had all this material before him in one book, especially the myths and legends.

It now became apparent to him that it would need at least two operas to follow the story of Siegfried from the beginning. In May and June he completed the libretto of a new opera which he called *Der junge Siegfried* (The Young Siegfried). He gave an account of this change of plan and much else besides in a long announcement to his friends (*Eine Mitteilung an meine Freunde*) later that summer. Afterwards, on 20 November, he explained to Liszt in a letter that in order to do justice to the material it would need three full-length operas and in addition a short introductory opera. By the end of 1852 Wagner had completed the entire libretto of the *Ring* and he had 50 copies printed for his friends and relations in February 1853, when he was not quite forty (see *Dokumente* 46–54, 60; Gregor-Dellin 1995, 359).

Wagner did not, however, get round to composing music for the *Ring* immediately. His health was not good, though he went on long tramps in the mountains that summer with Liszt and the poet Herwegh. After that he undertook a month's trip to northern Italy and saw the Mediterranean for the first time. One day at a hotel in La Spezia by the Gulf of Genoa he was lying in a doze with a fever when he had a kind of hallucination: he heard the opening sound of *Das Rheingold* (The Rhinegold), the first of the four operas of the *Ring*-cycle, the long drawn-out chord on E flat (*Mein Leben*, II 60).

At the end of April 1857 he and Minna were lodgers in a house in the grounds of the newly-built mansion belonging to the Wesendoncks near Zürich. Otto Wesendonck was a wealthy silk-merchant of thirty-five who greatly admired Wagner and had among other things given him financial help for his journey to Italy the previous year. His wife Mathilde was thirteen years younger than her husband and devoted to poetry. She and Wagner came to be united in their souls, whether or not they were ever so in their bodies; but he was 'poetically' in love with her, as some romantic poets have claimed to be with all womankind.

During the preceding years Wagner had been working conscientiously on the music for the *Ring*, though for a few months in the winter of 1855 he was a guest conductor in London. He had completed *Das Rheingold* and the second opera of the *Ring*-cycle, *Die Walküre* (The Valkyrie), and had also made some progress on the third, *Siegfried*

Mathilde Wesendonck

Wagner at forty (from a water-colour by C. Stockar-Escher, 1853)

From a watercolour of Zürich in 1857. The Wesendoncks' house is on the far left.

The Wesendoncks' house in Zürich. To the right is the house occupied by Richard and Minna Wagner from April 1857.

(as *Der junge Siegfried* was now called), when in mid-1957 he put this work aside and began to compose *Tristan and Isolde*. It seems also to have come about that Wagner's inward yearning failed to distinguish clearly between the situation of himself and Mathilde Wesendonck on the one hand and the fatal love of Tristan and Isolde on the other. He wrote Mathilde a passionate letter in the spring of 1858 which fell into Minna's hands and offended both Mathilde and Otto. Minna went to Dresden, while Wagner himself drifted to Venice and went on with *Tristan and Isolde*, which he finished in Lucerne in the summer of 1859.

Wanderings

That autumn Wagner went once again to Paris and stayed there for most of the following two years. He did some conducting in Paris and Brussels, and Minna came back to him. In March 1861 *Tannhäuser* was performed three times at the Paris Opera, and on each occasion the performance was subjected to intolerable disturbance organised by Wagner's enemies. This sort of loutish behaviour in opera houses was by no means unknown in the nineteenth century if composers did not conform to the expectations of some particular pressure groups. This opera hooliganism can be compared with the football hooliganism of the present day.

For the next year or two Wagner had no settled home, and he and Minna finally split up in 1862. He conducted orchestras in various places, St Petersburg among them, and managed now and again to do some work on *The Mastersingers*, but he was in continual flight from his creditors.

Munich — Ludwig II

At the end of April 1864, Wagner was half in hiding with his friends in Stuttgart when a royal messenger asked for him. Wagner presumed that some representative of his creditors had tracked him down, but unexpectedly it turned out to be a messenger from an unsuspected admirer, the new and very youthful king of Bavaria, Ludwig II, who wanted to offer the master gold and a life in clover. Wagner was now fifty-one (*Mein Leben*, II 330–32).

Ludwig II was the grandson of Ludwig I, who was king of Bavaria from 1825 to 1848 but was forced to abdicate, among other things because of a liaison with a notorious Irish dancer called Lola Montez.

Photograph of Wagner at fifty (1864–65)

Drawing of Wagner playing the piano for Ludwig II of Bavaria at the palace at Hohenschwangau in the autumn of 1865.

Wagner among his friends in Munich, 17 May 1865. At his feet lies the dog, Pohl, and behind him stands Hans von Bülow.

His son Maximilian II, who died in 1864, succeeded. Ludwig II was only 18 when he became king. He was said to be too highly gifted and perfect for any ordinary person to regard him as quite sane. He did not care about his subjects, despised affairs of state, and most of all wanted to live in the world of poetry and romance. The monument to this is the renowned series of fairy palaces that he began to have built, now visited by millions of tourists to the immense benefit of the exchequer. But the king's extravagance and various schemes led in the end to his being confined by the government to the castle of Berg on Starnberger See in 1886. There he was found a little later drowned in the lake.

Wagner's music was one of the great artistic undertakings that Ludwig II considered worth promoting and supporting, so that the composer could devote himself to his creative work untroubled by physical worries. The king offered to pay all Wagner's debts, give him an annuity and defray the production costs of his compositions, and in return he was to get the holographs and performance rights of the master's works. It goes without saying that Wagner accepted this offer with open arms. He got rid of his debt problems, and a secure future seemed to welcome him. The king allowed him to live in Haus Pellet, a villa on Starnberger See, so that they could meet every day when the king was staying in that area. In the autumn the king put at his disposal a mansion in central Munich, and subsequently bought it for him.

Cosima

The opposition of authorities other than the king, however, meant that Wagner could only stay in Munich for a year and a half under the wing of his powerful friend, who could actually be rather capricious and unpredictable. There were two main reasons for this. The high life, for which Wagner had a great weakness, with its constant coming and going of visitors and its other extravagances, greatly upset Ludwig's narrow-minded ministers and officials. They thought it preposterous that state money should be squandered like this on artists. In addition, Wagner's private life was a source of great scandal. In the summer of 1864, he and Liszt's daughter Cosima, who was married to the conductor Hans von Bülow, Wagner's great admirer, became lovers. This liaison did not remain secret for long.

Richard and Cosima first met when she was sixteen and he was exactly forty. She was married to Hans von Bülow at twenty and had

Photograph of Wagner in 1865

Wagner knocking at the door of Ludwig's treasurer, 1867 (front page of *Münchener Punsch*, 17 March 1867).

two daughters by him. In late November 1863 she and Wagner saw each other, as they often did in Berlin, he being now fifty and she twenty-five. They then seem to have arranged a meeting together and acknowledged their mutual love. At the beginning of July Cosima went to stay with him by Starnberger See with her daughters, and on 10 July 1865 their daughter Isolde was born. Isolde was of course, nevertheless, according to the law counted as the daughter of Hans von Bülow. Ironically, it was on the very day that she was born that von Bülow began orchestral rehearsals of *Tristan and Isolde*; two months later in Munich he conducted the first performance of this love-opera of Wagner's.

In Munich Wagner succeeded in finishing the second act of *Siegfried*, compiled the outline of the libretto of *Parsifal* and began to dictate to Cosima his memoirs for King Ludwig, who wanted to know everything about this demi-god of his. The king commissioned the well-known architect Gottfried Semper, who had planned the opera-house in Dresden, to design a theatre where Wagner's operas could be performed according to his own ideas. Nothing came of this, however, apart from drawings and a model, and it really looks as though Wagner did not want all his work to be at the mercy of the king's caprices (*Mein Leben*, I 5; Gregor-Dellin 1995, 529–50, 593–602).

Tribschen near Lucerne

Wagner moved from Munich to Switzerland at the end of 1865, though he continued to receive all his financial support from the king. Minna died in Dresden in January 1866. Cosima stayed alternately with her husband and with Wagner. They acquired Tribschen, a house near Lucerne, in the summer of 1866, and lived there for the next six years. Their daughter Eva was born in 1867 and their son Siegfried in 1869. Cosima did not, however, go to live permanently with Wagner until 1868, and was not formally divorced from Hans von Bülow until 1870, after which she and Wagner were publicly married.

In Switzerland Wagner finished *The Mastersingers*, and the opera was first performed in Munich on 21 June 1868, with von Bülow conducting. In Leipzig during the same year he met the 24-year-old philosopher Nietzsche, with whom he began a friendship which was very rewarding for both men, though in the end it caused them much pain. King Ludwig, who now held the performing rights of Wagner's

View of Vierwaldstätter See in Switzerland with Mt Pilatus in the background, after a lost water-colour. Beyond the lake can be seen Triebschen, Wagner's house near Lucerne where he lived 1866–72.

operas, had *Das Rheingold* performed for the first time in Munich in 1869, and *Die Walküre* in 1870, both despite the unwillingness of Wagner himself, who had quite another style of production and a much larger stage in mind.

Bayreuth

In February 1871 Wagner finally completed *Siegfried*, and he now began with the king's permission to look about for a place where he wanted to have his own opera-house built. He liked the look of the small town of Bayreuth north of Nuremberg. He did not care for large cities where there was so much else that might put his own palace of music in the shade. Germany had now at last become a single *Reich* and Wagner immediately set about founding a society of supporters over the whole country which was to finance the music festival that was now proposed. In 1872 he and Cosima moved to Bayreuth and in the same year the foundation-stone was laid of the festival theatre. The money, however, came in slowly, and at the end of 1873 the whole enterprise seemed about to fail. Wagner was now just sixty.

King Ludwig had up to now not wished to give any support and was presumably offended that Wagner had not wanted to have the theatre built in Munich. Besides, from time to time Ludwig's whole behaviour was becoming ever more odd. Now, when the project seemed to be in real trouble, he suddenly responded to the news with: 'No, no, and once again, no. It must not end like that.' To be sure, he did not actually finance either the building or the festival directly, but he underwrote a huge loan for it and for a private house for Wagner himself. The Wagner family paid back this loan over many decades (Gregor-Dellin 1995, 676).

During the years 1872 to 1874 Wagner composed the music for the fourth opera in the *Ring*-cycle, *Götterdämmerung* (The Twilight of the Gods, the drama corresponding to the original *Siegfrieds Tod*) and in 1874 the family moved into the newly-built mansion to which Wagner gave the name Wahnfried. On the front of the house he explains the name in lines of verse which apparently mean that here his unrealistic yearnings have finally found peace. The meaning of the word *Wahn* has gradually changed over the last century from 'yearning' to 'madness'.

Rehearsals for the complete *Ring*-cycle took place in 1875 and the first performance was given in the new festival theatre in Bayreuth in

August 1876 in the presence of Emperor Wilhelm I. King Ludwig had now become such a reclusive person that he stole at night on a private train from Munich to see a few rehearsals that were arranged specially for His Majesty. The work was in fact not fully rehearsed and some stage properties had not arrived; for instance the neck of the dragon Fafner had apparently been sent to Beirut. Even so it was not thought practicable to delay the first performance when so many important people had announced their coming long in advance.

At the premières Wagner noticed a great deal that he thought might have been done better and needed more rehearsal, and he seems to have been considerably disappointed in his own work. He straight away began to speak of the necessity of a repeat performance of the *Ring* the next year, in which the main defects would be put right. This, however, turned out to be impossible, because the festival had made an enormous loss which took many years to repay. The *Ring* was not given another complete performance in Bayreuth until 1896, thirteen years after Wagner's death. The family kept the composer's criticisms of his own production secret and they were not revealed until it was decided to publish nearly all his correspondence and Cosima's diaries, long after the death of both. Until then producers at Bayreuth tried to keep performances as much as possible on the original questionable lines.

A Controversial Figure

Richard Wagner is one of those figures about whom people have quickly taken sides with firm positions, for and against. Such figures seem to have been endowed with a sort of charisma which operates on different people in quite opposing ways. Those who have been affected by it are then filled either with unbounded adoration or bitter hatred. Figures with this propensity are inclined to let fly with all kinds of opinions on the spur of the moment and can unawares turn into some kind of religious leader. Their followers always become far more dogmatic than their master. They seize on every little detail which dropped from his pen or his lips and make it into an article of faith. Their opponents do the same but use such details to condemn him. As examples of countrymen of Wagner who have had to suffer similar treatment after their deaths one might mention Martin Luther and Karl Marx. This taking of sides in relation to Wagner is not yet over.

When Wagner is being discussed it is usually not long before one of the controversial aspects of his life outside his works is mentioned, since people have made a great deal of these matters in speech, writing and films. These are principally his love-affairs, economic difficulties and antisemitism. The main reason for this is assuredly that he is a world-renowned man, not that he was in these respects very different from others of his time or even from people nowadays. It is therefore important to try to give an objective account of these aspects.

Wagner's love-affairs were actually not more extensive than those of many others. The love-life of his father-in-law Liszt, for example, was far more colourful. After Minna stopped running off from Wagner there seem to have been no serious problems between them for the first decade and a half. Their lack of children, however, was always a source of some regret for them, and Minna found it hard to put up with her husband's financial recklessness. In the latter part of his life Wagner had a few romantic escapades, but probably the most remarkable thing was that he fell in love with the wives of two of his friends and benefactors. His liaison with Mathilde Wesendonck seems, however, never to have been a very physical one, and Cosima von Bülow clearly took the initiative in her relationship with him.

Antisemitism

Wagner's antipathy to certain racial characteristics that he believed he could see in the conduct of Jews has had far greater consequences. It was nevertheless far from being anything exceptional. Antisemitism has been endemic in Europe since the Middle Ages. Its origin can be traced to the fear felt by various classes of workpeople about competition from immigrant Jews, whose numbers had increased greatly during the Middle Ages with the advent of refugees from the expansion of Islamic power. Jews were not permitted either to own land or to practise crafts outside their own communities. Trade and money-lending were almost the only businesses they could engage in openly, and moreover these activities were considered beneath the dignity of free-born men in the Middle Ages, and in some places they were forbidden by the Church.

The authorities were able to profit greatly by this arrangement, for they put high taxes on these activities engaged in by Jews, who themselves frequently got a bad reputation as usurers. In propaganda the

Jews were among other things blamed for Christ's crucifixion, and in times of unrest they were often made scapegoats to provide some kind of outlet for public anger, as during the Crusades, the Black Death and other plagues, the Reformation and the Thirty Years' War.

During the Enlightenment period and after the French Revolution of 1789, Jews in Europe gradually gained ordinary human rights, for instance in Prussia in 1812. After that they began to take an active part in all aspects of intellectual, secular and artistic life, and because of their centuries-long experience they became especially influential in the fields of banking and trade. Their continually defensive position had also fostered among Jews an international fellow-feeling from which they now benefited in business life. The old in-grown antagonism was not uprooted in one generation either, but found a new outlet.

There is no reason to think that this antagonism was all that deeply rooted in Wagner, any more than in most others of his time, but his position seems to have been somewhat ambivalent and to have varied according to his changing moods and the expedience of the moment. Apart from the notorious article about Judaism in music of 1850, traces of his antagonism appear most strongly in some fragments of memoirs written by Cosima. Even so, his attitudes were to a large extent bound up with his reactions to individual Jews. Many of his chief acquaintances and colleagues to the end of his life were in fact Jewish, and he entrusted the conductor Hermann Levi, son of a Jewish rabbi, with the direction of his 'sacred' final work, *Parsifal*, in 1882.

Round about 1880 there was an organised anti-Jewish movement in Germany which soon spread to Austria, Russia, France and Britain. The background to it, as before, was competition and fear of the ever-increasing influence of the Jews, especially in commerce. Wagner took no part in this movement and he avoided putting his name to a special petition which this faction sent to the emperor urging that the rights of Jews should be restricted again.

Nowhere in Wagner's poetry is any anti-Jewish feeling to be found either, though attempts have been made to interpret unpleasant characters in his works, like Alberich, Mime and Beckmesser, as personifications of Jewishness. If one were to apply such criteria one could with far more certain justification brand Shakespeare and Dickens as anti-semitic because of works like *The Merchant of Venice* and *Oliver Twist*.

Wagner, however, suffered the misfortune half a century after his death that one of his dogmatic admirers came to power as chancellor of Germany. This was Adolf Hitler. There is a long and complex series of events relating to the connexions between Hitler and Wagner's son-in-law, daughter-in-law and descendants. But it is hardly fair to blame the composer personally for the Holocaust in the twentieth century as some have wanted to do. Certainly it is the case that he expressed horrible opinions in his envy and anger; he can be blamed for these, but not for the fact that some Nazi murderers admired his musico-dramatic works and interpreted them in their own way.

Because of these matters, the public in Germany was still shy and half afraid of Wagner's music long after the Second World War. The same can in fact be said of the attitude of ordinary people to Old Icelandic literature and everything else that the Nazis had prized as part of Germanic cultural inheritance. Neither of these artistic achievements has even now fully recovered from this burden of association. It is still the case, for instance, that orchestras in Israel are afraid to play works by Wagner because of the fear of extremists, even though musicians themselves there are less than happy with this unofficial ban. In Iceland itself it has been people of German-Jewish origin, like Victor Urbancic and Róbert Abraham Ottósson, who have taken the initiative in having the national Symphony Orchestra perform Wagner's music.

Death

When the first Bayreuth festival was over, Wagner went to Italy to recuperate. In 1877 he visited London as a conductor in order to reduce the debts the festival had incurred. In the same year he began work on *Parsifal* but did not complete it until 1882, when it was given its première at the second Bayreuth festival. During these years Wagner spent much of his time in Italy for the sake of his health, and was in Venice at the time of his death, 13 February 1883. He was buried in the garden of his Bayreuth home, Villa Wahnfried, which today houses a large museum of his life and work, celebrating the triumphal progress of his operas. Wahnfried is now also the home of the Richard Wagner Foundation.

Das Rheingold. Drawing by Theodor Pixis, *Illustrierte Zeitung*, Leipzig, 23 October 1869. Top: Alberich steals the gold from the Rhine Maidens. Centre: Fafner and Fasolt take Freia from the gods; Walhall in the background. Bottom: Wotan and Loge visit Alberich and Mime in Nibelheim.

The final scene of *Das Rheingold*. Drawing by Theodor Pixis, 1869. The gods enter Walhall, Loge looks towards the Rhine Maidens.

Die Walküre. Drawing by Theodor Pixis, 1869, for the production in Munich in 1870. Brünnhilde warns Siegmund of his approaching death.

Die Walküre. Drawing by Joseph Hoffman, 1876. Siegmund with Nothung.

Das Rheingold. Drawing by K. Ekwall (1843–1912) inspired by the production in Bayreuth of 1876. *Illustrierte Zeitung*, Leipzig, 16 September 1876. The Rhine Maidens with the glowing gold; Alberich creeps up on them.

Alberich, Bayreuth 1876. Photograph by Joseph Albert.

Brünnhilde (Amalia Materna) with her horse, Grane, Bayreuth 1876. Photograph by Joseph Albert.

Die Walküre. Drawing by K. Ekwall (1843–1912). Siegmund's death.

Götterdämmerung. The three Norns, Bayreuth 1876.
Photograph by Joseph Albert.

Siegfried. Drawing by Joseph Hoffmann, 1876. Siegfried kills the dragon Fafner.

Götterdämmerung. The Gibichung vassals, Bayreuth 1876.

Götterdämmerung. Drawing by K. Ekwall (1843–1912). Siegfried's body being carried back to the hall of the Gibichungs.

The ride of the valkyries. Drawing on glass by Carl Emil Doepler. Part of the scenery at Bayreuth, 1876.

Wagner in December 1871, after an oil painting by Franz von Lenbach.

Richard and Cosima Wagner in Vienna in 1872. Photograph by Fritz Luckhardt.

Festival Theatre in Bayreuth. Drawing by Ludwig Bechstein,
Allgemeine Illustrierte, 1876.

'The new mythology. Wagner's apotheosis in Bayreuth.' *Der Ulk*, Berlin, 1876. Wagner as Wotan, valkyries carry exhausted listeners.

Richard Wagner im Himmel.

'Richard Wagner in heaven.' *Der Floh*, Vienna 1883. Angels blow Wagner horns, Wagner teaches Mozart and Beethoven and roasts Offenbach, St Peter announces that the Ring shall be performed daily.

Wahnfried, the house in Bayreuth where Wagner lived from 1874 until his death. Photograph by Mark Kemming. In front is a bust of Ludwig II, above the entrance is a depiction of Wotan and his ravens (see next page) and the inscription 'Hier wo mein Wähnen Frieden fand – Wahnfried – sei dieses Haus von mir benannt' (Here where my longing found peace – Wahnfried – be this house named by me'). Richard and Cosima's graves are in the garden behind.

The panel above the entrance to Wahnfried, Wagner's house in Bayreuth, which shows Wotan and his ravens between two of the muses. Cut by Robert Kraus, 1873–74.

Photograph of Wagner at sixty (1873)

The first conductors at the Bayreuth Festival. Left: Hermann Levi, who worked with Wagner from 1871 onwards and conducted Parsifal on its first performance in 1882 and until 1894. Centre: Hans Richter, a close friend of Wagner from 1866, he conducted the Ring at Bayreuth in 1876 and on until 1912. Right: Felix Mottl, who assisted Wagner at the Festival of 1876 and was conductor at it for the next two decades.

Wagner with Cosima and friends in 1881. Left to right: Richard, Cosima, the author von Stein, the painter Joukovsky and the sisters Daniela and Blandine von Bülow.

Wagner crossing the rainbow bridge from the Festival Theatre to Walhall

Aeschylus und Shakespeare, nach Porges die beiden einzigen Bühnendichter, welche Wagner an die Seite gestell werden können, machen im vorschriftsmäßigen Frack dem Meister ihre Aufwartung.

Aeschylus and Shakespeare do honour to Wagner

Letzte Bitte
an meine lieben Genossen.

! Deutlichkeit !

– Die grossen Noten kommen von selbst;
die kleinen Noten und ihr Text sind die
Hauptsache. –

Nie dem Publikum etwas sagen, sondern
immer dem Andren; in Selbstgesprächen
nach unten oder nach oben blickend, nie
gerad'aus. –

Letzter Wunsch:

Bleibt mir gut, ihr Lieben!

Bayreuth, 13 August 1876. Richard Wagner

Wagner's final requests to the singers at the first performance of the *Ring*, hung up at the stage entrance to the Festival Theatre: 'Last request to my dear colleagues. ! Clarity ! – The great notes look after themselves; the little notes and their text are the main thing. – Never address yourselves to the public, but always to each other; in soliloquies looking downwards or upwards, never straight forwards. – Last request: Let us never quarrel, my friends! Bayreuth, 13 August 1876. Richard Wagner.'

Bayreuth 1876. Emperor Wilhelm I of Germany greets Wagner at the Festival Theatre

Wagner at rehearsals of the *Ring* at Bayreuth. Drawing by Adolf von Menzel, 1875.

Wagner as conductor. Cartoon by K. Klic, *Humoristische Blätter*, Vienna 1873.

Palazzo Vendramin-Calergi in Venice, where Wagner lived from 18 September 1882 until his death on 13 February 1883.

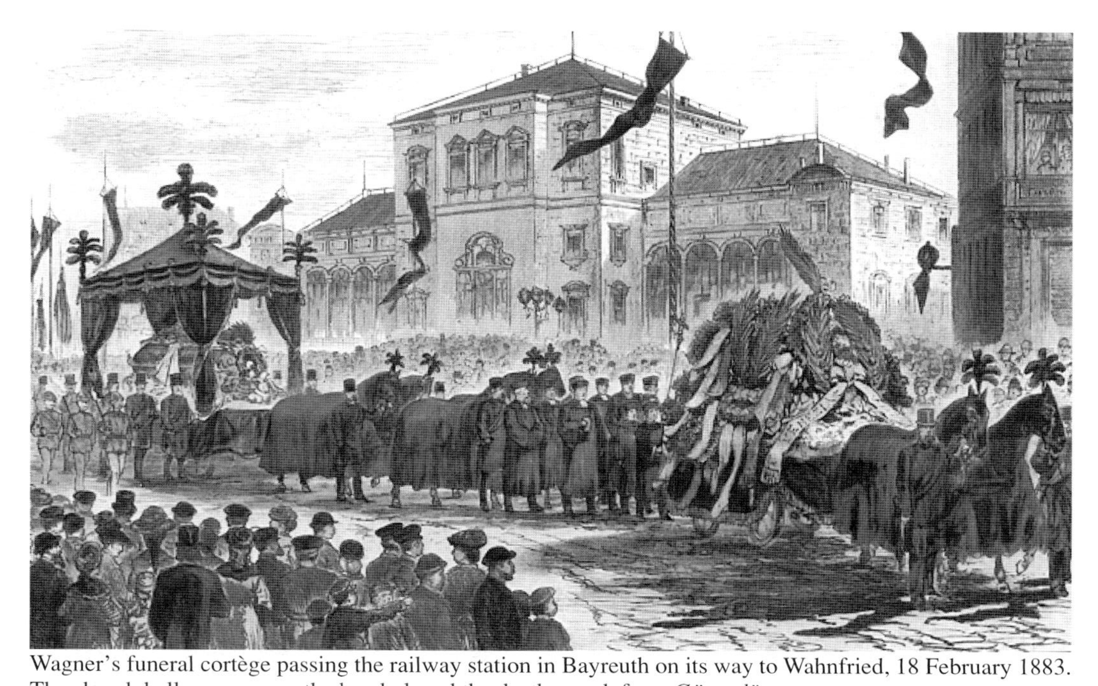

Wagner's funeral cortège passing the railway station in Bayreuth on its way to Wahnfried, 18 February 1883. The church bells were rung, the band played the death march from *Götterdämmerung*.

Richard and Cosima Wagner's graves in the garden of Wahnfried in Bayreuth. Photograph by Mark Kemming.

CHRONOLOGY

In the first column are listed the chief events of Wagner's life, in the second contemporary events of political and cultural significance for it.

Wagner's life	Contemporary events
1811 Birth of Ottilie Wagner (later Brockhaus).	1811 Birth of Liszt.
1813 Birth of Richard Wagner 22 May in Leipzig. Death of his father Friedrich in the autumn.	1812 Napoleon's disastrous campaign in Russia.
1814 Marriage of his mother Johanna Rosine to the artist Ludwig Geyer. They settle in Dresden.	1813 Great battle with Napoleon's army near Leipzig in October. Birth of Verdi.
1815 Birth of his half-sister Cäcilie.	1814 Vienna Convention on the division of Europe.
1817 Weber frequent guest at Geyer's.	1815 Battle of Waterloo.
1820 Wagner learns of Mozart's life-story.	1816 Weber appointed director of the Dresden opera.
1821 Death of Geyer. Richard goes for a time to Eisleben.	1817 Student festival in Wartburg castle.
1822 He attends Kreuzschule (Holy Cross School) in Dresden.	1818 Birth of Karl Marx.
1823 He begins reading Greek and Roman mythology.	1819 Publication of Schopenhauer's chief work, *Die Welt als Wille und Vorstellung* (The World as Will and Idea).
1825 Performs *Der Freischütz* with his school-fellows.	1820 Liszt gives his first concert at the age of nine.
1826 Translates parts of the *Odyssey*.	1821 Births of Dostoevsky and Flaubert.
1827 Is confirmed and writes the play *Leubald und Adelaïde*.	1822 Schubert's Unfinished Symphony composed.
1828 The family moves to Leipzig. Richard attends grammar school and frequents his uncle Adolf's library.	1823 First performance of Weber's *Euryanthe* in Vienna.
1829 He sees Beethoven's *Fidelio* and decides to be a composer.	1824 First performance of Beethoven's Ninth Symphony. Birth of Bruckner.
1830 Composes an overture. Gets to know Schumann in Leipzig.	1825 Death of the poet Jean Paul (Richter) at the age of 62.
1831 Enrolled in an academy of music.	1826 Death of Weber at the age of 40.
1832 Composes Symphony in C and a draft libretto for *Die Hochzeit*.	1827 Death of Beethoven at the age of 57.
1833 Goes to Würzburg. Composes his first opera, *Die Feen*.	1828 Births of Ibsen and Tolstoy. Death of Schubert at the age of 31.
1834 Conductor at Bad Lauchstädt and Magdeburg. Gets to know Minna Planer.	
1835 Composes *Das Liebesverbot*.	

1836 *Das Liebesverbot* performed in Magdeburg. Goes to Königsberg. Marries Minna.

1837 Conductor in Riga.

1838 Works on *Rienzi.*

1839 Flees his creditors in Riga by sea to London and Paris.

1840 Gets to know Heine, Liszt and Meyerbeer in Paris. Completes *Rienzi.*

1841 Composes *The Flying Dutchman.* Begins the libretto for *Tannhäuser.*

1842 Moves to Dresden. First performance of *Rienzi.* Meets Mendelssohn in Berlin.

1843 First performance of *The Flying Dutchman* in Dresden. Becomes *hofkapellmeister.*

1844 Works on *Tannhäuser.*

1845 First performance of *Tannhäuser* in Dresden. Begins the librettos of *Mastersingers* and *Lohengrin.*

1846 Begins the music for *Lohengrin.*

1847 Works on *Lohengrin.*

1848 Death of his mother. Wagner begins the libretto of the *Ring.*

1849 Writes the libretto for an opera on Jesus of Nazareth. Gets to know Mikhail Bakunin. Takes part in the May uprising in Dresden. Flees to Zürich.

1850 First performance of *Lohengrin* in Weimar. Writes the 'anti-Jewish' article.

1851 Works on the libretto of the *Ring.* Writes *Oper und Drama* and *Eine Mitteilung an meine Freunde.*

1829 Rossini composes *William Tell.*

1830 July revolution in France. Riots in German states. Birth of Hans von Bülow. Berlioz composes Symphonie Fantastique.

1831 Heine goes into exile in Paris.

1832 Death of Goethe at the age of 82.

1833 Birth of Brahms in Hamburg.

1834 Liszt gets to know Marie, Countess d'Agoult.

1835 First edition of Jakob Grimm's *Deutsche Mythologie.*

1836 Meyerbeer composes *Les Huguenots.*

1837 Daguerre and Talbot discover photography.

1838 Schubert composes *Kinderzenen* etc.

1839 Birth of Mussorgsky.

1840 Births of Zola and Tchaikovsky.

1841 Opening of Semper's opera-house in Dresden.

1842 Liszt appointed conductor in Weimar.

1843 Feuerbach's *Philosophie der Zukunft* published.

1844 Birth of Nietzsche.

1845 Birth of Ludwig II of Bavaria.

1846 Berlioz composes *Faust.*

1847 Death of Mendelssohn in Leipzig at the age of 38.

1848 February revolution in France. *Communist Manifesto* published. German national assembly in St Paul's church in Frankfurt (Frankfurt Diet).

1849 German constitution agreed in Frankfurt.

1852 Completes the libretto of the *Ring*. Gets to know the Wesendoncks.

1853 Travels to Italy. Vision of the music for *Das Rheingold*. Sees the sixteen-year-old Cosima.

1854 Composes the music for of *Das Rheingold* and *Die Walküre*. First conceives *Tristan and Isolde*.

1855 Guest conductor in London. Continues with the music for *Die Walküre*.

1856 Completes *Die Walküre* and begins *Siegfried*.

1857 The Wagners take up lodgings with the Wesendoncks. Music for the *Ring* broken off in the middle of *Siegfried*. Begins *Tristan and Isolde*.

1858 Travels to Venice because of quarrel with the Wesendoncks. Minna goes to Dresden.

1859 Completes *Tristan and Isolde* in Lucerne. Moves to Paris. Minna returns to him.

1860 Concerts in Paris and Brussels. Visits Rossini in Paris.

1861 *Tannhäuser* a failure in Paris. Travels widely. Begins *The Mastersingers*.

1862 Minna and Richard part for good.

1863 Visit to Russia. Cosima and Richard declare their love in Berlin.

1864 Flees from his creditors to Vienna. Ludwig II summons Wagner to Munich. Cosima becomes his lover. Resumes work on *Siegfried*.

1865 Birth of Richard and Cosima's daughter Isolde. First performance of *Tristan and Isolde* in Munich conducted by von Bülow. Act II of Siegfried finished. Begins to dictate memoirs.

1850 Death of Balzac at the age of 51.

1851 First performance of Verdi's *Rigoletto* in Venice.

1852 Napoleon III becomes emperor in France.

1853 First performances of Verdi's *La Traviata* and *Il Trovatore*.

1854 Trades Unions banned in Germany.

1855 Freytag publishes *Soll und Haben*.

1856 Deaths of Heine in Paris at the age of 59 and of Schumann at the age of 46. Births of Sigmund Freud and G. B. Shaw.

1857 Cosima Liszt and Hans von Bülow married in Berlin.

1858 Birth of Puccini in Lucca.

1859 Darwin publishes *The Origin of Species*. Battle of Solferino.

1860 Birth of Mahler. Death of Schopenhauer at the age of 72. Cosima gives birth to Daniela von Bülow.

1861 Liszt goes to Rome to take orders. American Civil War begins.

1862 Bismarck prime minister of Prussia. Birth of Gerhart Hauptmann.

1863 German worker's union founded. Cosima gives birth to Blandine von Bülow.

1864 German–Danish war over Schleswig. Birth of Richard Strauss.

1865 Taine publishes *La Philosophie de l'Art*.

1866 The Austro-Prussian War. Austrian defeat at Königgrätz. Siemens invents the dynamo.

1866 Death of Minna. Richard and Cosima move to Tribschen near Lucerne.

1867 Birth of Richard and Cosima's second daughter, Eva.

1868 First performance of *The Mastersingers* in Munich. Gets to know Nietzsche. Cosima goes to live permanently with Wagner.

1869 First performance of *Das Rheingold* in Munich. Birth of Siegfried Wagner.

1870 First performance of *Die Walküre* in Munich. Cosima divorced from Hans von Bülow and married to Wagner. *Siegfried Idyll.*

1871 Bayreuth chosen as site of music festival. *Siegfried* completed.

1872 Moves to Bayreuth. Foundation-stone of opera-house laid. Draft score of *Götterdämmerung* finished.

1873 Full score of *Götterdämmerung* begun.

1874 Moves into the the house Wahnfried. *Götterdämmerung* completed.

1875 Rehearsals of the *Ring* at Bayreuth.

1876 First performance of the complete *Ring*-cycle at Bayreuth. Stay in Italy.

1877 Conducting in London. Begins *Parsifal.*

1878 Works on *Parsifal.*

1879 Works on the full score for *Parsifal.*

1880 Health cure in Italy.

1881 Stay in Sicily.

1882 Completes *Parsifal.* First performance at the second Bayreuth festival.

1883 Death of Wagner 13 February in Venice. Burial in Bayreuth.

1867 Ludwig II becomes engaged but breaks it off within a year.

1868 Death of Rossini in Paris at the age of 76. Wagner and Nietzsche become known to each other.

1869 First Vatican Council opens. Death of Berlioz in Paris at the age of 66.

1870 Franco-Prussian War begins. Death of Charles Dickens at the age of 58.

1871 German Empire founded with Wilhelm I as emperor. The Paris commune.

1872 Birth of Scriabin in Moscow.

1873 Ludwig II builds fairy palaces with most zeal.

1874 Birth of Schoenberg.

1875 Birth of Thomas Mann.

1876 Tolstoy's *Anna Karenina* published. Brahms publishes his first symphony. Tchaikovsky composes *Swan Lake.*

1877 Ibsen's *Pillars of Society* published. Saint-Saëns composes *Samson et Dalila.* Edison invents the phonograph.

1878 Bruckner composes his Fifth Symphony.

1879 Dostoevsky's *The Brothers Karamazov* published.

1880 Death of Flaubert at the age of 59.

1881 Death of Dostoevsky at the age of 60. Births of Bartók and Picasso.

1882 Birth of Stravinsky.

1883 Bismarck takes measures for the introduction of a social security system. Death of Marx at the age of 65. Birth of Kafka.

Germanic Barbarians

Today we tend to think of Germany as one of the old-established great powers, like the nation familiar to us in twentieth-century history. Yet this image of Germany originates from no longer ago than 1871, when the king of Prussia became *Kaiser* of all Germany. Before that, the German-speaking area was divided into a large number of independent kingdoms and duchies, over which the spoken language varied considerably. The most powerful of the kingdoms were Prussia, Saxony and Bavaria. This was quite different from the situation in their strong and long-unified neighbours, France and Great Britain. From the time when the German-speaking peoples began to develop a sense of nationhood, it took four centuries for them to achieve unification as a single nation.

Ever since the days of Julius Caesar, two thousand years ago, when the Roman empire first confronted Germanic military forces north of the Alps, the Romans, and after them the heirs of Roman culture, had always called the Germans 'barbarians'. The word *barbarian* had originally been used by the Ancient Greeks of anyone who did not speak Greek, but gradually they and others began to apply it to foreigners in general, and especially those whom the Romans regarded as uncivilised, immoral and crude. This narrow-minded attitude to the unfamiliar, or to those who are to be exploited, is widespread in all periods. One need only recall how colonists and slave-traders referred to black Africans as animals in the eighteenth and nineteenth centuries.

Around AD 100, the Roman historian Tacitus compiled a book, *Germania*, on the culture, religion and customs of the Germanic tribes. In fact Tacitus himself never travelled to Germania, but based his book on the accounts of Roman soldiers. The book describes the Germans, admittedly, as a coarse people, heavy drinkers, with little learning, but on the other hand as lovers of freedom, uncorrupted by civilisation, honest, upright, brave, strong, self-sacrificing and moderate in their wants, and their women as particularly chaste. It has been a matter of debate whether the interpretations of the Roman mercenaries and the

Roman horse-soldier fighting Germanic barbarians. Roman relief from Trier.

The Battle of Teutoburger Wald in AD 9, when the Romans were defeated by Germans. Painting from 1903.

book itself are entirely reliable as history. Some even believe that Tacitus was trying to convince his fellow-Romans of their wickedness by drawing attention to and exaggerating these qualites of the Germans, as a contrast to the corrupt sensuality of the ease-loving Romans.

Resurrection of Tacitus

In the Renaissance period, around the middle of the fifteenth century, Tacitus's book was rediscovered after centuries of oblivion, and published in Venice in 1470 and in Nuremberg in 1473. The publication of this ancient book marks the beginning of a serious German counter-attack on the cultural dominance of the Romance-speaking world, and Germans made full use of Tacitus in their campaign. One aspect of this campaign was opposition to the power and corruption of the Pope and the Vatican, which came to a head with the Reformation and the spread of Protestantism in the wake of Martin Luther. Conversely, Tacitus's ancient work was also used as a weapon against the Germans themselves, or to spur them on in the struggle with the Ottoman Empire (Böldl 2000, 15–17; Schulze 1996, 43–5; Arthúr Björgvin Bollason 1990, 28–34).

This revived concept of the Germanic peoples, meaning the Cimbri, Teutons and Goths, was, however, for a long time only regarded as applicable to their courage, physical strength and uprightness. They were still deemed uncivilised by the standards of the high culture of Paris or Rome. Promoters of ancient Germanic culture therefore sought out various, sometimes fantastic, devices for refuting this attitude, and for demonstrating that the ancient Germans, or at least their chieftains, had indeed been concerned about culture, and that the Germans themselves were of honourable descent.

One of these theories was that Druids (spiritual leaders of the Celts), fleeing from Britain, had in early times taught the Germans about Greek, and even Egyptian, culture. Another was on the lines that the Germans were descended from one of Noah's numerous sons, called Tuyscon (i.e. German). After the Flood, the ark came to rest, of course, on Mt Ararat in the Caucasus. It was in this area, in Scythia by the Black Sea, that Noah's issue were supposed to have first settled, and this was precisely where the Goths were believed at the time to have come from.

In the sixteenth and seventeenth centuries Germanic scholars tried harder and harder to glorify their languages. Some Dutch scholars maintained that their forefathers, the Cimbri, had spoken the language of Adam, and that this had escaped the confusion of tongues in the Tower of Babel. Others claimed that German was the world's second-oldest language, after Hebrew, and still others said that Greek and Latin had developed from Germanic languages.

In order to reinforce their self-image in the face of the heroic legends of the Greeks and Romans, such scholars began at the same time to glorify and exaggerate the importance of Germanic heroes, especially the chieftain Arminius, who, according to Roman histories, defeated the Roman legions at the renowned Battle of Teutoburger Wald in AD 9. In the mid-sixteenth century his name was Germanicised to create the national hero Hermann. He became a symbol for resistance to the power of southern Europe and when King Gustavus Adolphus of Sweden in the early seventeenth century intervened in the Thirty Years' War between Catholics and Protestants, this was interpreted as a repetition of the triumphal march of the ancient Germanic Goths against the decadent Roman Empire (Magnus 1554; Lohenstein 1689; Böldl 2000, 17–23).

Climate Theories

The efforts of Germanic scholars to promote national consciousness did not go unnoticed by their neighbours in the south, and not all were impressed. In the seventeenth and eighteenth centuries, interesting exchanges of opinion took place between French and German thinkers about the interpretation of the so-called 'climate theory'. According to this theory, climate and weather were important influences on the development of human behaviour both physical and mental. Such theories had in fact been known already among the Ancient Greeks, and they have actually still been used by some scholars right on into the twentieth century (Heiberg 1920, 453–64; Huntington 1915).

The classification of nations according to the climate theory began in the late seventeenth century, when French writers claimed that those who lived at Germany's latitudes were incapable of any refined learning, though they could be endowed with fine physical powers. Half a century later an opposing German view was set forth in an

Gustavus Adolphus, king of Sweden
1611–32

Baron Charles de Montesquieu (1689–1755)

encyclopaedia of philosophy. There the division of the world into climate zones — cold, temperate and hot — is linked with a classification of mankind and human qualities into three corresponding types. The Latin nations — the French, Italians and Spanish — are assigned to the hot zone. They have their virtues, but tend to be foolish, illogical in thought, frivolous, arrogant, libidinous and vengeful. In the temperate zone, people are perceptive, far-seeing, sensible and logical. In this zone live the Germans and the English, for instance. Yet the authors do not deny the Germans' weakness for drink, which Tacitus had deemed their major vice. In the cold zone are, among others, the Scandinavians, who are considered to be slow of understanding in spiritual things, avaricious and emotionally frigid, but to have a high tolerance of cold and hunger. Scandinavians, not surprisingly, were not over-pleased with this description, especially the Swedes (Bouhour 1671; Walch 1726, I 24; Bonstetten 1825, 226).

In the German-speaking area, people began to express criticism of Tacitus and other ancient writers, casting doubt on their knowledge and understanding of the ancient Germans. Those writers had never themselves visited the area, and their informants understood neither the language of the Germans nor the basis of their organisation. Thus all their conclusions were in the light of the standards of Roman society. Some people suggested that Tacitus's information related only to Germanic peasants, and not their civilised leaders (Zschackwitz 1743; Schütze 1746, 31–49; Majer 1798, 24; Böldl 2000, 30–32).

The climate theory reached a scientific milestone when Montesquieu published his major work *De l'esprit des lois* in 1748. He put forward physiological arguments to show how a cold climate could strengthen the tissues of the human body and at the same time enhance moral power. In spite of his own nationality, he regarded the Germanic peoples as superior to the Romance ones in this respect, and the more so the further north they lived. He saw the Nordic peoples as particularly well fitted to promoting and preserving the freedom and equal rights of the individual.

Montesquieu did not, however, directly contradict the prevailing view that in the field of higher culture the Germans and other Nordic nations were uncivilised in comparison with the French, who were the inheritors of classical culture. Various other writers in southern Europe took quite an extreme view of this, and continued to look down on the

Germans, believing that the cold climate constricted the spiritual and aesthetic senses. Nor did the ideas of Montesquieu and his followers about ancient Nordic freedom and equality give rise to any criticism of the absolutism of the time, until around 1800, after Napoleon Bonaparte had begun his attempt to conquer Europe (Espiard 1752; Kleffel 1749, 11; von See 1975, 12–14; Böldl 2000, 27–30).

Desire for Unification of Germany

In the latter half of the eighteenth century there was growing pressure to reduce the number of small German states by unification; many influences were at work here. Technical progress had increased productivity in agriculture and industry, and so merchants, farmers and manufacturers wanted the multitude of import duties imposed by each small state abolished. The bloody Seven Years' War of 1756–63, waged by Frederick II of Prussia against the 'three petticoats' (*der Krieg mit den drei Röcken*, i.e. Maria Theresa of Austria, Catharine the Great of Russia and Mme de Pompadour in France, as he called it), also lent weight to the argument that a strong united Germany should be formed, which could stand against the other major powers (Schulze 1996, 49–62; Böldl 2000, 34–35).

Visionaries who sought to promote a sense of German nationality and to diffuse knowledge of ancient Germanic culture were, of course, supported by those who wanted unification for economic reasons; some of these were fairly wealthy. Thus publication of books and periodicals supporting unification and German nationalism increased greatly after the mid-eighteenth century.

In 1760–80, James Macpherson and Thomas Percy published collections of early Scottish and English poetry in Britain. (Some years later it was discovered that most of the poems attributed to the third-century Ossian, relating to a prehistoric Scottish Heroic Age, had in fact been written by the young Macpherson himself.) In Germany their example was soon followed. Many Germans felt that the British were far more akin to them than the French, and since 1714 England had been ruled by Hanoverian monarchs of German descent (Macpherson 1760; Percy 1765; Meynert 1797; Böldl 2000, 35–37).

The most influential of the Germans in this field was the polymath Johann Gottfried Herder (1744–1803), one of the pioneers of the *Sturm und Drang* movement, which developed towards Romanticism. He believed that all poetry originated with the people, regardless of national boundaries, and he was deeply interested in folk-poetry independent of conventional 'culture'. Thus he took a particular interest in the poetry of those peoples whom Europeans regarded as primitive, and published folk-poetry from various countries in 1778–79 (*Volkslieder* I–II).

This was a novel idea at this time, according to which folk-poetry deserved as much respect as that of recognised poets and the Greeks and Romans were not the only ones that could boast of fine ancient poetry and culture. This boosted the confidence and self-respect of those peoples who had hitherto been despised by the self-styled cultural élite of the Romance world, though it did not, of course, stop the people of southern Europe from continuing to feel superior. Others followed Herder's line, like Schiller, who demanded full respect for German folk-culture (1958, 473–76).

Rediscovery of Early German Literature

In spite of the efforts of individual intellectuals to raise the status of German antiquarian studies before the late eighteenth century, they cannot be said to have influenced national life very deeply, or to have sparked off any mass movement. In the first years of the nineteenth century, however, there was a significant change. The obvious reasons for this were the German defeat by Napoleon's armies in 1806 and the French occupation that followed. The French arrogantly trumpeted to the world the humiliating defeat of the Germans by removing the statue of Victory in her carriage from the top of the Brandenburg Gate in Berlin, and transporting it to Paris. At this time, the spirit and triumphalism of the French were attributed by many to the fact that they had a united fatherland, which they loved, and to their pride in their culture, ancient and modern, while the Germans were manifestly lacking such a coherent ideology.

After the defeat at the hands of the French, more and more voices called for unification of the fragmented German states. At the same time, the Germans were urged to nurture the Germanic cultural heritage and the memory of their own ancient heroes, rather than enviously contemplating the ancient glories of Greece, Rome and France. Early German poems of chivalry and courtly love began to be published, and translated into contemporary High German verse, or into prose, to make them more accessible. Before this, such poetry had mainly been

The Brandenburg Gate in Berlin

Das Nibelungenlied. Kriemhilt and Prünhilt quarrel while Sîfrit stands by. Illustration from the Hundeshagen manuscript.

Das Nibelungenlied. Gunther sails to Prünhilt's castle in Islande. Illustration by Eduard Bendemann and Julius Hübner from the edition of Leipzig 1840.

Das Nibelungenlied. Death of Sîfrit. Illustration from the Hundeshagen manuscript.

the domain of scholars. Now poets and other artists began to create poems, stories, plays and visual art inspired by this early literature (Haymes and Samples 1996).

Das Nibelungenlied

The longest and most famous of the early German poems is *Das Nibelungenlied*, composed in Middle High German around AD 1200 or a little later. The poem exists in various fragments and versions of different length in over 30 manuscripts dating from the thirteenth to sixteenth centuries. It comprises in all 39 sections (*Aventiure*) and nearly 2,400 stanzas.

The characters of the poem coincide to some extent with those in Old Icelandic poems and stories about Sigurðr Fáfnisbani, Brynhildr, Guðrún and Hǫgni. As it has generally (and mistakenly) been believed that Wagner's *Ring* is mainly based upon the first part of this poem, it will be best to summarise briefly the main contents of the first 19 *Aventiure*. Parallels will be discussed later on in the order that they appear in Wagner's librettos.

1. The fair Kriemhilt grows up at the Burgundian court at Worms on the Rhine. She dreams of training up a beautiful falcon, which is then torn to pieces by two eagles.
2. Sîfrit grows up in the palace of Xanten, about 250 km further down the Rhine. He is regarded as the finest of young lads.
3. Sîfrit travels to Worms to ask for Kriemhilt's hand. Hagene, a follower of her brother Gunther, briefly recounts Sîfrit's previous exploits, i.e. winning a hoard of gold from the Nibelungs (in this poem a race of human heroes) and slaying a dragon, after which he bathes in the dragon's blood, making his skin invulnerable to weapons. Sîfrit challenges Gunther, but their fight is avoided, and Sîfrit becomes a guest of the Burgundians.

4–5. Sîfrit defeats the Saxons for Gunther. He is welcomed with a victory parade, where he and Kriemhilt see each other for the first time.

6. Prünhilt is a beautiful, and strong, queen in Islande. Gunther sets out to sail to Islande and ask for her hand.

7–8. Prünhilt challenges Gunther to a trial of strength. Sîfrit, who had in his youth acquired a cape of invisibility from the Nibelungs, stands unseen by Gunther's side and defeats Prünhilt. Prünhilt gathers forces, while Sîfrit seeks reinforcements in the land of the Nibelungs.

9–10. Sîfrit rides ahead to Worms to herald the arrival of Gunther and Prünhilt.

A double wedding is celebrated. Kriemhilt and Sîfrit make love on their wedding night, but Prünhilt denies Gunther intercourse, and hangs him up on a peg. On Gunther's behalf, Sîfrit breaks down her resistance, and takes away from her a ring and a belt, which he gives to Kriemhilt.

11–14. Sîfrit and Kriemhilt go to Xanten. Both queens give birth to sons, each named after the other's husband. Ten years later Sîfrit and Kriemhilt accept an invitation to Worms. The two queens argue fiercely about the heroism and reputation of their husbands. The dispute grows more and more rancorous until Kriemhilt discloses that Sîfrit has made love to Prünhilt. Sîfrit denies this, and the parties make peace on the surface. But Sîfrit's fate is sealed.

15. Hagene pretends he wishes to guard Sîfrit in battle, and Kriemhilt tells him of the one place on Sîfrit's body where he can be wounded.

16–17. Gunther, Sîfrit and Hagene go hunting. Hagene murders Sîfrit, and his body is transported to Worms. When Hagene approaches the catafalque, the body bleeds; this is regarded as evidence of his guilt. Sîfrit is given a royal funeral.

18–19. Kriemhilt remains in Worms. Her brothers manage to achieve a reconciliation, and she agrees to bring the gold of the Nibelungs from Xanten to Worms. Hagene steals the treasure and hides it in the river Rhine.

This first half of the poem contains no parallels with *Das Rheingold*, or with *Die Walküre*, and reference to Sîfrit's youth is very slight. He gains neither ring nor gold from a dragon, for instance. The main parallels are with the latter part of *Götterdämmerung*, though Prünhilt largely disappears from the action after *Aventiure* 14, as soon as the murder of Sîfrit has been planned. There is no shared funeral pyre.

The latter half of the poem deals with the revenge of Kriemhilt, who marries King Etzel (Attila), and betrays her brothers. This is in fact the main part of *Das Nibelungenlied*, but has no relevance to the story told in the *Ring*.

The poem was not published until 1755, and for a long time after that remained largely unknown outside a small group of scholars. After 1800, however, it was published frequently in contemporary German versions, and it began to be glorified as a treasure of German cultural heritage, and was extensively used to promote German national consciousness. Artists made illustrations, and it provided inspiration for many poems, stories and plays. The poet Ernst Raupach published a play on the Nibelung treasure, in a prelude and five acts, in 1834.

Plans for an Opera on the Nibelungs

There were various plans about for composing an opera on the Nibelungs around the middle of the nineteenth century. Mendelssohn and Schumann both played with the idea about 1840, though nothing came of it. In 1844 the German writer on aesthetics Friedrich Theodor Vischer published a detailed proposal for a libretto which was to be based on *Das Nibelungenlied.*

In the following years the poetess Louise Otto tried repeatedly to get a composer to write music for a libretto based on *Das Nibelungenlied*, to be written by herself. Among those she approached was Wagner, but he declined. She also made the acquaintance of the Danish composer Niels W. Gade, who started on a draft of such an opera, but this came to nothing. She succeeded in interesting Schumann in the idea once again, but about this time his health began to fail. The first complete opera on the subject of the Nibelungs was *Die Nibelungen* by Heinrich Dorn, which was first performed in Weimar in 1854, conducted by Liszt (*Dokumente*, 15–17, 19–26, 75–7).

ICELANDIC STUDIES IN GERMANY

Early Acquaintance

German writers and scholars first made the acquaintance of Old Icelandic literature in Latin translations. The first of these were of the Prose Edda (a treatise on poetics and mythology originally written by Snorri Sturluson in the thirteenth century) and the first two poems, *Vǫluspá* and *Hávamál*, of the Poetic Edda (a thirteenth-century collection of traditional heroic and mythological poems); all three were published by the Danish scholar Peder Hansen Resen in Copenhagen in 1665. The Icelandic text of the first of these (*Edda Islandorum*) was based on a greatly altered redaction of Snorri Sturluson's *Edda* made by Magnús Ólafsson (born *c.*1573, from 1622 until his death in 1636 priest at Laufás in northern Iceland) in 1609, and was accompanied by an anonymous Danish translation (perhaps partly the work of S. J. Stephanius) and a Latin version mainly by Magnús Ólafsson, but with some chapters by Torfæus (Þormóður Torfason). *Vǫluspá* and *Hávamál* were printed in Icelandic and Latin; both texts of *Vǫluspá* were based on the work of Stefán Ólafsson of Vallanes, those of *Hávamál* on that of an anonymous interpreter, and notes to both poems by Guðmundur Andrésson were also included (see Faulkes 1977–79).

Secondly, in 1685 a German translation was published of a famous description of Norway compiled about 1600 by the Norwegian cleric Peder Claussøn (Friis) and published by the Danish scholar Ole Worm in Copenhagen in 1632 (*Norriges oc omliggende Øers sandfærdige Bescríffuelse*). Peder Claussøn had also made a Danish adaptation of Snorri Sturluson's *Heimskringla* (a history of Norway from the earliest times down to 1177), which was published in 1633, also by Ole Worm, and his description of Norway was of course largely based on Icelandic sources.

Thirdly, some Heroic Sagas (*fornaldarsögur*, sagas that supposedly took place before the settlement of Iceland in the late ninth century) were published in Sweden with Swedish and/or Latin translations in 1664–1737; these included *Hervarar saga ok Heiðreks* in 1672, *Gríms saga Loðinkinna*, *Ketils saga hœngs*, *Ǫrvar-Odds saga* and *Sǫrla þáttr* in 1697, *Þiðreks saga* in 1715 and *Vǫlsunga saga* in 1737 (on these last two see pp. 105–06 below).

In 1746 the text of *Gylfaginning* from the Uppsala manuscript of the Prose Edda was published by J. Göransson with Swedish and Latin translations. In the seventeenth and eighteenth centuries, the title pages of books were as wordy as the 'blurb' on a modern book's wrapper. The title page of this edition (*De Yfverborna Atlingars, eller, Sviogötars ok Nordmänners, Edda . . . Hyperboreorum Atlantiorum, seu, Suiogothorum et Nordmannorum Edda*) exemplifies the persistent urge to fit the Prose and Poetic Eddas into some kind of mythological European Union. It clearly states, for instance, that the book is written in 'Gothic', which the Swedes regarded as an ancient form of Swedish. Small differences may be seen beween the Swedish and the Latin of the title page: in addition to Goths, Swedes, Norwegians and Scythians, the Latin makes reference to the Germanic *Cimbri* and the Celtic *Galli*.

This tendency is in fact quite understandable, as no comparable medieval sources exist from other nations of northern and central Europe. Few people from these regions, however, had the audacity to lay claim to the mythology of the Greeks and Romans, although many parallels exist between it and Scandinavian mythology.

For a long time, only a small number of German scholars took an interest in this field, and until the latter half of the eighteenth century these scraps of eddic verse (that is, poetry of the type found in the Poetic Edda and *Gylfaginning*, the mythological section of the Prose Edda) and Scandinavian mythology were hardly accorded the dignified name of literature. They were primarily valued as sources for the history and religious practices of Scandinavian and other Germanic peoples, and did not always meet with the approval of strict Lutheran writers. The first publication of what may be called a 'Germanic mythology' in Hamburg in 1703 exemplifies such disapproving attitudes; it was edited by a preacher named Trogullis (Troels) Arnkiel with the title *Cimbrische Heyden-Religion*.

By the latter half of the eighteenth century, however, old Nordic culture and religion was beginning to be elevated to a position of respect in the Germanic cultural region, in competition with the Classical southern-European culture which had hitherto been regarded as the only 'correct' standard. One of the first writers to express this attitude was the Swiss historian Paul Henri de Mallet (1730–1807), who taught

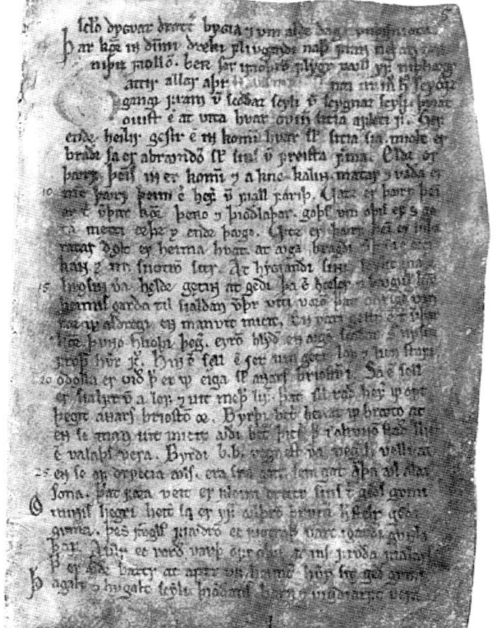

The beginning of *Hávamál* in the Codex Regius of the Poetic Edda.

EDDA. ISLANDORUM
AN. CHR. M. CC. XV
ISLANDICE. CONSCRIPTA
PER
SNORRONEM. STURLÆ
ISLANDIÆ. NOMOPHYLACEM
NUNC. PRIMUM
ISLANDICE. DANICE. ET. LATINE
EX. ANTIQVIS. CODICIBUS. M. SS
BIBLIOTHECÆ. REGIS. ET. ALIORUM
IN. LUCEM. PRODIT
OPERA. ET. STUDIO
PETRI. JOHANNIS. RESENII. I. V. D
JURIS. AC. ETHICES. PROFESSORIS. PUBL
ET. CONSULIS. HAVNIENSIS
FRIDERICI. III
REGUM. PRINCIPUM. SAPIENTUM
SUMMI. OPTIMI. MAXIMI
GLORIOSO. NOMINI. MEMORIÆ. IMMORTALI
D. D. D.

HAVNIÆ
TYPIS. HENRICI. GÖDIANI. REG. ET. ACAD
TYPOGR. M. DC. LX. V

Title page of the first printed edition of the Prose Edda, Copenhagen 1665.

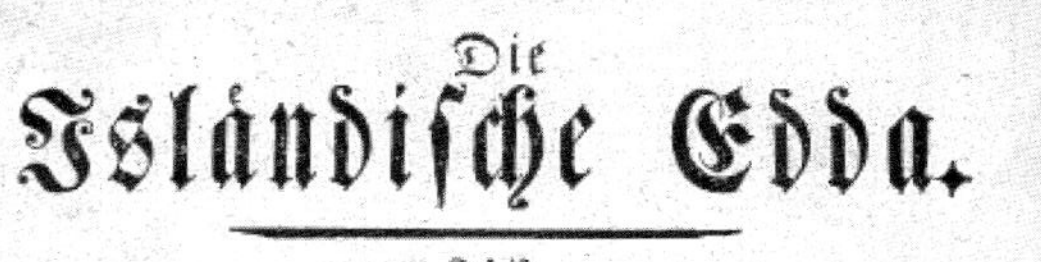

Die
Isländische Edda.

Das ist:
Die geheime Gottes=Lehre
der ältesten Hyperborder, der Norder, der Veneten, Gethen, Gothen, Vandaler, der Gallier, der Britten, der Skoten, der Sueven, ꝛc. kurz des ganzen alten Kaltiens, oder des Europäischen Skytiens
enthaltend.

I. Das sybillinische Karmen die Voluspáh genannt,
so eine poetische Weissagung von dem Anfang der Welt bis zu ihrem Untergange.

II. Des Odins Sitten=Lehre, Hava oder Hars Mál,
d. i. Odins Gottes=Lehre.
Wobey verschiedene alte Oden aus dem X. und XI. Sec. angehänget sind.

III. Drey und Dreyßig Dömosagen oder Fabeln,
so eine Erklärung der Voluspáh in Beyspielen, oder eine historische und rhetische Beschreibung von dem Gott Thor und seinen persönlichen Verrichtungen und Reisen in die Welt.

Im Jahr 1070 bis 1075
aus alten runischen Schriften mit lateinischen Buchstaben zuerst edirt
von
Sämund Froden;
Hiernächst im Jahr 1664 von dem Königl. Dänischen Rath Resen aus den ältesten Handschriften, in die Dänische und lateinische Sprache übersetzt besorget;
Und nun in die Hochteutsche Sprache,
mit einem Versuch zur rechten Erklärung übersetzt und edirt,
von
Jacob Schimmelmann
Königl. Preußischer Consistorialrath in Stettin.

Daselbst gedruckt bey Johann Franz Struck, Königl. Preuß. privil. Buchdrucker, 1777.

LANDSBÓKASAFN ÍSLANDS

Title page of the first printed German translation of the Prose Edda, Stettin 1777.

Ásgarðr, the citadel of the gods. Illustration from the first printed German translation of the Prose Edda, 1777, which seems to be based on contemporary villages in northern Germany.

for a time at the University in Copenhagen, and in 1755 and 1756 published *Introduction à l'histoire de Dannemarc* and *Monumens de la mythologie et de la poésie des Celtes*, which include a good deal of material derived from the Prose Edda, including most of the narratives of *Gylfaginning*; he deemed Scandinavian religious ideas less extreme than those of more southerly regions.

In this, Mallet followed Montesquieu's theory of climate, without drawing much distinction between Nordic, Celtic and Germanic. This was a common view at the time. Unlike his scholarly predecessors, he regarded eddic verse as fully valid poetry in its own right, which contradicted the age-old assumption that the Celts and Scandinavian peoples were nothing but crude barbarians. Mallet's book was soon translated into German and was published in two volumes in 1765 by Gottfried Schütze.

The Prose Edda was first published in German as *Die isländische Edda* in Stettin in 1777, although it would be more accurate to call this a summary or retelling of *Gylfaginning* along with *Vǫluspá* and *Hávamál*, largely derived from Resen's editions. In this book, several Germanic and Celtic races are added to those listed in the Swedish edition of 1746, i.e. Wends, Britons, Scots and Swabians. The work was edited by Jakob Schimmelmann, a Lutheran Enlightenment man, who viewed thirteenth-century reality through eighteenth-century spectacles. He saw the author, Snorri Sturluson, for instance, as an enlightened ruler, governor and judge who had rescued the Edda manuscripts from the 'barbarism' of the Popish church, rather than as an aristocratic politician, poet and historian who cultivated pagan poetry as part of the cultural heritage of the Nordic world.

Schimmelmann also sought to demonstrate that the doctrines of the Eddas and the Bible were in fact the same, as a beneficent God does not discriminate between humans, and loved the ancient Nordic peoples, just as he loves the Jews. Schimmelmann regarded *Vǫluspá* and the mythology recounted in the Prose Edda as Scandinavian variants of the Old Testament prophetic books, needing only to be cleansed of the taint of heathenism.

Gradually, however, Old Icelandic poetry began to be studied in its own right, and not just as a historical source. In 1766 translations of Egill Skalla-Grímsson's poems *Sonatorrek* and *Hǫfuðlausn* were published by the poet and critic Heinrich von Gerstenberg (1737–1823).

His volume (*Briefe über die Merkwürdigkeiten der Litteratur*, 1766–70) contained the first notes in German on the names and various other aspects of Nordic mythology that occur in these poems, along with an essay on verse forms (pp. 153–57). Gerstenberg, like Mallet, regarded these and other old poems as evidence of quite a sophisticated culture. He believed, however, that this culture had been brought from the East by Óðinn and the Ases — the gods of Old Norse mythology (Icelandic Æsir, plural of Áss), who were thought to have originated historically as a race of people from Azerbaijan by the Black Sea.

Next on the scene was an Austrian Jesuit priest, Michael Denis, who was a professor of aesthetics for a time, and subsequently director of the Imperial Library in Vienna. He was regarded as a leading bibliographer, but was also a poet, who translated, or more accurately rewrote, many of the spurious Celtic poems of Ossian written by the Scot Macpherson.

The main character in Denis's work (*Ossian und Sineds Lieder,* 4 vols, 1784) is the warrior-poet Sined. He also brought into his compilation, and rewrote, some Old Icelandic poetry, such as *Vǫluspá* and *Vegtamskviða* (i.e. *Baldrs Draumar*), Eyvindr skáldaspillir's *Hákonarmál* (from *Heimskringla)*, and Egill Skalla-Grímsson's *Hǫfuðlausn*. In this he was following the same procedure as the Englishman Thomas Percy, who translated some Old Icelandic poems (*Five Pieces of Runic Poetry*, 1763) and added them to the mythological section of the second edition of his translation of Mallet's *Introduction à l'histoire de Dannemarc* and *Monumens de la mythologie et de la poésie des Celtes* (*Northern Antiquities*, 1809).

Poetry about the ancient Celtic and Nordic world by Denis, Klopstock and other German poets of the late eighteenth century, expressed nostalgia and idealised notions of a virtuous primitive life. This was also one aspect of the quest in the many small states of Germany for a shared Germanic heritage as impressive as that of the Latin (i.e. French and Italian) world. This was a major contributory factor in the Germans' growing interest in Icelandic and other Scandinavian literature throughout the nineteenth and well on into the twentieth century.

But Michael Denis was far from regarding these Nordic writings as great art. The old poems were clearly far too crude for this contemporary of Haydn and Mozart, and indeed for the Rococo period in general. His versions of the poems were therefore made consistent with the refinement and sensibility of the time. He was far from alone in his views. In the theatres of Copenhagen at this time, Scandinavian heroes and gods might appear wearing fanciful costumes and powdered wigs.

The poet and cultural guru Johann Gottfried Herder (see pp. 74–75 above) held different views. He felt that the poetry of the so-called savage or barbarian nations should not be beautified, but should be allowed to speak in its own uncouth manner. This difference of views is exemplified, for instance, in the way that the oldest translations of *Vǫluspá* had interpreted this poem on the creation and end of the world as a sibylline prophecy, or as a key to the secrets of the universe, derived from a long-extinct class of priests. Herder, on the other hand, regarded *Vǫluspá* and other eddic poetry as folk-verse from a time when the world was perceived as poetry, as this pioneer of the Romantic movement put it. In a review of the German edition of Mallet's *Introduction à l'histoire de Dannemarc*, Herder also upheld Montesquieu's theory of climate to some extent, and suggested that Norse mythology could provide ammunition for a new Germanic philosophy.

In spite of initially taking an internationalist view of folk poetry, in his later years Herder began to distinguish between southern and northern poetry, in a broad sense. This attitude was to be influential when Romantic scholars began to formulate theories about Germanic myths and legends, and poets and composers were also inspired by these subjects (J. G. Herder, *Iduna, oder der Apfel der Verjüngung*, 1796; Böldl 2000, 136–45).

Not all of those who were interested in Scandinavian culture shared this polemic attitude. Friedrich David Gräter (1768–1830) has been dubbed the godfather of the field of studies called *Nordistik* in German. In 1789 he published *Nordische Blumen* (Nordic Flowers), containing eight eddic poems in German translation, along with excerpts from another two, and four essays on mythology. He was, however, by no means the first to translate Icelandic poetry into German, as mentioned above (pp. 85–86). Gräter was equally interested in early German culture and contemporary Scandinavian, especially Danish, literature. He continued to pursue these interests all his life, and co-edited various periodicals. He held the view, however, that Graeco-Roman culture was superior to the Nordic, as witness for instance his attempt to put eddic poetry into Greek hexameters. In his later years he found himself at loggerheads with those whose views were more nationalistic (Ernst

Johann Gottfried Herder (1744–1803)

Volkslieder.

ausgegeben von Herder

— Sind Veilchen in des Jahres Jugend, sind Erstlinge der Natur, früh und nicht dauernd, Süß, aber bald dahin: der Duft, die Blüthe Von wenigen Minuten —

Shakespear's Hamlet.

Erster Theil.

Leipzig,
in der Weygandschen Buchhandlung
1778.

Title page of volume I of Herder's *Volkslieder*, published in 1778–79.

Jakob and Wilhelm Grimm

DEUTSCHE MYTHOLOGIE

VON JACOB GRIMM.

DRITTE AUSGABE

ERSTER BAND.

GÖTTINGEN

DIETERICHSCHE BUCHHANDLUNG

1854.

Title page of volume I of Jakob Grimm's *Deutsche Mythologie*, first published in 1835.

Arndt 1814, 430; Jakob Grimm, *Deutsche Mythologie*, 1835; Böldl 2000, 145–51).

Whatever form it took, this dissemination of Old Icelandic literature at least constituted a first attempt to present the Nordic heritage; this may perhaps be compared to the modern idea that people can learn to appreciate classical music through TV and 'pop' versions.

Pan-Germanism

The medieval German *Minnesänge*, poems of chivalry and fair maidens which had been composed at royal courts of various sizes in the period of the Crusades, were not regarded as constituting a sufficiently rich or ancient cultural heritage (cf. pp. 75–78 above). Efforts were therefore made to expand the boundaries of what was perceived as the Germanic cultural region. One of the most extreme proponents of this was Johann Gottlieb Fichte, who, along with Hegel and Schelling, was among the most renowned philosophers of the German cultural period sometimes identified with the writer Johann Wolfgang von Goethe.

In 1808, for instance, Fichte maintained in a series of *Reden an die deutsche Nation* (Addresses to the German People; see especially p. 423) that all the Germanic tribes that had not been subject to extended Roman rule were in fact 'German'. They had remained untouched by Roman cultural influence, as witness the purity of the Germanic languages, which were largely untainted by the pollution of Latin. He was followed by poets and scholars such as Ernst Moritz Arndt and the brothers Grimm, who may be regarded, more than any others, as the inventors of pan-Germanism. According to this theory, all Nordic peoples and Norse culture could be counted as parts of the Germanic cultural heritage.

Wilhelm Grimm subscribed to this view in his 1811 edition of ancient Danish epics, ballads and tales (*Altdänische Heldenlieder, Balladen und Märchen*, 1811, ix–x, xvi–xxii, 427–30). He also favoured the view that in essence all the heroic tales of the Eddas were German (*Deutsche Heldensage*, 1829, 4, 436). The title of his brother Jakob's book *Deutsche Mythologie* (German Mythology; 1835) clearly follows the same principle, since it largely comprises, of course, mythological material from the Prose and Poetic Eddas. But Jakob Grimm interprets the Eddic accounts in his own manner, and makes many and diverse comparisons with phenomena drawn from such sources as the Ancient

Greeks and Romans, Indian myths and latter-day German oral traditions. The principal idea of both Grimm brothers was that in ancient times there had in every case been *one* myth and *one* story, from which all variants had subsequently developed.

As a direct consequence of this pan-German ideology, Icelandic and other Norse studies were given a huge boost in German cultural life. German and Norse culture was said to share a common origin, and efforts were made to discover as many Germanic heroes as possible, in order to promote German national pride. Superhuman warriors were most likely to be found in the romantic Heroic Sagas, such as *Vǫlsunga saga* and *Ragnars saga loðbrókar*.

Publications of Old Icelandic Literature

It was not long before both scholarly and popular editions of Old Icelandic poetry and sagas began to be published, together with translations, such as the publications of Friedrich von der Hagen (*Die Edda-Lieder von den Nibelungen*, 1814; *Altnordische Sagen und Lieder*, 1814; *Nordische Heldenromane*, 1814–15; *Lieder der älteren oder Sämundischen-Edda*, 1812) and his rivals, the brothers Grimm (*Lieder der alten Edda*, 1815). Here German readers first had the opportunity to read the originals of many eddic poems and Icelandic sagas, together with translations. For the next few decades such publications continued without a break, along with many writings inspired by this ancient literature. It was as if German writers and scholars had been given thrilling new toys to play with, and were almost beside themselves at the wealth they were able to choose from.

Not all scholars subscribed to this glorification of Nordic literature, feeling that it was undeserved, as the ideas behind it were both crude and immoral. Heated disputes were carried on in writing, between, for instance, the historian Friedrich Rühs on the one hand and Peter Erasmus Müller and the brothers Grimm on the other (see Böldl 2000, 159–69).

It is interesting that a hundred years after Old Icelandic culture was first diffused on a large scale in Germany, a new trend of similar nature began with the publication of twenty-four volumes of translations of Old Icelandic literature in Eugen Diederichs's *Thule* edition of 1911–30. Selected passages from the Icelandic sagas were, in addition, published in small format for German soldiers in World War I, not least to teach them the art of dying with stoicism. Some scholars had already begun to add racial mysticism to their admiration for warriors and heroism — which was to reach its zenith in Nazism (see Óskar Bjarnason, 'Þegar Íslendingar urðu forfeður Þjóðverja', *Skírnir* 1999, 53–88).

Enter Sigurðr Fáfnisbani

Friedrich Schlegel, a writer and literary historian, appears to have been the first to draw the attention of Germans to the Icelandic versions of the legends of the Burgundians and Nibelungs. In the tenth of a series of lectures on classical and romantic literature that he gave in 1802, he compared these versions with *Das Nibelungenlied* (*Geschichte der alten und neuen Literatur*, 1961 (Kritische Friedrich-Schlegel-Ausgabe VI), 232–35).

These Icelandic legends first provided inspiration for new writings in the work of a Prussian baron of French descent named Friedrich Baron de la Motte Fouqué (1777–1843). As early as 1808 he began publication of a trilogy of plays, *Sigurd der Schlangentödter, Sigurds Rache* and *Aslauga* (Sigurðr the Dragon-slayer, Sigurðr's Revenge and Áslaug). These plays were dedicated to the philosopher Fichte (see p. 90 above) and his nationalism.

In 1810 the entire trilogy was published under the title *Held des Nordens* (Hero of the North). This was a drama-cycle intended for reading aloud — a common form at that time, not meant for full stage production. The plays are largely based upon events recounted in *Vǫlsunga saga* and *Ragnars saga loðbrókar*, although Fouqué adds some personal touches. The high-flown language of the plays led to immediate popularity, not only among the public but also among respected writers such as Richter (Jean Paul) and E. T. A. Hoffmann. Beethoven himself, at the beginning of 1816, specifically urged Fouqué to compile for him a libretto for a grand opera, which he said would be a great boon for himself and for the German theatre (Beethoven 1907, II 63–64). Beethoven's request seems never to have been fulfilled. The translation of Sigurðr's Icelandic nickname *Fáfnisbani* (Slayer of Fáfnir) as *Schlangentödter* (Dragon-slayer) seems to have been Fouqué's own (see Jakob and Wilhelm Grimm, *Deutsches Wörterbuch* 1854–1971, IX 471).

Though Fouqué never visited Iceland, he became an impassioned admirer of all things Icelandic. He gathered gifts of books from wealthy

Germans, for instance, to help stock the newly founded library (*Stiftsbókasafn*) in Iceland, forerunner of the present National Library. In 1821 he was made an honorary member of the Icelandic Literary Society (*Hið Íslenska bókmenntafélag*), and on this occasion he wrote an encomium on Iceland. The Icelandic poet Bjarni Thorarensen (1786–1841) responded with a tribute in verse, *Íslands riddari* (Knight of Iceland), and also translated one-third of Fouqué's poem. The first publication of one of the sagas of Icelanders in its entirety in German was by Fouqué, *Gunnlaugs saga ormstungu*, 1826. Finnur Magnússon (1781–1847), a renowned scholar in Copenhagen, thanked Fouqué in verse in 1827 (see Ulrich Groenke, 'Fouqué und die isländische Literaturgesellschaft', *Island-Berichte* 20, 1979, 94–101; Bjarni Thorarensen, *Ljóðmæli*, 1935, I 110–16; II 118–24).

Fouqué wrote many dramas and novels, some of them based on Icelandic literature, which enjoyed great popularity in their time. In his novels, the heroes were all splendid and chivalrous medieval knights — even Egill Skalla-Grímsson, the medieval saga about whom depicts him as a very rough diamond indeed. He also sets the stories of Sigurðr Fáfnisbani in the High Middle Ages and not in the migration age (fourth to fifth century of the Christian era). The only one of his works which has stood the test of time is the tale of *Undine*, which is older than Hans Christian Andersen's famous *Little Mermaid*, but on a similar theme. *Undine* has provided several composers with inspiration for ballets and operas.

However posterity judges Fouqué and his writings, he must be acknowledged as the first person to have promoted Old Icelandic literature vigorously in Germany (see Böldl 1996, 366–67).

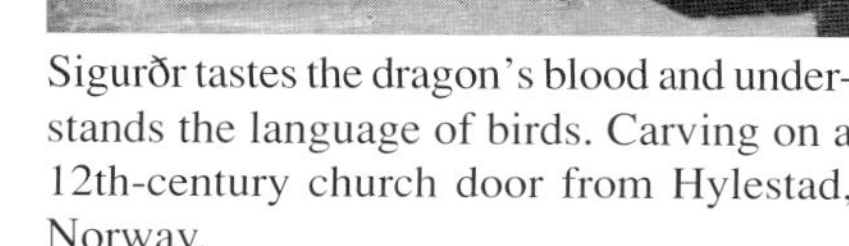

Sigurðr tastes the dragon's blood and understands the language of birds. Carving on a 12th-century church door from Hylestad, Norway.

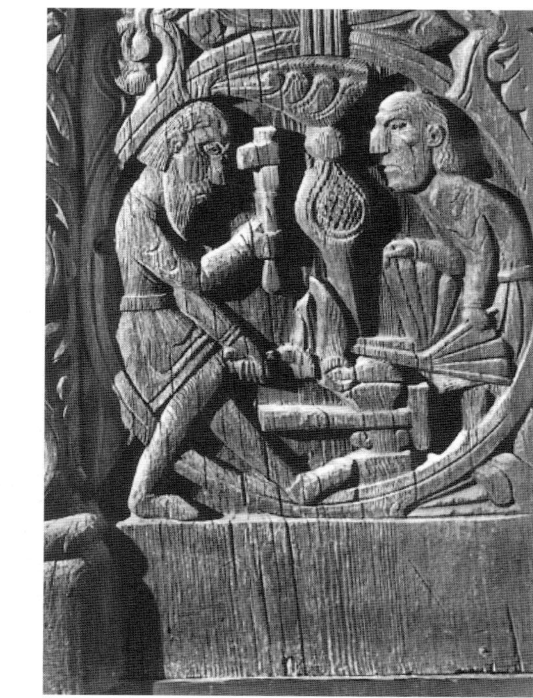

Reginn forges a sword for Sigurðr. Carving on a 12th-century church door from Hylestad, Norway.

A dragon being killed by a man on horseback. Carving on a church door from Valþjófsstaðir, Iceland, made about 1200.

Young man sounding a horn in a forest. 16th-century carving on a seat-panel from Grund, Eyjafjörður, Iceland.

Sigurd,
der Schlangentödter.
Ein Heldenspiel in sechs Abentheuern
von
Friedrich Baron de la Motte Fouqué.

Berlin 1808.
Bei Julius Eduard Hitzig.
(Schützenstraße No. 10.)

Cover of Fouqué's *Sigurd, der Schlangentödter*, Berlin 1808.

Adolf Wagner (1774–1735), Richard's uncle. Drawing made in 1832.

Wagner Looks North

From the discussion in the previous chapter, it should be clear that many of the Icelandic myths, heroic legends and ancient poems which were to occupy Richard Wagner in the latter part of his life had already appeared in German when he was still a child. They were published by some of the foremost scholars in the field at the time. An avid reader like him could therefore easily have got to know this fount of stories during his childhood and youth. It has already been mentioned (p. 17) that during his schooldays in Leipzig (1828–30) Wagner spent long hours in the library of his uncle Adolf, a man who took a keen interest in the classics and linguistics. Wagner says (*Mein Leben* I, 30; *My Life*, 1983, 23):

> His huge library had excited me to feverish reading in all directions, so that I jumped avidly from one area of literature to another, without achieving a basic grounding of any of them.

Unfortunately no catalogue exists of the library of uncle Adolf, comparable with that of his nephew Richard. Adolf is, however, known to have been acquainted with Fouqué, and owned copies of his plays (see p. 92 above), which were largely based on *Vǫlsunga saga*. It is very likely that a man like Adolf Wagner would have owned the majority of the relatively few books on Old Norse literature that had been published from the early nineteenth century onwards, such as the translations published by Friedrich von der Hagen of *Vǫlsunga saga* and *Ragnars saga loðbrókar* (*Altnordische Sagen und Lieder*, 1814) and *Þiðreks saga* (*Nordische Heldenromane*, 1814).

After Richard had reached adulthood, one of the most important publishers of Old Icelandic writings in German was his friend Ludwig Ettmüller, whom Wagner called 'Edda-Müller'. In 1830 he published *Vǫluspá* with a glossary, and later, in 1837, his own translation of *Die Lieder der Edda von den Nibelungen* (including most of the heroic poems of the Poetic Edda). He even attempted to use the Icelandic system of alliteration in his translations. In 1851, the publication of Karl Simrock's translation of the Poetic Edda and the greater part of the Prose Edda marked a milestone. Wagner therefore certainly had plenty of material to choose from when he entered this field about the middle of the nineteenth century.

At this time Wagner owned four editions of *Das Nibelungenlied*, and during the years 1844–48 he borrowed many books on the subject from the Royal Library in Dresden. Yet he frankly says in *Eine Mitteilung an meine Freunde* (A Communication to my Friends) in the summer of 1851 (*AWF* 357–59) that he has never been able to see how to create an opera about Siegfried on the basis of *Das Nibelungenlied* (see also p. 7 above):

> To all our wishes and warm impulses, which in truth transport us to the *Future*, we seek to give a physical token by means of pictures from the Past, and thus to win for them a form the modern Present never can provide. In the struggle to give the wishes of my heart artistic shape, and in the ardour to discover *what* thing it was that drew me so resistlessly to the primal source of old home Sagas, I drove step by step into the deeper regions of antiquity, where at last to my delight, and truly in the *utmost* reaches of old time, I was to light upon the fair young form of *Man*, in all the freshness of his force.
>
> My studies thus bore me, through the legends of the Middle Ages, right down to their foundation in the old-Germanic Mythos; one swathing after another, which the later legendary lore had bound around it, I was able to unloose, and thus at last to gaze upon it in its chastest beauty. What here I saw, was no longer the Figure of conventional history, whose garment claims our interest more than does the actual shape inside; but the real naked Man, in whom I might spy each throbbing of his pulses, each stir within his mighty muscles, in uncramped, freest motion: the type of the true *human being* . . .
>
> Although the splendid type of *Siegfried* had long attracted me, it first enthralled my every thought when I had come to see it in its purest human shape, set free from every later wrappage. Now for the first time, also, did I recognise the possibility of making him the hero of a drama; a possibility that had not occurred to me while I only knew him from the medieval *Nibelungenlied*.

Wagner, admittedly, does not here state unequivocally what the 'primal source' and 'old-Germanic Mythos' are. But he can hardly be meaning anything other in this connection than Icelandic sagas and poems. He had quite simply nothing else to choose from. Moreover, the Danish composer Niels W. Gade recalled in his old age that in April 1846 he had met Wagner, who was conducting Beethoven's Ninth Symphony in Dresden. Wagner said to Gade: 'I must study these Old Norse eddic poems of yours; they are far more profound than our medieval poems' (*Dokumente*, 26).

In his autobiography Wagner also states directly that his reading of Franz Joseph Mone's bold studies of German heroic stories led him to turn his attention to other 'German' heroic legends than those about the Nibelungs and German re-tellings of heroic stories (*Mein Leben* I, 394–95; *My Life* 1983, 343; *Dokumente*, 27):

> I became especially attracted to the unusually rich pages of Mone's investigations of these heroic legends, even though stricter scholars have criticized them as overly audacious. This drew me irresistibly to the nordic sources of these myths, and to the extent that it was possible without fluent knowledge of the Scandinavian languages, I now tried to get to know the Eddas, as well as the prose fragments comprising the basis for large parts of these legends. Viewed in the light of Mone's comments, the *Wälsunga saga* exerted a decisive influence on the manner in which I began to form this material to my own purposes. The consciousness of the close primeval kinship of these old myths, which had been shaping within me for some time, thus gradually gained the power to create the dramatic forms which governed my subsequent works.

It is clear that the verse-form of eddic poems and the setting of *Vǫlsunga saga* had appealed to Wagner, and that he felt that these works bore witness to a more fundamental stage of culture than *Das Nibelungenlied* and other medieval German poems. The characters and their qualities, as well as many aspects of the stories, certainly differ considerably from what one finds in *Das Nibelungenlied.*

Wagner says that he read these works during the period 1847 to 1848, at the same time as he was working on the music for *Lohengrin*, which he completed in April 1848. The theatre-goer Eduard Devrient noted in his diary on 1 April 1848 that Wagner had walked with him in the Grosser Garten in Dresden, and told him of a new idea for an opera based on the story of Siegfried and the Nibelungs (*Dokumente*, 29).

Composition of Libretto and Music

Wagner started on the libretto of the *Ring* in the autumn of 1848, constructing his own myth under the influence, which will be traced as far as possible in detail in the chapter on Comparison with Sources below, of the various ancient writings he had read. The first outline,

VAULU-SPÁ.

Das älteste

Denkmal germanisch-nordischer Sprache,

nebst

einigen Gedanken über Nordens Wissen und Glauben

und

nordische Dichtkunst

von

Ludwig Ettmüller.

Leipzig, 1830.

Weidmannsche Buchhandlung.

819.1 Ett

Title-page of Ettmüller's edition of *Vǫluspá*, Leipzig 1830, 'The earliest monument of Germanic-Nordic language'.

Die Edda

die ältere und jüngere

nebst den

mythischen Erzählungen der Skalda

übersetzt und mit Erläuterungen begleitet

von

Karl Simrock.

Zweite, vermehrte und verbesserte Auflage.

Stuttgart und Augsburg.

J. G. Cotta'scher Verlag.

1855.

819.1 Edd

Title page of Simrock's translation of the Poetic and Prose Eddas, first published in Stuttgart in 1851.

which he completed on 4 October, is only about eight pages long, and yet it actually contains the framework for the whole of *Der Ring des Nibelungen*. At this period, however, Wagner had only one opera in mind, *Siegfrieds Tod* (The Death of Siegfried), which would later become *Götterdämmerung*. *Der Nibelungen-Mythus* was thus at this stage just the backcloth for this eventual opera.

Only two weeks later, on 20 October, he completed the first prose draft of a libretto for *Siegfrieds Tod*, and shortly afterwards an outline for the scene with the Norns intended for the opening of the same opera. After this the libretto was shelved for two and a half years. At this time Wagner was forced to flee the country because of his part in the Dresden uprising in the spring of 1849, and settled in Switzerland. He might never have pursued the project any further, any more than he did with his drafts for music dramas on Frederick Barbarossa, Jesus of Nazareth and Vǫlundr (Wayland the Smith), all of which he compiled during the years 1848–50, but which he got no further with (see pp. 24–27 above).

In the spring of 1851, however, he returned to the Siegfried material. The most likely incentive for this seems to be the publication at the end of February of Karl Simrock's new translation of almost all the eddic poems and most of the narratives of the Prose Edda. This gave Wagner an excellent overview of the Eddas and Norse mythology. Before long he realised that it would be necessary to compose another opera, on Siegfried's youth, in order to explain better what led up to the hero's death. His friend Eduard Devrient had in fact already pointed this out to him in the winter of 1848–49. So in May 1851 Wagner wrote two versions in prose for *Der Junge Siegfried* (The Young Siegfried), and finally one in verse in June. This was to be a comic opera, and a deliberate contrast to what followed (*Dokumente*, 28).

In the autumn of 1851 Wagner came to the conclusion that two further operas would be required in order to accommodate all the material he wanted to include. He mentions this in letters to Theodor Uhlig on 12 October and 11–12 November, and to Franz Liszt on 20 November, 1851. So from early November 1851 to late May 1852, he was compiling the libretto for *Das Rheingold* and *Die Walküre*.

Wagner published fifty copies of the entire libretto in February 1853, and presented them to friends and relatives. Ten years later, in 1863, it was published on a commercial scale, with the revisions he had made up to that time (see *Dokumente*, 57–60, 77–78; Strobel 1930, 262).

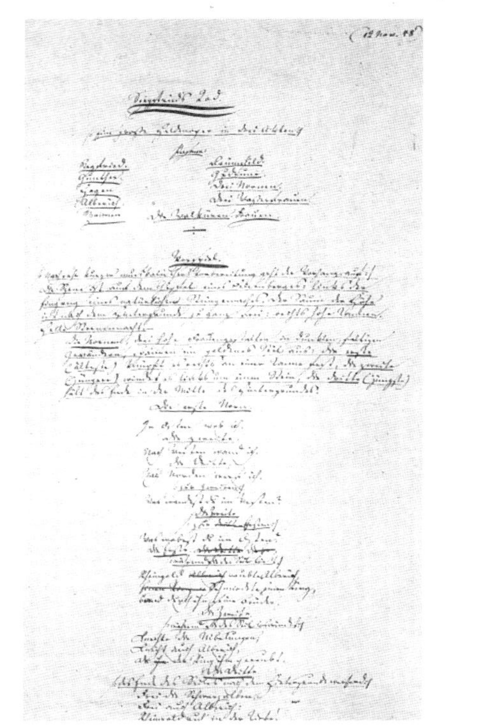

Draft of *Siegfrieds Tod*, 1848

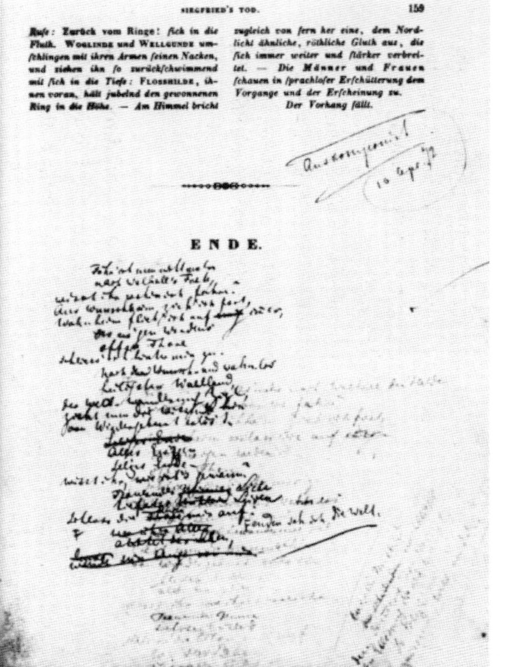

SIEGFRIED'S TOD. 159

Rufe: Zurück vom Ringe! sich in die Fluth. WOGLINDE und WELLGUNDE umschlingen mit ihren Armen seinen Nacken, und ziehen ihn so zurückschwimmend mit sich in die Tiefe: FLOSSHILDE, ihnen voran, hält jubelnd den gewonnenen Ring in die Höhe. — Am Himmel bricht zugleich von fern her eine, dem Nordlicht ähnliche, röthliche Gluth aus, die sich immer weiter und stärker verbreitet. — Die Männer und Frauen schauen in sprachloser Erschütterung dem Vorgange und der Erscheinung zu.

Der Vorhang fällt.

ENDE.

Last page of *Siegfrieds Tod* (p. 159 of the libretto of *The Ring*, privately printed in 1853) with Wagner's handwritten alterations. The work eventually became *Götterdämmerung*.

Here the original titles of the last two operas, *Der junge Siegfried* and *Siegfrieds Tod*, have been changed to *Siegfried* and *Götterdämmerung* (The Twilight of the Gods).

From the above it can be seen that Wagner wrote the librettos of the four parts of the *Ring* in reverse order, starting with the last. After this he began to compose the music, starting now at the beginning of the story (cf. pp. 28 and 39 above). Between November 1853 and August 1857 he completed the music for *Das Rheingold* and *Die Walküre*, and began work on *Siegfried*. After this he put the opera cycle aside for seven years while he composed *Tristan and Isolde* and *The Mastersingers*. He then completed *Siegfried* in 1864–71 and *Götterdämmerung* in 1869–74.

Icelandic Literature and Wagner

The Icelandic writings Wagner clearly made most use of, directly or indirectly, in writing *Der Ring des Nibelungen*, are the Prose Edda, the Poetic Edda, *Vǫlsunga saga* and *Þiðreks saga*, along with a few details from *Heimskringla, Egils saga* and *Gísla saga*. These sources will be briefly discussed here. Direct links between these and other books and the text of *Der Ring des Nibelungen* will be discussed later as they arise.

1. The Prose Edda was, as early as 1300, attributed to Snorri Sturluson, who probably compiled it at his home in Reykholt between about 1220 and 1230. The meaning of the word *edda* is not entirely clear; it can, for instance, mean great-grandmother. But as the title of a book it probably means 'poetics' and the Prose Edda is essentially a handbook for poets. In order to understand the ancient poetic language, however, it was necessary to know something of various ancient myths of gods and heroes, and so the Prose Edda has often been seen as a guide to Norse mythology. Versions of the book survive in three vellum manuscripts and a number of vellum fragments from the fourteenth and fifteenth centuries, which are preserved in Copenhagen, Uppsala and Reykjavik. A paper copy of a lost vellum manuscript, from around 1595, is preserved in Utrecht, Holland. Since it was first compiled, additions to and adaptations of the original text have often been made, and the Prose Edda was first published, based on a much altered seventeenth-century version with Latin and Danish translations, in Copenhagen in 1665 (see p. 81 above).

Snorri Sturluson's warm pool at his home at Reykholt. Photograph by Mats Wibe Lund.

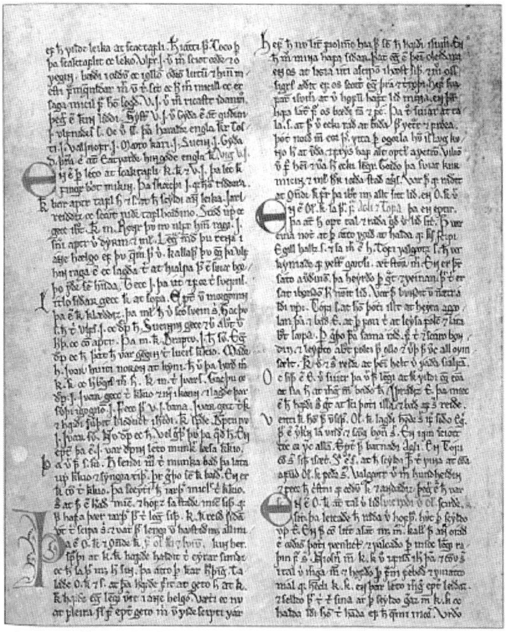

A page from Kringla, the oldest manuscript fragment of Snorri Sturluson's history of the kings of Norway, *Heimskringla* (Lbs frg. 82, c. 1258–1264).

2. The Poetic Edda is a collection of mythological and heroic poems. The oldest extant manuscript, which dates from about 1270, contains about 30 poems. This came into the possession of Bishop Brynjólfur Sveinsson in 1643. The bishop believed that the collection was the work of the eleventh-century scholar Sæmundr the Wise, and so he called it 'Sæmundr's Edda,' just as the Prose Edda is known as 'Snorri's Edda' in Icelandic. Although this was a misunderstanding, the name 'Sæmundr's Edda' has continued to be used. In 1662 Bishop Brynjólfur gave the book to the king of Denmark, since when it has been known as the *Codex Regius of the Eddic Poems* or *Konungsbók eddukvæða* (the king's book of eddic poems). This manuscript is now in the keeping of Stofnun Árna Magnússonar in Reykjavik. Some of the poems in it are found in other medieval books and fragments, and further comparable poems of rather later date are preserved in various other manuscripts, so that the eddic poems in all may be said to total about 1600 stanzas.

The poems are probably of varied date, and are likely to have evolved gradually in oral tradition. The oldest of them may date back to long before the settlement of Iceland. This is all speculation, however, and there is no hard evidence other than the late-thirteenth-century Icelandic written versions of the poems, which do, nevertheless, appear to contain many ancient motifs. *Vǫluspá* (The Seeress's Prophecy) and *Hávamál* (Words of the High One) were published with Latin translations in Copenhagen in 1665; the first volume of a complete edition of eddic poems was published by the Árni Magnússon Foundation in Copenhagen in 1787 and the second in 1818, but this work was not completed until 1828, when the third and final volume appeared, and the first complete text was that edited by Rasmus Rask in 1818.

3. *Vǫlsunga saga* is one of the so-called Heroic Sagas (*fornaldarsögur*, 'sagas of ancient time'), which are set in prehistoric times outside Iceland. Its historical background in general is the period of migrations in Europe, that is the fourth to sixth centuries, and the story reflects warfare between Burgundians, Huns and Goths. The god and goddess, Óðinn and Frigg, also appear at the beginning of the saga. *Vǫlsunga saga* was largely written on the basis of the heroic poems of the Edda, probably in the late thirteenth century. It also contains material from poems which have not been preserved in the actual Edda manuscript. The oldest extant manuscript of *Vǫlsunga saga* dates from about 1400.

The saga was first printed in Stockholm in 1737, together with Latin and Swedish translations.

4. *Þiðreks saga af Bern* is something between a Heroic Saga and a *chanson de geste* in prose. It is disjointed, comprising many diverse episodes, and indeed the foreword states that the saga was written down from German oral stories and poems. 'Bern' is not Berne in Switzerland but Verona in Italy, and 'Þiðrekr' is Theodoricus, king of the Ostrogoths around AD 500. In the thirteenth century many German merchants visited Bergen in Norway, and it is probable that the saga was written down there. The oldest extant manuscript dates from about 1300. Although preserved in Stockholm, this manuscript appears to have been written by Norwegians and Icelanders. A slightly different version is preserved in later Icelandic manuscripts. The saga was first printed in Stockholm with Swedish and Latin translations in 1715.

5. *Heimskringla* is a history of the kings of Norway from legendary times until 1177. It was written in Iceland in the first half of the thirteenth century, but most of the surviving manuscripts are later copies. Since the sixteenth century *Heimskringla* has been attributed to Snorri Sturluson. The first publication of the bulk of the book was in Stockholm with Swedish and Latin translations in 1697.

6. *Egils saga Skalla-Grímssonar* and *Gísla saga Súrssonar* belong to the actual Sagas of Icelanders, which are principally concerned with Icelandic farmers and travellers, and take place mainly in Iceland. These sagas were consequently not printed and translated into foreign languages until later than the sagas whose subjects were less restricted. *Egils saga* was first printed on Hrappsey in Iceland in 1782, and a Danish translation of the whole saga was published in Denmark in 1839 by N. M. Petersen (*Historiske Fortællinger om Islændernes Færd hjemme og ude* I). *Gísla saga* was first printed at Hólar in Iceland in 1756, and a Danish translation appeared in 1845. In 1816 a selection from the Icelandic sagas translated into German by Karl Lachmann was published in Berlin (*Sagaenbibliothek des skandinavischen Alterthums in Auszügen)*. It contains brief selections and retellings from 66 sagas, 50 of them from Sagas of Icelanders and the shorter tales (*þættir*). Each chapter is usually only a few pages in length. Wagner owned a copy of this book.

Verse-Form

In *Eine Mitteilung an meine Freunde* (1851), Wagner declared that he did not find a verse-form with the right metre for the light-footed Siegfried until he discovered the alliterative form in the same 'primal myth' where he had found the young Siegfried (*AWF* 375–76; *Dokumente* 51–52; cf. the Preface to the proposed publication of *Siegfrieds Tod* in 1850, *Dokumente* 34):

> When I sketched my *Siegfried* — for the moment leaving altogether out of count its form of musical completion — I felt the impossibility, or at least the utter unsuitability, of carrying-out that poem in modern verse . . . Just so as this Human Being moved, must his spoken utterance need to be. Here sufficed no more the merely *thought-out* verse, with its hazy, limbless body; the fantastic cheat of terminal Rhyme could no longer throw its cloak of seeming flesh above the total lack of living bony framework, above the viscid cartilage, here stretched capriciously and there compressed, that verse's hulk still holds within as makeshift. I must have straightway let my 'Siegfried' go, could I have dressed it only in such verse. Thus I must needs bethink me of a Speech-melody quite other. And yet, in truth, I had not to bethink, but merely to resolve me; for at the primal mythic spring where I had found the fair young Siegfried-man, I also lit, led by his hand, upon the physically-perfect mode of utterance wherein alone that man could speak his feelings. This was the *alliterative* verse, bending itself in natural and lively rhythm to the actual accents of our speech, yielding itself so readily to every shade of manifold expression, — that *Stabreim* which the Folk itself once sang, when *it* was still both Poet and Myth-Maker.

Wagner had discovered alliteration, of course, in the eddic verse forms, which are still used today in Icelandic poems. But it is not unreasonable to call this alliterative form 'Old Germanic', since examples of such poetry are known in German from before AD 900. Best known is a fragment of *Das Hildebrandslied*, of which the first half exists in an early ninth-century manuscript (W. Braune, *Althochdeutsches Lesebuch*, 1958, no. XXVIII). The subject is not Sigurðr Fáfnisbani, but is closer in content to *Ásmundar saga kappabana* ('slayer of warriors'; *Fornaldar sögur Norðurlanda* I, 383–408).

Before Wagner, attempts had been made, by Fouqué (1810), Friedrich von der Hagen (1814) and Ludwig Ettmüller (1837) among others, to imitate the alliterative form in translations and retellings. In the introduction to his edition of the heroic poems of the Poetic Edda in 1837, Ettmüller had also written at length about eddic verse-forms. Wagner is known to have been in touch with Ettmüller in Zürich around the time when he was working on the libretto of the *Ring* in 1851–52. The old scholar offered him advice, though Wagner himself says little of this. Finally, it is worth reiterating that when Wagner wrote *Eine Mitteilung an meine Freunde* in the summer of 1851, he had recently acquired Karl Simrock's new translation of both Eddas, which was a milestone in the promulgation of Old Icelandic literature in German, and also served as an excellent model for alliterative writing, as Simrock himself was a talented versifier (see Wille 1935, 27; Magee 1990, 50–52).

As far as Wagner's use of alliteration is concerned, it must be admitted that he would not earn a high grade were he an Icelandic high-school student today. He tends to over-alliterate, by the standards of the formal Icelandic alliterative system, which has strict rules regarding the position and number of the alliterating sounds. For example, look at Alberich's first words in Scene 1 of *Das Rheingold*, when he intervenes in the game of the Rhine Maidens, with alliteration on the letter *n* (lines 20–25; on the text used and form of reference to Wagner's librettos see p. 128 below):

He he! Ihr **N**icker!	Ha, ha! You nixies!
Wie seid ihr **n**iedlich,	How dainty you are,
neidliches Volk!	you delectable creatures!
Aus **N**ibelheim's Nacht	From Nibelheim's night
naht' ich mich gern,	I'd gladly draw near
neigtet ihr auch zu mir.	if only you'd look on me kindly.

Still, he would not actually fail the test of alliterative skill, and in fact the eddic forms are much less strict than the rules of prosody invented in later times by literary scholars. In any case, Wagner was not actually trying, rather incompetently, to *imitate* eddic verse structure. He developed his own verse-forms after putting a good deal of thought into the kind of line that would be suitable for music drama in German, and concluded that he needed short lines that could be driven forward by alliteration in units of varying length and rhythm. Plasticity was always the major concern of Wagner's mature work, and consequently the eddic 'long line' as such, end-stopped and balanced about its caesura, did not have the quality he wanted. Nevertheless he seems to have drawn from his encounter with this poetry the idea of functional (rather than ornamental) alliteration, and a general economy of syllables.

Overall, Wagner did an excellent job, considering that the alliterative form was quite foreign to him. He generally alliterates in a graceful manner, for added emphasis. An example of this is in Brünnhilde's exhortation to Sieglinde in Act III Scene 1 of *Die Walküre* when she tells her that she carries in her womb the world's noblest hero, which is reminiscent of the eddic verse-form *ljóðaháttr* 'song-form' (lines 3644–48):

Denn eines **w**iss'	Know this alone
und **w**ahr' es immer:	and ward it always:
den **h**ehrsten **H**elden der Welt	The world's noblest hero
heg'st du, o Weib,	O woman, you harbour
im **sch**irmenden **Sch**oß!	within your sheltering womb.

It would be an interesting project for a composer with an ear for Icelandic verse forms to consider whether Wagner's interest in alliterative forms had an influence upon the nature of his music (cf. Wiessner 1924; Þorsteinn Gylfason 1995; Jóhannes Jónasson 1998, 20).

An example of a minor change of wording made by Wagner to accommodate alliteration is a line from Act II Scene 4 of *Götterdämmerung*, when Hagen urges the court to listen to Brünnhilde's complaint. The first version is from November 1848, the second from December 1852 (*SSD* II 199; Huber 1988, 8035–36):

Merket wohl, was die Frau euch klagt! Jetzt merket **k**lug, was die Frau euch **k**lagt!	Mark closely now What the woman discloses!

Wagner's Sources

It is unusual for writers to record precisely in footnotes where they found inspiration for every aspect of their work, and indeed they may not see the process in these terms; rather, they use a variety of ingredients to cook up their own literary brew.

For a writer, Wagner is in fact rather explicit regarding his sources and models, although he does not go into detail. And even if we had no other evidence than Wagner's own remarks quoted above, it seems clear that Old Icelandic poems and sagas made a far greater contribution to the *Ring* than did *Das Nibelungenlied*. The story and wording of the *Ring* also demonstrate this clearly, when the works are compared.

Hardly any episode from *Das Nibelungenlied* has been used as a model, except in the latter part of the final opera of the cycle, *Götterdämmerung*, for which Wagner had completed a detailed first draft,

Siegfried's Tod, two and a half years before he got access to Karl Simrock's Edda translations. Most of the relevant episodes, however, also occur in *Þiðreks saga*, and could just as well well have been derived from there.

Many names in other parts of the *Ring* are also drawn from *Das Nibelungenlied* (using Modern German, not Middle High German spellings), though they are also found in Old Icelandic texts, generally in a rather different form, or in another role, such as Alberich (Álfrekr), Brünnhilde (Brynhildr), Gunther (Gunnarr), Hagen (Hǫgni), Siegfried (Sigurðr), Sieglinde (Sigrlinn), Siegmund (Sigmundr).

In many cases, however, Wagner's knowledge of Old Icelandic texts was via secondary sources such as books by the German scholars and writers Jakob Grimm, Karl Simrock and Fouqué. He made copious use of Grimm's *Deutsche Mythologie*, whence he derived most of his mythological name-forms. Eventually, however, Wagner altered many of the names to his own taste, in order to give them added significance and meaning in German, in accordance with Grimm's understanding of them. Wodan (Óðinn) thus became Wotan (cf. *Wut*, fury, wildness), Fro (Freyr) became Froh (= joyful) and Donar (Þórr) became Donner (= thunder). Gunther's sister was by Grimm named Gudrun, but Wagner changed this to Gutrune, to signify 'good rune(s)' in German. The name is still, however, clearly derived from the Guðrún of Icelandic texts, while Kudrun was the heroine of a medieval German poem of the same name, though the subject is very different. Wagner, naturally enough, also sought to use name-forms that were easily pronounced by German speakers — and singers.

On the other hand, there is no evidence that Wagner ever met Konrad Maurer, one of the leading German experts on Icelandic literature at that time (see p. 14 above), though they were both in and around Munich for eighteen months in 1864–65. This is perhaps not surprising. Maurer was ten years younger, and Wagner had finished writing the entire libretto of the *Ring* twelve years before he went to Munich.

At any rate, Wagner was clearly of the same view as the brothers Grimm and many others, that the culture of northwest Europe was essentially 'German' or Germanic, and so he probably felt that it was unnecessary to specify in which country or region a story originated. And at this time Iceland was, naturally enough, seen only as a Danish or Norwegian colony (cf. p. 10 above). Thirdly, Wagner was less interested in history as such than in myth, which he regarded as transcending time and place. For these reasons, the words *Iceland* and *Icelandic* never appear in his writings.

It is not always easy to discern how Wagner was influenced by his forerunners in the field of Norse literature and myth in the German-speaking world; one cannot always rely on his own statements, or on what he says he remembers, and no deductions can be drawn from his silences. His writings are often contradictory, depending on when they were written, and his autobiography is considered by some to be an unreliable source for his own life.

In 1856, at the request of Franz Müller, a government official in Weimar, Wagner made a note of the ten books that had provided him with most stimulus to write the *Ring*, which he had completed three years before. His list was as follows:

1. 'Der Nibelunge Noth u. die Klage.' Ed. Lachmann.
2. 'Zu den Nibelungen etc.' by Lachmann.
3. 'Grimm's Mythologie.'
4. 'Edda.'
5. 'Volsunga-saga' (translated by Hagen – Breslau).
6. 'Wilkina- und Niflunga saga' (ditto).
7. 'Das deutsche Heldenbuch.' Old edition, also revised by Hagen. Edited by Simrock in 6 volumes.
8. 'Die deutsche Heldensage' by Wilh. Grimm.
9. 'Untersuchungen zur deutschen Heldensage' by Mone (very important).
10. 'Heimskringla' translated by Mohnike (I think!) (*not* by Wachter — bad).

The list appears to have been jotted down in a hurry, giving no indication of how each of these books inspired the writer. It is impossible to say, for instance, what he means by the word 'Edda'. He probably means those editions and translations of the Poetic and Prose Eddas which were already in print. But this scrap of paper has, naturally enough, given rise to considerable debate, and views vary on its reliability.

There has arisen some surprise that the only book that Wagner specifically calls 'very important' is the work of the German historian Mone, published in 1836. In his autobiography Wagner says he read Mone's book in 1847, and that this first sparked his interest in the Norse version of the Nibelung story. He also indicates that, while Mone was not highly respected among language specialists, he himself liked his boldness and imagination. Perhaps this was where Wagner first saw the possibility of creating his own mythological world — as he eventually did — and this could explain the significance of Mone's book in his mind.

Wagner never, on the other hand, mentions Fouqué and his trilogy *Held des Nordens* of 1810 (see p. 92 above). Yet it is quite obvious that some aspects of the structure and story of the *Ring* bear a closer resemblance to Fouqué's version than to the originals in *Vǫlsunga saga* or the Prose Edda. But Wagner's silence regarding Fouqué is quite understandable. He may have been just so familiar with Fouqué's adventure stories that he felt it would be superfluous to mention them. He probably read them in his youth; as mentioned below (p. 117) there were copies of Fouqué's book in his uncle Adolf's library, where Richard read enthusiastically in his youth.

It was in Fouqué's trilogy that Wagner first saw a dramatisation of the Icelandic version of the story of Sigurðr in *Vǫlsunga saga*. The content of the first part of Fouqué's trilogy coincides almost exactly with that of Wagner's *Siegfried* and *Götterdämmerung*.

Special features shared by Fouqué and Wagner include, for instance, the three Norns who chant over Brünnhilde's resting place on the Valkyrie Rock before the second appearance of Siegfried. Fouqué also uses the Norns scene to fill in details about Hjálm-Gunnarr and his enemy Agnarr in the eddic poem *Sigrdrífumál* and in *Vǫlsunga saga* (see W II 4.3 and W III 2.1 below). The Norns do not appear at this point in the Eddas or in *Vǫlsunga saga* and it would seem that their appearance at the beginning of *Götterdämmerung* is drawn from Fouqué (see *Dokumente*, 19; Fouqué 1808, 45–47; Böldl 1996, 366–69; Kühnel 1991, 26).

Nor does Wagner make any reference in his list to the influence of Greek tragedy, though especially Aeschylus's *Oresteia* and *Prometheus Bound* contain various parallels to the myths in the Prose Edda (see Sørensen 1989, 1–24; Sabor 1997, 78–79).

Das Lied vom Hürnen Seyfrid

This Early New High German poem, whose title may be rendered as 'Siegfried of the Horny Skin', has sometimes been regarded as one of Wagner's sources for his concept of Siegfried, though he never says so himself. A version of the poem appears to have been published in Nuremberg around 1530 (the first edition is undated). In 1557 the famous writer and mastersinger Hans Sachs dramatised the story in

Hans Sachs. Lead coin from 1576, the year of his death.

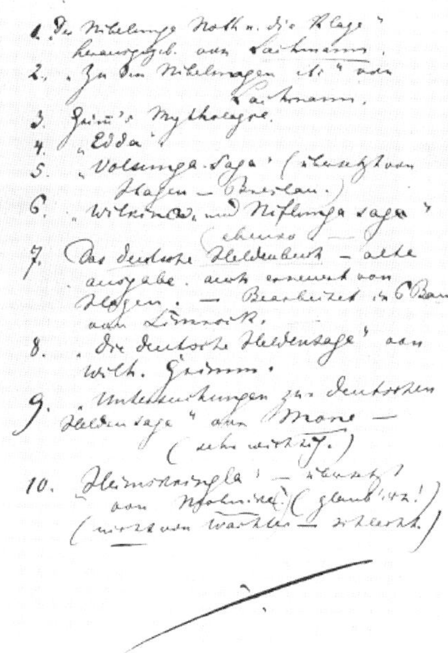

1. „Der Nibelungen Noth u. die Klage"
herausgegeb. von Lachmann.
2. „Zu den Nibelungen etc" von
Lachmann.
3. Grimm's Mythologie.
4. „Edda"
5. „Volsunga-saga" (übersetzt von
Hagen — Breslau.)
6. „Wilkina- und Niflunga saga"
(ebenso —)
7. Das deutsche Heldenbuch — alte
ausgabe. auch erneuert von
Hagen. — Bearbeitet in 6 Bän.
von Simrock.
8. „Die deutsche Heldensage" von
Wilh. Grimm.
9. „Untersuchungen zur deutschen
Heldensage" von Mone —
(sehr wichtig.)
10. „Heimskringla" — übersetzt
von Mohnike (glaub' ich!)
(nicht von Wachter — schlecht.)

Wagner's memorandum of his chief sources for the *Ring*. Among them he names 'Edda', 'Volsunga-saga', 'Wilkina- und Niflunga saga' (i.e. *Þiðreks saga*) and 'Heimskringla'.

seven acts. The poem was published in modern German in 1811, and in Early New High German in 1825. It was also published in a cheap popular edition before the middle of the nineteenth century. It comprises 179 stanzas. Since a role in the making of the *Ring* has been attributed to it, a brief summary of the poem follows:

> King Sigmund and Queen Siglinge of Niderlant have a difficult son, Seyfrid. He is sent away to see the world, finds work with a blacksmith and breaks his anvil. The smith sends him to fetch coals from near the den of a dragon, hoping that the dragon will kill him. Seyfrid kills the dragon, burns the body and smears the fat from the dragon's corpse on his own body. This makes his skin invulnerable ('horny') all over, except for a place he cannot reach, between his shoulder-blades.
>
> He then goes to the court of King Gybich, at Worms on the Rhine. The king has three sons, Günther, Gyrnot and Hagen, and a fair daughter, Krimhilt. Another dragon steals her away to his cave. Gybich announces that he who rescues Krimhilt from the dragon shall receive her hand in marriage.
>
> Dwarves offer to give Seyfrid their gold if he slays the dragon which has stolen it from them. Their king is Eugel, and his father was Nibelung. Eugel tells Seyfrid of Krimhilt in the dragon's cave and the giant Kuperan, who keeps the key to the cave. Eugel makes Seyfrid invisible in a cape (or cap) of mist and he fights the giant. The giant is defeated and Seyfrid finds Krimhilt.
>
> The dragon, who turns out to be a man under a spell, spews fire. Seyfrid slays him, together with another sixty smaller dragons. Eugel accompanies Seyfrid and Krimhilt towards Worms. Seyfrid turns back, fetches the dwarves' gold and sinks it in the Rhine. King Gybich rides to meet Seyfrid and prepares the wedding, which lasts fourteen days. Gybich's sons begin to envy Seyfrid, and Hagen stabs him to death by a spring in Odenwald.

In Wagner's *Nibelungen-Mythus*, three items from the poem may be recognised. First, the name of the dwarf Nibelung, first owner of the gold. Second, the enmity and mutual fear of dwarves and giants. This hostility has no real parallel in Wagner's other sources. Third, Siegfried's behaviour towards the smith in Wagner's work bears some resemblance to that of Seyfrid in the poem, though a similar motif may be seen in *Þiðreks saga*, and even in the fairytale (in the Grimms' *Kinder- und Hausmärchen*, 1850, no. 4, 27–28) of the boy who went out into the world to learn fear.

Use of Sources

From all his sources, Richard Wagner synthesised his own myth, which is integrated and independent. His intention was not to set *Das Nibelungenlied* or the Eddas to music. Instead he used material from many different sources and melded it together in his own crucible. Even so, scholars have long been comparing the librettos of the *Ring* with the early literature that contains models for certain episodes, in order to show which sources are likely, and which highly unlikely. This quest has sometimes, of course, led scholars to extremes. Some cannot see the wood for the trees, while others get lost in it (see, for instance, Golther 1902; Huber 1988; Magee 1990).

As far as is known, no attempt has ever been made before to examine the making of the *Ring* from a primarily Icelandic viewpoint in the search for prototypes and parallels. There are plenty of these to be found in Icelandic literature, however, not least in terms of episodes, wording, and references familiar to Icelanders but not recognised or deemed important by others.

Yet it is not easy to display these parallels, as Wagner gathers material from many different sources and uses the motifs in different places in his writing. Direct borrowings, while they exist, are relatively rare. It is worth reiterating that Wagner's librettos are his own independent creation, though he makes copious use of Old Icelandic literature. In this context, it should be made clear, once and for all, that whether Wagner derived his ideas directly from reading Icelandic sagas and poems, or via versions and retellings by German writers and scholars, the ultimate source is Old Icelandic literature.

Elizabeth Magee's excellent book, published in 1990, is mainly concerned with Wagner's intermediate sources between the primary sources and his own final version. She feels that Wagner's links to the primary sources have been sufficiently explored, as she says in her introduction (p. 15):

> It will also be noted that our subject is the influence of the Nibelung activity of Wagner's contemporaries, not of the primary sources — the *Völsunga saga* and Eddas, *Das Nibelungenlied*, *Das Lied vom Hürnen Seyfrid*, and *Thidreks saga* — themselves. These latter have already been widely, if not fully comprehensively, dealt with by others.

The present author is not in agreement with this last assertion. An attempt will be made here to point out far more cases of prototypes in the primary sources than have hitherto been identified, while less attention will be paid to the intermediaries. Elizabeth Magee has dealt excellently with that subject. Wagner's ideology and interpretation will also largely be left alone, not to mention the music itself.

The chapter on Comparison with Sources will cite examples of medieval Icelandic and German material being used in *Der Nibelungen-Mythus* and early drafts of the *Ring* librettos, even where Wagner later omitted them. They clearly demonstrate how much Wagner had already in 1848 absorbed from the literary sources, even if he subsequently made changes during the development of his work, omitting some things, adding others, abbreviating or expanding, in accordance with his own changing ideology or with the requirements of the music, stage direction or verse-form. As time passed, Wagner appears to have used a freer hand, adding more of his own original ideas.

The Old Icelandic literature considered here comprises the Poetic Edda, Prose Edda, *Vǫlsunga saga* and *Þiðreks saga*, along with a handful of items from *Heimskringla*, *Egils saga* and *Gísla saga* (see pp. 103–06), *Ragnars saga loðbrókar*, and possibly *Sǫrla þáttr*. The German primary sources are principally *Das Nibelungenlied*, *Das Lied vom Hürnen Seyfrid* and the Grimms' *Kinder- und Hausmärchen* (see pp. 78–79, 114). Various versions of older sources compiled by nineteenth-century German writers and scholars (cf. pp. 92–93, 110–12) will be mentioned from time to time. The correspondences will be summarised in tabular form at the end of the discussion of each opera.

Wagner's Reading on the Volsungs and Niflungs

A. In his youth, Wagner spent a good deal of time in his uncle Adolf Wagner's library, which must have included most of the writings that had come out in German about Old Icelandic and other Old Norse literature, as well as those about medieval German literature. It is known that Adolf owned Fouqué's *Sigurd der Schlangentödter* (1808) and *Held des Nordens* (1810). It is very likely that he owned translations of both *Vǫlsunga saga* and *Þiðreks saga*.

B. The following works on relevant topics were in Richard Wagner's own library before 1849:

1. Parts of the Poetic Edda and Prose Edda translated by Friedrich Rühs, Friedrich von der Hagen, C. F. Meyer, Ludwig Ettmüller and the brothers Grimm.
2. Translations of *Heimskringla* by Ferdinand Wachter and Gottlieb Mohnike.
3. Extracts from sixty-six Icelandic sagas translated by Karl Lachmann.
4. Editions of *Nibelungenlied* by A. J. Vollmer, Gustav Pfizer, Karl Simrock and a fourth from 1840 with no editor named.
5. Editions of *Das Lied vom Hürnen Seyfrid* by Karl Simrock and A. J. Vollmer.
6. Editions of *Kudrun* by Adolf Ziemann, Karl Simrock and A. J. Vollmer.
7. L. Frauer, *Die Walkyrien der skandinavisch-germanischen Götter- und Heldensaga*, 1846.
8. W. Grimm, *Deutsche Heldensage*.
9. Jakob Grimm, *Deutsche Mythologie*, *Deutsche Grammatik*, *Geschichte der deutschen Sprache*.
10. J. and W. Grimm, *Deutsche Sagen*.
11. F. Hagen, *Heldenbuch*.
12. Karl Lachmann, *Zu den Nibelungen und zur Klage*.
13. F. Mone, *Untersuchungen zur Geschichte der teutschen Heldensage*.
14. C. Russwurm, *Nordische Sagen*.
15. Hans Sachs, *Der hörnen Seufrid*.
16. Karl Simrock, *Das kleine Heldenbuch*, *Das Amelungenlied*.
17. Ludwig Uhland, *Gedichte*.
18. Karl Weinhold, *Die Sagen von Loki*.

C. The following books were borrowed by Wagner from the Royal Library in Dresden during the years 1844–49:

1. Editions of *Nibelungenlied* by F. Hagen, J. Hinsberg, C. W. Göttling and Karl Lachmann.
2. Editions of and books about the Eddas by J. and W. Grimm, G. T. Legis, J. L. Studach and L. Ettmüller.
3. *Vǫlsunga saga*, ed. F. Hagen.
4. J. Grimm, *Deutsche Rechtsalterthümer*.
5. J. and W. Grimm, *Altdeutsche Wälder*.

D. Finally, it is clear that Wagner made a great deal of use of Karl Simrock's translation of both Eddas after it came out early in 1851, just before he started to work with his full energy on the compilation of the complete libretto of the *Ring*.

FROM DRAFT TO *RING*-CYCLE

Der Nibelungen-Mythus

In order to understand some of the observations in the next chapter on Wagner's librettos, it is useful to have his first draft of the *Ring* at hand. It was written in the autumn of 1848 and originally called *Die Nibelungensage (Mythus)*. This version is to be found in Strobel 1930, 26–33. It was subsequently published as *Der Nibelungen-Mythus. Als Entwurf zu einem Drama* (The Nibelungen-Myth. As Sketch for a Drama) in *GSD* II 156–66 (second edition, 1887–88). Wagner completed the draft on 4 October 1848. It was conceived as the background to *Siegfrieds Tod*, the opera that Wagner had in mind at that time and that became the last opera of the *Ring*-cycle, eventually being renamed *Götterdämmerung*. Nearly two thirds of this draft contain material for the prospective opera, and indeed he completed the libretto of this opera only two weeks later (cf. pp. 101–03 above). The first third of the draft provided the framework for all the other three operas of the cycle: *Das Rheingold, Die Walküre* and *Siegfried*.

Der Nibelungen-Mythus is quoted here from the rather quirky translation by William Ashton Ellis printed in *Pilgrimage to Beethoven and other Essays by Richard Wagner* (reprinted from *Richard Wagner's Prose Works* VII, 1898), 1994, 299–311, which is based on the *GSD* II version. Some adjustment has been made to the spelling and punctuation in the interest of consistency, and the names of the operas to which the episodes of the draft refer appear at the head of each section in square brackets.

[*Das Rheingold*]

From the womb of the Night and Death was spawned a race that dwells in Nibelheim (Nebelheim), i.e. in gloomy subterranean clefts and caverns: *Nibelungen* are they called; with restless nimbleness they burrow through the bowels of the earth, like worms in a dead body; they smelt and smith hard metals. The pure and noble Rhine-gold *Alberich* seized, divorced it from the waters' depth, and wrought therefrom with cunning art a ring that lent him rulership of all his race, the Nibelungen: so he became their master, forced them to work for him alone, and amassed the priceless *Nibelungen-Hoard*, whose greatest treasure is the Tarnhelm, conferring power to take on any shape at will, a work that Alberich compelled his own brother Reigin (Mime = Eugel) to weld for him. Thus armoured, Alberich made for mastery of the world and all that it contains.

The race of *Giants*, boastful, violent, ur-begotten, is troubled in its savage ease: their monstrous strength, their simple mother-wit, no longer are a match for Alberich's crafty plans of conquest: alarmed they see the Nibelungen forging wondrous weapons, that one day in the hands of human heroes shall cause the Giants' downfall. — This strife is taken advantage of by the race of *Gods*, now waxing to supremacy. *Wotan* bargains with the Giants to build the Gods a Burg from whence to rule the world in peace and order; their building finished, the Giants ask the Nibelungen-Hoard in payment. The utmost cunning of the Gods succeeds in trapping Alberich; he must ransom his life with the Hoard; the Ring alone he strives to keep: — the Gods, well knowing that in it resides the secret of all Alberich's power, extort from him the Ring as well: then he curses it; it shall be the ruin of all who possess it. Wotan delivers the Hoard to the Giants, but means to keep the Ring as warrant of his sovereignty: the Giants defy him, and Wotan yields to the counsel of the three Fates (Norns), who warn him of the downfall of the Gods themselves.

Now the giants have the Hoard and Ring safe-kept by a monstrous Worm in the Gnita- (Neid-) Haide [the Grove of Grudge]. Through the Ring the Nibelungs remain in thraldom, Alberich and all. But the Giants do not understand how to use their might; their dullard minds are satisfied with having bound the Nibelungen. So the Worm lies on the Hoard since untold ages, in inert dreadfulness: before the lustre of the new race of Gods the giants' race fades down and stiffens into impotence; wretched and tricksy, the Nibelungen go their way of fruitless labour. Alberich broods without cease on the means of gaining back the Ring.

In high emprise the Gods have planned the world, bound down the elements by prudent laws, and devoted themselves to most careful nurture of the Human race. Their strength stands over all. Yet the peace by which they have arrived at mastery does not repose on reconcilement: by violence and cunning was it wrought. The object of the higher ordering of the world is moral consciousness: but the wrong they fight attaches to themselves. From the depths of Nibelheim the conscience of their guilt cries up to them: for the bondage of the Nibelungen is not broken; merely the lordship has been reft from Alberich, and not for any higher end, but the soul, the freedom of the Nibelungen lies buried uselessly beneath the belly of an idle Worm: Alberich thus has justice in his plaints against the Gods. Wotan himself, however, cannot undo the wrong without committing yet another: only a free Will, independent of the Gods themselves, and able to assume and expiate itself the burden of all guilt, can loose the spell; in Man the Gods perceive the faculty of such free-will. In Man they therefore seek to plant their own divinity, to raise his strength so high that, in full knowledge of that strength, he may rid him of the Gods' protection, to do of his free will what his own mind inspires. So the Gods bring up Man for this high destiny, to be the canceller of their own guilt; and their aim would be attained even if in this human creation they should perforce annul themselves, that is, must part with their immediate influence through freedom of man's conscience. Stout human races, fruited by the seed divine, already flourish: in strife and fight they steel their strength; Wotan's Wish-maids shelter them as Shield-maids, as *Walküren* led the slain-in-fight to Walhall, where the heroes live again a glorious life of jousts in Wotan's company.

[*Die Walküre*]

But not yet is the rightful hero born, in whom his self-reliant strength shall reach full consciousness, enabling him with the free-willed penalty of death before his eyes to call his boldest deed his own. In the race of the *Wälsungen* this hero at last shall come to birth: a barren union is fertilised by Wotan through one of Holda's apples, which he gives the wedded pair to eat: twins, *Siegmund* and *Sieglinde* (brother and sister), spring from the marriage, Siegmund takes a wife, Sieglinde weds a man (Hunding); but both their marriages prove sterile: to beget a genuine Wälsung, brother and sister wed each other. Hunding, Sieglinde's husband, learns of the crime, casts off his wife, and goes out to fight with Siegmund. Brünnhild, the Walküre, shields Siegmund counter to Wotan's commands, who had doomed him to fall in expiation of the crime; already Siegmund, under Brünnhild's shield, is drawing sword for the death-blow at Hunding — the sword that Wotan himself once had given him — when the god receives the blow upon his spear, which breaks the weapon in two pieces. Siegmund falls. Brünnhild is punished by Wotan for her disobedience: he strikes her from the roll of the Walküren, and banishes her to a rock, where the divine virgin is to wed the man who finds and wakes her from the sleep in which Wotan plunges her; she pleads for mercy, that Wotan will ring the rock with terrors of fire, and so ensure that none save the bravest of heroes may win her. —

[*Siegfried*]

After long gestation the outcast Sieglinde gives birth in the forest to *Siegfried* (he who brings Peace through Victory): Reigin (Mime), Alberich's brother, upon hearing her cries, has issued from a cleft and aided her: after the travail Sieglinde dies, first telling Reigin of her fate and committing the babe to his care. Reigin brings up Siegfried, teaches him smithery, and brings him the two pieces of the broken sword, from which, under Mime's directions, Siegfried forges the sword Balmung.

Then Mime prompts the lad to slay the Worm, in proof of his gratitude. Siegfried wishes first to avenge his father's murder: he fares out, falls upon Hunding, and kills him: only thereafter does he execute the wish of Mime, attacks and slays the Giant-worm. His fingers burning from the Worm's hot blood, he puts them to his mouth to cool them; involuntarily he tastes the blood, and understands at once the language of the woodbirds singing round him. They praise Siegfried for his glorious deed, direct him to the Nibelungen-hoard in the cave of the Worm, and warn him against Mime, who has merely used him as an instrument to gain the Hoard, and therefore seeks his life. Siegfried thereon slays Mime, and takes the Ring and Tarnhelm from the Hoard: he hears the birds again, who counsel him to win the crown of women, Brünnhild. So Siegfried sets forth, reaches Brünnhild's mountain, pierces the billowing flames, and wakes her; in Siegfried she joyfully acclaims the highest hero of the Wälsung-stem, and gives herself to him: he marries her with Alberich's Ring, which he places on her finger. When the longing spurs him to new deeds, she gives him lessons in her secret lore, warns him of the dangers of deceit and treachery: they swear each other vows, and Siegfried speeds forth.

[*Götterdämmerung*]

A second hero-stem, sprung likewise from the Gods, is that of the *Gibichungen* on the Rhine: there now bloom *Gunther* and *Gudrun*, his sister. Their mother, Grimhild, was once overpowered by Alberich, and bore him an unlawful son, *Hagen*. As the hopes and wishes of the Gods repose on Siegfried, so Alberich sets his hope of gaining back the Ring on his hero-offspring Hagen. Hagen is sallow, glum and serious; his features are prematurely hardened; he looks older than he is. Already in his childhood Alberich had taught him mystic lore and knowledge of his father's fate, inciting him to struggle for the Ring: he is strong and masterful; yet to Alberich he seems not strong enough to slay the Giant-worm. Since Alberich has lost his power, he could not stop his brother Mime when the latter sought to gain the Hoard through Siegfried: but Hagen shall compass Siegfried's ruin, and win the Ring from his dead body. Toward Gunther and Gudrun Hagen is reticent, — they fear him, but prize his foresight and experience: the secret of some marvellous descent of Hagen's, and that he is not his lawful brother, is known to Gunther: he calls him once an Elf-son.

Gunther is being apprised by Hagen that Brünnhild is the woman most worth desire, and excited to long for her possession, when Siegfried speeds along the Rhine to the seat of the Gibichungs. Gudrun, inflamed to love by the praises he has showered on Siegfried, at Hagen's bidding welcomes Siegfried with a drink prepared by Hagen's art, of such potence that it makes Siegfried forget his adventure with Brünnhild and marriage to her. Siegfried desires Gudrun for wife: Gunther consents, on condition that he helps him win Brünnhild. Siegfried agrees: they strike blood-brothership and swear each other oaths, from which Hagen holds aloof. — Siegfried and Gunther set out, and arrive at Brünnhild's rocky fastness: Gunther remains behind in the boat; Siegfried for the first and only time exerts his power as Ruler of the Nibelungen, by putting on the Tarnhelm and thereby taking Gunther's form and look; thus masked, he passes through the flames to Brünnhild. Already robbed by

Siegfried of her maidhood, she has lost alike her superhuman strength, and all her runecraft she has made away to Siegfried — who does not use it; she is powerless as any mortal woman, and can only offer lame resistance to the new, audacious wooer; he tears from her the Ring — by which she is now to be wedded to Gunther — , and forces her into the cavern, where he sleeps the night with her, though to her astonishment he lays his sword between them. On the morrow he brings her to the boat, where he lets the real Gunther take his place unnoticed by her side, and transports himself in a trice to the Gibichenburg through the power of the Tarnhelm. Gunther reaches his home along the Rhine, with Brünnhild following him in downcast silence: Siegfried, at Gudrun's side, and Hagen receive the voyagers. — Brünnhild is aghast when she beholds Siegfried as Gudrun's husband: his cold civility to her amazes her; as he motions her back to Gunther, she recognises the Ring on his finger: she suspects the imposture played upon her, and demands the Ring, for it belongs not to him, but to Gunther who received it from her: he refuses it. She bids Gunther claim the Ring from Siegfried: Gunther is confused, and hesitates. Brünnhild: 'So it was Siegfried that had the Ring from her?' Siegfried, recognising the Ring: 'From no woman I had it: my right arm won it from the Giant-worm; through it I am the Nibelungen's lord, and to none will I cede its might.' Hagen steps between them, and asks Brünnhild if she is certain about the Ring? If it be hers, then Siegfried gained it by deceit, and it can belong to no one but her husband, Gunther. Brünnhild loudly denounces the trick played on her; the most dreadful thirst for vengeance upon Siegfried fills her. She cries to Gunther that he has been duped by Siegfried: 'Not to thee — to this man am I wed; he won my favour.' — Siegfried charges her with shamelessness: Faithful had he been to his blood-brothership, — his sword he laid between Brünnhild and himself: — he calls on her to bear him witness. — Purposely, and thinking only of his ruin, she will not understand him. — The clansmen and Gudrun conjure Siegfried to clear himself of the accusation, if he can. Siegfried swears solemn oaths in confirmation of his word. Brünnhild taxes him with perjury: All the oaths he swore to her and Gunther, has he broken: now he forswears himself, to lend corroboration to a lie. Everyone is in the utmost commotion. Siegfried calls Gunther to stop his wife from shamefully slandering her own and husband's honour: he withdraws with Gudrun to the inner hall. — Gunther, in deepest shame and terrible dejection, has seated himself at the side, with hidden face: Brünnhild, racked by the horrors of an inner storm, is approached by Hagen. He offers himself as the venger of her honour: she mocks him, as powerless to cope with Siegfried: One look from his glittering eye, which shone upon her even through that mask, would scatter Hagen's courage. Hagen: He well knows Siegfried's awful strength, but she will tell him how he may be vanquished? So she who once had hallowed Siegfried, and armed him by mysterious spells against all wounding, now counsels Hagen to attack him from behind; for, knowing that that the hero ne'er would turn his back upon the foe, she had left it from the blessing. — Gunther must be made a party to the plot. They call upon him to avenge his honour: Brünnhild covers him with reproaches for his cowardice and trickery; Gunther admits his fault, and the necessity of ending his shame by Siegfried's death; but he shrinks from committing a breach of blood-brotherhood. Brünnhild bitterly taunts him: What crimes have not been wreaked on her? Hagen inflames him by the prospect of gaining the Nibelung's Ring, which Siegfried certainly will never part with until death. Gunther consents; Hagen proposes a hunt for the morrow, when Siegfried shall be set upon, and perhaps his murder even concealed from Gudrun; for Gunther was concerned for her sake: Brünnhild's lust-of-vengeance is sharpened by her jealousy of Gudrun. So Siegfried's murder is decided by the three. — Siegfried and Gudrun, festally attired, appear in the hall, and bid them to the sacrificial rites and wedding ceremony. The conspirators feigningly obey: Siegfried and Gudrun rejoice at the show of peace restored.

Next morning Siegfried strays into a lonely gully by the Rhine, in pursuit of quarry. Three mermaids dart up from the stream: they are the soothsaying Daughters of the waters' bed, whence Alberich once had snatched the gleaming Rhine-gold to smite from it the fateful Ring: the curse and power of that Ring would be destroyed, were it re-given to the waters, and thus resolved into its pure original element. The Daughters hanker for the Ring, and beg it of Siegfried, who refuses it. (Guiltless, he has taken the guilt of the Gods upon him, and atones their wrong through his defiance, his self-dependence.) They prophesy evil, and tell him of the curse attaching to the Ring: Let him cast it in the river, or he must die today. Siegfried: 'Ye glib-tongued women shall not cheat me of my might: the curse and your threats I count not worth a hair. What my courage bids me, is my being's law; and what I do of mine own mind, so is it set for me to do: call yet this curse or blessing, it I obey and strive not counter to my strength.' The three daughters: 'Wouldst thou outvie the Gods?' Siegfried: 'Shew me the chance of mastering the Gods, and I must work my main to vanquish them. I know three wiser women than you three; they wot where once the Gods will strive in bitter fearing. Well for the Gods, if they take heed that then I battle *with* them. So laugh I at your threats: the Ring stays mine, and thus I cast my life behind me.' (He lifts a clod of earth, and hurls it backwards over his head.) — The Daughters scoff at Siegfried, who weens himself as strong and wise as he is blind and bond-slave. 'Oaths has he broken, and knows it not: a boon far higher than the Ring he's lost, and knows it not: runes and spells were taught to him, and he's forgot them. Fare thee well, Siegfried! A lordly wife we know; e'en to-day will she possess the Ring when thou art slaughtered. To her! She'll lend us better hearing.' — Siegfried, laughing, gazes after them as they move away singing. He shouts: 'To Gudrun were I not true, one of you three had ensnared me!' He hears his hunting-comrades drawing nearer, and winds his horn: the huntsmen — Gunther and Hagen at the head — assemble round Siegfried. The midday meal is eaten: Siegfried, in the highest spirits, mocks at his own unfruitful chase: But water-game had come his way, for whose capture he was not equipped, alack! or he'd have brought his comrades three wild water-birds that told him he must die today. Hagen takes up the jest, as they drink: Does he really know the song and speech of birds, then? — Gunther is sad and silent. Siegfried seeks to enliven him, and sings him songs about his youth: his adventure with Mime, the slaying of the Worm, and how he came to understand bird-language. The train of recollection brings him back the counsel of the birds to seek Brünnhild, who was fated for him; how he stormed the flaming rock and wakened Brünnhild. Remembrance rises more and more distinct. Two ravens suddenly fly past his head. Hagen interrupts him: 'What do these ravens tell thee?' Siegfried springs to his feet. Hagen: '*I* rede them; they haste to herald thee to Wotan.' He hurls his spear at Siegfried's back. Gunther, guessing from Siegfried's tale the true connection of the inexplicable scene with Brünnhild, and suddenly divining Siegfried's innocence, had thrown himself on Hagen's arm to rescue Siegfried, but without being able to stay the blow. Siegfried raises his shield, to crush Hagen with it; his strength fails him, and he falls of a heap. Hagen has departed; Gunther and the clansmen stand round Siegfried, in sympathetic awe; he lifts his shining eyes once more: 'Brünnhild, Brünnhild! Radiant child of Wotan! How dazzling bright I see thee nearing me! With holy smile thou saddlest thy horse, that paces through the air dew-dripping: to me thou steer'st its course; here is there Lot to choose (*Wal zu küren*)! Happy me thou chos'st for husband, now lead me to Walhall, that in honour of all heroes I may drink All-father's mead, pledged me by thee, thou shining Wish-maid! Brünnhild, Brünnhild! Greeting!' He dies. The men uplift the corpse upon his shield, and solemnly bear it over the rocky heights, Gunther in front.

In the Hall of the Gibichungs, whose forecourt extends at the back to the bank of the Rhine, the corpse is set down: Hagen has called out Gudrun; with strident tones he tells her that a savage boar had gored her husband. — Gudrun falls horrified on Siegfried's body: she rates her brother with the murder; Gunther points to Hagen: he was the savage boar, the murderer of Siegfried. Hagen: 'So be it; an I have slain him, whom no other dared to, whatso was his is my fair booty. The Ring is mine!' Gunther confronts him: 'Shameless Elf-son, the Ring is mine, assigned to me by Brünnhild: ye all, ye heard it.' — Hagen and Gunther fight: Gunther falls. Hagen tries to wrench the Ring from the body, — it lifts its hand aloft in menace; Hagen staggers back, aghast; Gudrun cries aloud in her sorrow; — then Brünnhild enters solemnly: 'Cease your laments, your idle rage! Here stands his wife, whom ye all betrayed. My right I claim, for what must be is done!' — Gudrun: 'Ah, wicked one! 'Twas thou who brought us ruin.' Brünnhild: 'Poor soul, have peace! Wert but his wanton: his wife am I, to whom he swore or e'er he saw thee.' Gudrun: 'Woe's me! Accursed Hagen, what badest thou me, with the drink that filched her husband to me? For now I know that only through the drink did he forget Brünnhild.' Brünnhild: 'O he was pure! Ne'er oaths were more loyally held, than by him. No, Hagen has not *slain* him; for Wotan has he marked him out, to whom I thus conduct him. And I, too, have atoned; pure and free am I: for he, the glorious one alone, o'erpowered me.' She directs a pile of logs to be erected on the shore, to burn Siegfried's corpse to ashes: no horse, no vassal shall be sacrificed with him; she alone will give her body in his honour to the Gods. First she takes possession of her heritage; the Tarnhelm shall be burnt with her; the Ring she puts upon her finger. 'Thou froward hero, how thou held'st me banned! All my rune-lore I bewrayed to thee, a mortal, and so went widowed of my wisdom; thou usedst it not, thou trustedst in thyself alone: but now that thou must yield it up through death, my knowledge comes to me again, and this Ring's runes I rede. The ur-law's runes, too, know I now, the Norns' old saying! Hear then, ye mighty Gods, your guilt is quit: thank him, the hero, who took your guilt upon him! To mine own hand he gave to end his work: loosed be the Nibelungs' thraldom, the Ring no more shall bind them. Not Alberich shall receive it; no more shall he enslave you, but he himself be free as ye. For to you I make this Ring away, wise sisters of the waters' deep; the fire that burns me, let it cleanse the evil toy; and ye shall melt and keep it harmless, the Rhinegold robbed from you to weld to ill and bondage. One only shall rule, All-father thou in thy glory! As pledge of thine eternal might, this man I bring thee: good welcome give him; he is worth it!' — Midst solemn chants Brünnhild mounts the pyre to Siegfried's body. Gudrun, broken down with grief, remains bowed over the corpse of Gunther in the foreground. The flames meet across Brünnhild and Siegfried: — suddenly a dazzling light is seen: above the margin of a leaden cloud the light streams up, shewing Brünnhild, armed as Walküre on horse, leading Siegfried by the hand from hence. At like time the waters of the Rhine invade the entrance to the Hall: on their waves the three Water-maids bear away the Ring and Helmet. Hagen dashes after them, to snatch the treasure, as if demented, — the Daughters seize and drag him with them to the deep.

Draft and Final Version

One can see that most of the major events in the story of the *Ring* are already included in this short draft. Wagner may have taken account of an attempt made by the renowned scholar Karl Lachmann (1836, 339–45) to recreate the original Nibelung myth, but his approach was quite different.

In the final version of *Das Rheingold*, the main additions to the original *Nibelungen-Mythus* are the role of the Rhine Maidens, the struggle over Freia and the apples of youth, and Erda's prophecy. In *Die Walküre*, the only major addition is Fricka's intervention, which forces Wotan to kill Siegmund and throws the god into despair. In

Siegfried, the main additions are Wotan's visit to Mime and their contest of wisdom, the awakening of Erda, and Wotan's attempt to hinder Siegfried's journey to Brünnhilde. Finally, the role of Alberich is developed considerably, both in *Siegfried* and in *Götterdämmerung*. He becomes Wotan's main adversary.

The final part of the draft, the original version of *Götterdämmerung*, is the most developed, containing complete sections of dialogue. More episodes than before are inspired by *Þiðreks saga* or *Das Nibelungenlied*. Wagner, however, treats this material with a free hand, and many of his changes have a greater resemblance to *Vǫlsunga saga* or the Eddas, especially at the ending.

Wagner's first draft contains so many items that resemble *Vǫlsunga saga* that one must question Elizabeth Magee's assertion (1990, 60–61; cf. 44–46) that Wagner had not read this saga before writing *Der Nibelungen-Mythus*. She bases this view on the fact that records do not show him borrowing the saga from the Royal Library in Dresden until three weeks after he completed the draft. But this does not preclude the possibility that a fast reader like Wagner, observant and with an excellent memory, may have quickly read a copy of *Vǫlsunga saga*, belonging to a friend, at some point; Friedrich von der Hagen's translation had been published as early as 1814. Wagner could easily have read it in a single evening. And let us not forget Wagner's hours spent in the library of his uncle Adolf in his youth (see p. 117 above). Or he could have read the book in the reading-room of the Royal Library, without borrowing it.

As mentioned above (p. 99), Wagner wrote in his autobiography that he had read *Vǫlsunga saga* in early 1848, more than six months before he wrote *Der Nibelungen-Mythus* (*Mein Leben* I 30, 394–95). In a letter to Theodor Uhlig of 1851, he describes his efforts to buy a copy of the book while he was still in Dresden; his detailed description of its appearance and size clearly indicate that he knew the book and had handled it, before trying to buy a copy and finally finding it in the library. When he borrowed it, it turned out that he did not need it, as he had remembered everything correctly! (*Dokumente* 57–58, 64)

A multitude of small departures from the original *Nibelungen-Mythus* will be discussed as they arise below. Special mention will be made of those cases where a concept from the Old Icelandic sources that appears in the draft is omitted in the final version.

THE COMPOSITION OF THE RING — OVERVIEW

Wagner wrote the librettos for the four operas of the *Ring* in reverse order (*Götterdämmerung* first, *Das Rheingold* last), though the music for them was composed in the order in which they were intended to be performed, sometimes with long breaks while Wagner turned his mind to other things. The words were compiled always in the same stages, first a rough draft, then a text in prose, and finally the text in verse, though this last sometimes underwent changes before it reached its final form. Below is a schematic overview of the stages of composition. The first sketch for the plot, *Die Nibelungensage (Mythus)*, was completed 4 October 1848.

NAME	AVERAGE LENGTH	DRAFT	PROSE TEXT	VERSE TEXT	DRAFT OF MUSIC	FINAL MUSIC
Das Rheingold	2′ 30″	Nov. 1851	March 1852	Sept.–Nov. 1852	Nov. 1853–Jan. 1854	Feb.–May 1854
Die Valkyrie						
Act I	1′ 10″					
Act II	1′ 30″					
Act III	1′ 10″					
Total	3′ 50″	Nov. 1851	May 1852	June 1852	June–Dec. 1854	Jan. 1855–Mar. 1856
Siegfried						
Act I	1′ 20″					
Act II	1′ 15″					
Act III	1′ 25″					
Total	4′ 00″	May 1851	May 1851	June 1851	Sept. 1856–Aug. 1869	Oct. 1856—Feb. 1871
Götterdämmerung						
Act I	2′ 00″					
Act II	1′ 10″					
Act III	1′ 20″					
Total	4′ 30″	Oct. 1848	Nov. 1848	Nov. 1848–Dec. 1852	Oct. 1869–Apr. 1872	May 1873–Nov. 1874
Whole cycle	14′ 50″					

COMPARISON WITH SOURCES

Method of reference

A. *Wagner's libretto*

Each item in the list of comparisons is identified by act (in roman numerals), scene (in arabic numerals) and item number (arabic numerals). G = *Götterdämmerung* (G. P. = Prologue), R = *Das Rheingold,* S = *Siegfried,* W = *Die Walküre.*

Quotations from the final version of the libretto of the *Ring*, and the translations of them, are from *Wagner's Ring* 1993 (reprinted 2000), except for the German text of the stage directions, which is not given in that edition and is taken from the edition of the relevant full score as published by Schott (Mainz): *Das Rheingold*, *Sämtliche Werke* 10, ed. Egon Voss, 1988; *Die Walküre*, 1874; *Siegfried*, 1876; *Götterdämmerung*, *Sämtliche Werke* 13, ed. Hartmut Fladt, 1981. These are the editions on which the text and translation in *Wagner's Ring* 1993 are based. Numbers in brackets refer to lines of the *Ring* in Huber 1988; in the case of stage directions, the number of the immediately preceding or following line of verse text is given.

References to early draft versions of Wagner's librettos are shown in square brackets [ ].These are generally taken from Strobel 1930, with references to page numbers, but references to the older version of *Siegfrieds Tod* (later *Götterdämmerung*) and other works are to volume and page of *SSD*.

References to Wagner's *Die Nibelungensaga (Mythus)* or *Der Nibelungen-Mythus* (also in square brackets) are made to the pages of the English translation, pp. 118–25 above.

B. Poetic Edda

Reference is made to individual eddic poems by stanza number. The edition generally used and quoted is *Edda. Die Lieder des Codex Regius nebst verwandten Denkmälern*, ed. Gustav Neckel, 4th edn rev. Hans Kuhn, 1962, but the spelling is normalised. For the poems *Grógaldr* and *Fjǫlsvinnsmál* the text used is that of *Norrœn Fornkvæði*, ed. S. Bugge, 1867 (repr. 1965), 338–51. The translations are by Anthony Faulkes.

C. Prose Edda

The text is quoted from Snorri Sturluson, *Edda.* Part 1, *Prologue and Gylfaginning*, 1988, and Part 2, *Skáldskaparmál*, 1998. Ed. Anthony Faulkes. The translations are generally from Snorri Sturluson, *Edda.* Trans. Anthony Faulkes, 1987, reprinted 1998. Both are cited by chapter number (*SnE* G = *Gylfaginning*,

SnE S = *Skáldskaparmál*; note that the first few chapters of *Skáldskaparmál* are conventionally numbered as a continuation of *Gylfaginning*).

D. *Vǫlsunga saga*

Text and translation (with some modification) cited by chapter number in *Vǫlsunga Saga. The Saga of the Volsungs*. Ed. and trans. R. G. Finch, 1965.

E. *Þiðreks saga*

Quoted by chapter numbers from the edition of Guðni Jónsson, 1951 (the same as in C. R. Unger's edition of 1853), with the chapter numbers of H. Bertelsen's edition (1905–11) in brackets. The translations are by Anthony Faulkes.

F. *Das Nibelungenlied (NL)*

Reference is made by stanza number and the number of the *Aventiure*, in the edition of Karl Bartsch, 1948. The translation used is that of A. T. Hatto, 1965.

G. *Das Lied vom Hürnen Seyfrid*

Reference is made to stanza numbers in the edition of Wolfgang Golther, 1911.

DAS RHEINGOLD

CHARACTERS	ICELANDIC EQUIVALENTS*
Rhine Maidens	
Flosshilde	[Fljóthildr]
Wellgunde	[Vellgunnr]
Woglinde	[Váglinda]
Nibelungs	
Alberich	Advari, Álfrekr
Mime	Reginn, Mímir
Gods	
Wotan	Óðinn
Fricka	Frigg, Lofn, Vár
Freia	Freyja, Iðunn
Donner	Þórr
Froh	Freyr
Loge	Loki, Logi
Erda	Jǫrð, Vala
Giants	
Fafner	Fáfnir
Fasolt	Reginn

*The names in brackets are those used in the surtitles for the production of the *Ring* in Reykjavik in 1994, which were presented in an Icelandic version by Þorsteinn Gylfason. They are not found in early Icelandic texts.

Wagner's Nibelungs

The plural word *Nibelungen* (Icelandic *Niflungar*) has various meanings in medieval sources. In the Prose Edda, Niflungar is a name for the Gjúkungar (the sons of Gjúki), Gunnarr and Hǫgni. In the first part of *Das Nibelungenlied* they appear as human heroes, living in Nibelunge lant, served by both giants and dwarves. In the latter part of the poem, and in *Þiðreks saga*, the name is used of the royal family of the Burgundians, as in several of the eddic poems. In *Das Lied vom Hürnen Seyfrid*, on the other hand, the Nibelungs are dwarves, whose ancestor was called Nibelung. Wagner appears to adopt this idea, although he also imbues his Nibelungs with various attributes of dark-elves and dwarves, as described in the Poetic and Prose Eddas. *Der Nibelungen-Mythus* says of the Nibelungs (p. 118 above):

> *From the womb of the Night and Death was spawned a race that dwells in Nibelheim (Nebelheim), i.e. in gloomy subterranean clefts and caverns: Nibelungen are they called.*

The genitive singular *Nibelungen* in the title of *The Ring* refers to Alberich.

Nibelheim or *Nebelheim* is a nineteenth-century Germanisation of the Icelandic *Niflheimr*, which often occurs in the Prose Edda, and is believed to mean 'world of mists' or 'world of darkness'.

Der Nibelungen-Mythus continues:

> *With restless nimbleness they burrow through the bowels of the earth, like worms in a dead body; they smelt and smith hard metals.*

The wording of this passage is clearly derived from the Prose Edda (*SnE* G14):

> *Þar næst settusk guðin upp í sæti sín ok réttu dóma sína ok mintusk hvaðan dvergar hǫfðu kviknat í moldunni ok niðri í jǫrðunni svá sem maðkar í holdi.*
>
> *(Next the gods took their places on their thrones and instituted their courts and discussed where the dwarfs had been generated from in the soil and down in the earth like maggots in flesh.)*

And in the Prose Edda, dwarves and black elves down in the earth are often said to own precious metals, and to be unusually skilful smiths. They were commissioned, for instance, to make various magical items for the gods.

Das Rheingold, Scene One

R.1.1

Three Rhine Maidens guard a hoard of gold at the bottom of the Rhine. Their names, all of which are reminiscent of water and waves, are invented by Wagner (*Ring*, 1–19).

[In *Der Nibelungen-Mythus* they do not appear until just before Siegfried's murder (G. III.1.1), where they are called 'weissagende Töchter der Wassertiefe' ('soothsaying Daughters of the waters' bed', p. 123 above). In the original draft of early October, 1848, *Die Nibelungensaga (Mythus)*, they were said to have swans' wings ('Drei Meerfrauen mit Schwanenflügeln', Strobel 1930, 30).]

The Rhine Maidens are largely Wagner's own creation, though they may have been based on various folk-tales.

A suggestion might also have come from *Þiðreks saga*, where Hǫgni speaks with *sjókonur* ('sea-women') who have come from the Rhine to a nearby lake, and kills two of them (364 (397)). In *Das Nibelungenlied*, Hagene also speaks with *merewîp* in the Danube (*NL* 1533–49, *Av*. 25). In both cases, however, the events take place long after the slaying of Sîfrit/Sigurðr, when the Nibelungs are making their final journey to King Etzel/Attila.

The swans' wings of the Rhine Maidens in *Die Nibelungensaga (Mythus)* are very likely derived from the eddic poem *Vǫlundarkviða* (1–2), the prose introduction of which says:

> *Snemma of morgin fundu þeir á vatnsstrǫndu konur þrjár, ok spunnu lín. Þar váru hjá þeim álptarhamir þeira. Þat váru valkyrjur.*
>
> *(Early in the morning, they found on the shore of the lake three women, and they were spinning linen. Near them were their swan-shapes; they were valkyries.)*

A little over a year later Wagner wrote an opera libretto on Wayland the Smith, which is partly based upon Karl Simrock's retelling of *Vǫlundarkviða* (see p. 27 above; *SSD* III 178–206).

R. 1.2

The dwarf Alberich intervenes in the game of the Rhine Maidens, and tries to grab one of them (*Ring*, 20–196).

Alberich's name is derived from the Albrîch of *Das Nibelungenlied*, who is first introduced as a strong dwarf in the service of the Nibelung kings. After Sîfrit has won the hoard of gold from the Nibelungs, he forces Albrîch to become guardian of the gold (*NL* 96–99, *Av*. 3; 493–502, *Av*. 8). His name is also reminiscent of the dwarf Álfrekr in *Þiðreks saga*, who was renowned for his skill and thievery (16 (28)).

R. 1.3

The luminous Rhinegold appears (*Ring*, 197):

Durch die Flut ist von oben her ein immer lichterer Schein gedrungen, der sich an einer hohen Stelle des mittlesten Riffes allmählich zu einem blendend hell strahlenden Goldglanze entzündet; ein zauberisch goldenes Licht bricht von hier durch das Wasser.

(An increasingly bright glow penetrates the floodwaters from above, flaring up as it strikes a point high up on the central rock and gradually becoming a blinding and brightly beaming gleam of gold; a magical golden light streams through the water from this point.)

The 'Rhinegold' name is Wagner's own idea, but all the sources used for comparison here, except *Þiðreks saga*, mention gold in the river Rhine, a prize which men strive to possess. In the Middle Ages the Upper Rhine deposited alluvium of golden sand. But the idea of luminous gold occurs only in the Prose Edda, in a description of a feast held for the gods by the giant Ægir (a personification of the ocean) in his hall under the sea (*SnE* S33):

> *En er goðin hǫfðu sezk í sæti þá lét Ægir bera inn á hallargólf lýsigull þat er birti ok lýsti hǫllina sem eldr ok þat var þar haft fyrir ljós at hans veizlu.*
>
> *(And when the gods had taken their places, Ægir had glowing gold brought into the middle of the hall which illuminated and lit up the hall like fire, and this was used as lights at his feast.)*

R. 1.4

Alberich hears the Rhine Maidens chattering about the power of the gold, and how it can be gained (*Ring*, 253–57, 269–74, 299–302, 314–17):

Wellgunde:	
Der Welt Erbe	*The world's wealth*
gewänne zu eigen,	*would be won by him*
wer aus dem Rheingold	*who forged from the Rhinegold*
schüfe den Ring,	*the ring*
der maaßlose Macht ihm verlieh'.	*that would grant him limitless power.*
. . .	
Woglinde:	
Nur wer der Minne,	*Only the man who forswears*
Macht versagt,	*love's sway,*
nur wer der Liebe	*only he who disdains*
Lust verjagt,	*love's delights*
nur der erzielt sich den Zauber	*can master the magic spell*
zum Reif zu zwingen das Gold.	*that rounds a ring from the gold.*
. . .	
Alberich:	
Der Welt Erbe	*The world's wealth*
gewänn' ich zu eigen durch dich?	*might I win through you?*
Erzwäng' ich nicht Liebe,	*Though love can't be gained by force,*
doch listig erzwäng' ich mir Lust?	*through cunning might I enforce its delights?*
. . .	
Das Licht lösch' ich euch aus,	*Your light I'll put out,*
entreiße dem Riff das Gold,	*wrench the gold from the rock*
schmiede den rächenden Ring:	*and forge the avenging ring:*

denn hör' es die Fluth –	*so hear me, you waters: –*
so verfluch' ich die Liebe!	*thus I lay a curse on love!*

In *Das Nibelungenlied* (1124, *Av.* 19) it is said that after the murder of Sîfrit, the hoard of the Nibelungs was taken from Nibelunge lant to Worms:

Der wunsch der lac dar under, von golde ein rüetelîn.
der daz het erkunnet, der möhte meister sîn
wol in aller werlde über ietslîchen man.

(In among the rest lay the rarest gem of all, a tiny wand of gold, and if any had found its secret he could have been lord of all mankind!)

This wand is not mentioned elsewhere in the poem and has no role in it. The idea seems, however, to have taken root in Wagner's mind and to have been applied to the ring itself. Cf. S. II.2.6.

The Poetic and Prose Eddas mention two magic rings, wrought by dwarves. One is the gold ring Draupnir (*SnE* S35, cf. *SnE* G49):

Þá bar fram Brokkr sína gripi. Hann gaf Óðni hringinn ok sagði at ina níundu hverja nótt mundi drjúpa af honum átta hringar jafnhǫfgir sem hann.
(Then Brokk brought out his precious things. He gave the ring to Odin and said that every ninth night there would drip from it eight rings equal to it in weight.)

The other is the ring which Loki takes from the dwarf Andvari (*SnE* S39; cf. R. 4.1):

Dvergrinn bað hann taka eigi bauginn af sér ok lézk mega œxla sér fé af bauginum ef hann heldi.
(The dwarf asked him not to take the ring from him, saying he could multiply wealth for himself from the ring if he kept it.)

In both cases, the power of the ring is solely that it can yield more wealth. There is no mention of forswearing love for wealth, which is Wagner's own idea, and indeed a common motif in Romantic literature.

Das Rheingold, Scene 2

R. 2.1
The gods Wotan, Fricka, Freia, Froh, Donner and Loge are introduced into the story one by one (*Ring*, 323–609).

The names and conduct of the gods are largely consistent with the descriptions given in the Prose Edda of Óðinn, Frigg, Freyja, Freyr, Þórr and Loki (*SnE* G20–35). The names have, however, existed in various different forms in Germanic dialects, and Wagner creates their characters with considerable freedom.

R. 2.2

Giants have built a mighty citadel for Wotan. In return they demand Freia, goddess of youth and love, as had been agreed. These terms were accepted on Loge's advice, and Wotan feels that he is bound by the contract, which is carved on the shaft of his spear (*Ring*, 332–47):

Wotan:

Vollendet das ewige Werk:	*The everlasting work is ended!*
auf Berges Gipfel	*On mountain peak*
die Götter-Burg,	*the gods' abode;*
prächtig prahlt	*resplendent shines*
der prangende Bau!	*the proud-standing hall!*

Fricka:

Dich freut die Burg,	*The stronghold delights you,*
mir bangt es um Freia.	*but I fear for Freia.*
Achtloser, laß dich erinnern	*Heedless husband, don't you recall*
des ausbedungenen Lohn's!	*the payment that was agreed?*

The Prose Edda's account of the citadel-builder includes the following (*SnE* G42):

> *Þat var snimma í ǫndverða bygð goðanna, þá er goðin hǫfðu sett Miðgarð ok gert Valhǫll, þá kom þar smiðr nokkvorr ok bauð at gera þeim borg á þrim misserum svá góða at trú ok ørugg væri fyrir bergrisum ok hrímþursum þótt þeir komi inn um Miðgarð. En hann mælir sér þat til kaups at hann skyldi eignask Freyju, ok hafa vildi hann sól ok mána. Þá gengu Æsirnir á tal ok réðu ráðum sínum, ok var þat kaup gert við smiðinn . . . En því réð Loki er þat var til lagt við hann.*
>
> *(It was right at the beginning of the gods' settlement, when the gods had established Midgard and built Val-hall, there came there a certain builder and offered to build them a fortification in three seasons so good that it would be reliable and secure against mountain-giants and frost-giants even though they should come in over Midgard. And he stipulated as his payment that he should get Freyja as his wife, and he wished to have the sun and moon. Then the Æsir went into discussion and held a conference, and this bargain was made with the builder . . . And it was Loki that was responsible for this being granted him.)*

R. 2.3

[*Der Nibelungen-Mythus* (1848) describes the race of Giants as *ur*-begotten, with 'monstrous strength' and 'simple mother-wit'. See p. 119 above.]

Giants as a separate race turn up in various places in the Poetic and Prose Eddas. Giants, male and female, live in Jǫtunheimar (the World of Giants), and the gods are often attracted to pretty Giant maidens. In other sources, such as *Das Nibelungenlied* (94, *Av.* 3; 487–502, *Av.* 8) Giants only appear as gigantic males, and no Giant maidens are mentioned.

R. 2.4

Fricka rebukes Wotan for believing his treacherous friend, Loge (*Ring*, 425–28):

Daß am liebsten du immer	*So you still prefer to trust*
dem listigen trau'st!	*in that cunning trickster?*
Viel Schlimmes schuf er uns schon,	*Much ill he has caused us already,*
doch stets bestrickt er dich wieder.	*yet ever again he ensnares you.*

The cunning Loki is one of the best-known characters of the Poetic and Prose Eddas; he appears to be a half-god, half-giant (*SnE* G33):

> *Sá er enn talðr með Ásum er sumir kalla rógbera Ásanna ok frumkveða flærðanna ok vǫmm allra goða ok manna. Sá er nefndr Loki eða Loptr, sonr Fárbauta jǫtuns . . . Loki er fríðr ok fagr sýnum, illr í skaplyndi, mjǫk fjǫlbreytinn at háttum. Hann hafði þá speki um fram aðra menn er slœgð heitir, ok vælar til allra hluta. Hann kom Ásum jafnan í fullt vandræði ok opt leysti hann þá með vélræðum.*

> *(That one is also reckoned among the Æsir whom some call the Æsir's calumniator and originator of deceits and the disgrace of all gods and men. His name is Loki or Lopt, son of the giant Farbauti . . . Loki is pleasing and handsome in appearance, evil in character, very capricious in behaviour. He possessed to a greater degree than others the kind of learning that is called cunning, and tricks for every purpose. He was always getting the Æsir into a complete fix and often got them out of it by trickery.)*

The enigmatic relationship between Loki and Óðinn is well known; at one point he is 'comrade and table-companion of Óðinn' (*SnE* S16). He also enters an eating contest with Logi, the personification of fire (*SnE* G46–47), who is also mentioned in *Orkneyinga saga* (ch. 1) and other Old Icelandic texts (see *SnE* S, p. 183). Wagner combines Loki and Logi into a single character of dual nature.

R. 2.5

The giants Fasolt and Fafner enter, and demand payment for their work (*Ring*, 449–67). [In the first version of *Das Rheingold* of November 1851, the giants are named Windfahrer and Reiffrost; four months later they had been renamed Fasolt and Fafner (Strobel 203, 209).]

The older names could be Germanised versions of Icelandic names for giants, such as Vindsvalr and Hrímnir. Fáfnir is of course familiar from the Poetic and Prose Eddas and *Vǫlsunga saga*. The name Fasolt is derived from the Fasold of *Þiðreks saga*, whence it was adopted in heroic poems and stories written by German writers and scholars in the nineteenth century. In these contexts, however, Fasolt/Fasold is simply a man of great strength, and not a giant. Wagner may have chosen the name to alliterate with Fafner. In Icelandic sources, Fáfnir's brothers are named Reginn and Otr.

R. 2.6

Wotan attempts to save Freia (*Ring*, 468–86):

Nennt, Leute, den Lohn: *was dünkt euch zu bedingen?*	*Name your due, good people;* *what are you minded to ask?*

Fasolt:

Bedungen ist, *was tauglich uns dünkt;* *gemahnt es dich so matt?* *Freia, die holde,* *Holda, die freie –* *vertragen ist's –* *sie tragen wir heim.*	*We already asked* *for what seems to us fitting;* *is your memory of it so faint?* *Freia the fair,* *Holda the free –* *it's already agreed:* *we carry her home.*

Wotan:

Seid ihr bei Trost *mit eurem Vertrag?* *Denkt auf andren Dank:* *Freia ist mir nicht feil.*	*Are you out of your minds* *with this contract of yours?* *Think of some other thanks:* *Freia isn't for sale.*

Fasolt:

Was sag'st du, ha! *Sinn'st du Verrath?* *Verrat am Vertrag?* *Die dein Speer birgt,* *sind sie dir Spiel,* *des berath'nen Bundes Runen?*	*What's that you say? Ha!* *You're plotting betrayal?* *Betrayal of our agreement?* *The runes of well-considered contract,* *safeguarded by your spear,* *are they no more than sport to you?*

The Prose Edda says (*SnE* G42):

En at kaupi þeira váru sterk vitni ok mǫrg særi, fyrir því at jǫtnum þótti ekki trygt at vera með Ásum griðalaust ef Þórr kvæmi heim, en þá var hann farinn í Austrveg at berja trǫll.

(But at their agreement there had been mighty witnesses invoked and many oaths, for the giants did not think it safe to be among the Æsir without a

guarantee of safety if Thor were to return home, but at the time he was gone away into eastern parts to thrash trolls.)

R. 2.7

Fafner points out to Fasolt that Freia's apples have more importance than the goddess herself (*Ring*, 530–47):

Freia's Haft	*Holding Freia*
hilft wenig;	*helps us little;*
doch viel gilt's	*much, however, will be gained*
den Göttern sie zu entreißen.	*if we wrest her away from the gods.*
Gold'ne Äpfel	*Golden apples*
wachsen in ihrem Garten;	*grow in her garden;*
sie allein	*she alone*
weiß die Äpfel zu pflegen:	*knows how to tend them;*
der Frucht Genuß	*the taste of the fruit*
frommt ihren Sippen	*confers on her kinsfolk*
zu ewig nie	*endlessly never-*
alternder Jugend;	*ageing youth;*
siech und bleich	*but, sick and wan,*
doch sinkt ihre Blüthe,	*their bloom will wither,*
alt und schwach	*old and weak*
schwinden sie hin,	*they'll waste away,*
müssen Freia sie missen:	*if Freia they have to forgo:*
ihrer Mitte drum sei sie entführt!	*so let her be plucked from their midst!*

The Prose Edda's account of Iðunn and her apples of youth is here transferred to Freia. The Edda says (*SnE* G26):

Bragi heitir einn . . . Kona hans er Iðunn. Hon varðveitir í eski sínu epli þau er goðin skulu á bíta er þau eldask, ok verða þá allir ungir, ok svá mun vera allt til ragnarøkrs.

(There is one called Bragi . . . Idunn is his wife. She keeps in her casket apples which the gods have to feed on when they age, and then they all become young, and so it will go on right up to the Twilight of the Gods.)

R. 2.8

Donner threatens the giants with his hammer (*Ring*, 557–59, 564–67):

Fasolt und Fafner,	*Fasolt and Fafner,*
fühltet ihr schon	*you've felt my hammer's*
meines Hammers harten Schlag?	*heavy blow before?*
. . .	
Schon oft zahlt' ich	*Often before I've*

Riesen den Zoll;	*paid giants their due;*
kommt her! des Lohnes Last	*come here, the debt's discharge*
wäg' ich mit gutem Gewicht!	*I'll weigh out in good measure.*

Such threats from Þórr have various prototypes in verses about the gods in the Poetic Edda, e.g. *Vǫluspá* 26:

Þórr einn þar vá,	*Thor alone there struck a blow,*
þrunginn móði,	*bursting with wrath,*
hann sjaldan sitr	*he seldom sits idle,*
er hann slíkt um fregn.	*when he learns of such things.*

R. 2.9

Wotan forbids Donner to use force, as the contract must be observed (*Ring*, 568–72):

Halt, du Wilder!	*Stop, you firebrand!*
Nichts durch Gewalt!	*Nothing by force!*
Verträge schützt	*My spearshaft*
meines Speeres Schaft:	*safeguards contracts:*
spar' deines Hammers Heft!	*spare your hammer's haft.*

Wotan's reference to the need to uphold rules and contracts is similar to what is said of Óðinn (here described as a king in Sweden) in Snorri Sturluson's *Heimskringla, Ynglinga saga* ch. 8:

Óðinn setti lǫg í landi sínu, þau er gengit hǫfðu fyrr með Ásum.

(Odin established in his land the same laws which had formerly been current among the Æsir.)

R. 2.10

Once Loge has arrived, he is alternately threatened and coaxed to find a way of freeing Freia (*Ring*, 610–24):

Wotan:

Arglistig	*Slyly*
weich'st du mir aus:	*you seek to elude me;*
mich zu betrügen	*take care, in truth,*
hüte in Treuen dich wohl!	*that you don't deceive me.*
Von allen Göttern	*Of all the gods*
dein einz'ger Freund,	*your only friend,*
nahm ich dich auf	*I took you*
in der übel trauenden Troß. –	*into the ill-trusting tribe. –*
Nun red' und rathe klug!	*Now speak and counsel wisely!*
Da einst die Bauer der Burg	*When the citadel's builders*
zum Dank Freia bedangen,	*demanded Freia by way of thanks,*

du weißt, nicht anders	*you know that*
willigt' ich ein,	*I only acquiesced*
als weil auf Pflicht du gelobtest	*because you promised on oath*
zu lösen das hehre Pfand.	*to redeem the noble pledge.*

The Prose Edda says (*SnE* G42):

> *En þat kom ásamt með ǫllum at þessu mundi ráðit hafa sá er flestu illu ræðr, Loki Laufeyjarson, ok kváðu hann verðan ills dauða ef eigi hitti hann ráð til at smiðrinn væri af kaupinu, ok veittu Loka atgǫngu.*
>
> *(And there was agreement among them all that he must have been responsible for this decision who is responsible for most evil, Loki Laufeyjarson, and declared he would deserve an evil death if he did not find a scheme whereby the builder would forfeit his payment, and they offered to attack Loki.)*

R. 2.11

Donner threatens Loge with his hammer (*Ring*, 637–38):

Verfluchte Lohe,	*Accursèd flame,*
dich lösch' ich aus!	*I'll snuff you out!*

In the eddic poem *Lokasenna* 63, Thor says to Loki:

Þegi þú, rǫg vættr!	*Be quiet, perverted creature!*
Þér skal minn þrúðhamarr,	*My mighty hammer, Mjollnir,*
Mjǫllnir, mál fyrnema.	*shall deprive you of speech.*

R. 2.12

The giants agree to accept the Rhinegold instead of Freia. The gold is said to be 'red' (*Ring*, 681–84, 730–33, 801–802):

Loge:

Nur einen sah ich,	*Only one man I saw*
der sagte der Liebe ab:	*who forswore love's delights:*
um rothes Gold	*for the sake of red gold*
entrieth er des Weibes Gunst.	*he forwent women's favours.*
. . .	

Wotan:

Von des Rheines Gold	*Of the gold in the Rhine*
hört' ich raunen:	*I've heard it whispered*
Beute-Runen	*that booty-runes*
berge sein rother Glanz.	*lie hid in its fiery glow.*
. . .	

Fafner:

Uns rauhen Riesen genügt	*We uncouth giants will be content*

des Niblungen rothes Gold.	*with the Niblung's bright red gold.*

Gold is not normally called 'red' in German (in that language the word is more often *gelb*, 'yellow'), but it was, and is, commonly so in Icelandic, for instance in the eddic poem *Reginsmál* 9:

'Rauðu gulli (kvað Hreiðmarr)	*'Red gold', said Hreidmar,*
hygg ek mik ráða munu,	*'I think I'll have at my disposal*
svá lengi sem ek lifi.'	*as long as I live.'*

R. 2.13

When the giants take Freia as their hostage, the gods grow pale and weak (*Ring*, 853–56, 893–97):

Loge:

Wie bang und bleich	*How fearful and wan*
verblüht ihr so bald!	*you wither away so soon!*
Euch erlischt der Wangen Licht;	*The bloom in your cheeks is fading;*
der Blick eures Auges verblitzt! –	*the light has gone from your eyes!*
. . .	
Ohne die Äpfel,	*Without the apples,*
alt und grau,	*old and grey,*
greis und grämlich,	*grizzled and grim,*
welkend zum Spott aller Welt,	*withered and scorned by the whole of the world,*
erstirbt der Götter Stamm.	*the race of gods will perish.*

The Prose Edda recounts the kidnapping of Iðunn and her apples thus (*SnE* G56):

En at ákveðinni stundu teygir Loki Iðunni út um Ásgarð í skóg nokkvorn ok segir at hann hefir fundit epli þau er henni munu gripir í þykkja, ok bað at hon skal hafa með sér sín epli ok bera saman ok hin. Þá kemr þar Þjazi jǫtunn í arnarham ok tekr Iðunni ok flýgr braut með ok í Þrymheim til bús síns. En Æsir urðu illa við hvarf Iðunnar ok gerðusk þeir brátt hárir ok gamlir.

(But at the agreed time Loki lured Idunn out through Asgard into a certain forest, saying that he had found some apples that she would think worth having, and told her she should bring her apples with her and compare them with these. Then giant Thjassi arrived in eagle shape and snatched Idunn and flew away with her to his home in Thrymheim. But the Æsir were badly affected by Idunn's disappearance and soon became grey and old.)

R. 2.14

Wotan and Loge set off for Nibelheim to try to take the gold from Alberich. Donner, Froh and Fricka bid them farewell (*Ring*, 925–28):

Donner:	
Fahre wohl, Wotan!	*Fare well, Wotan!*
Froh:	
Glück auf! Glück auf!	*Good luck! Good luck!*
Fricka:	
O kehre bald *zur bangenden Frau!*	*O come back soon* *to your worried wife!*

This is reminiscent, on the one hand, of two journeys made by Loki to black elves in order to gain their gold and talismans (*SnE* S35, 39). The farewell, on the other hand, is similar to that of Frigg to Óðinn in the eddic poem *Vafþrúðnismál* 4, when he goes in search of the all-wise giant:

Heill þú farir, *heill þú aptr komir,* *heill þú á sinnum sér.*	*Fare thee well!* *Come back safe!* *Be safe on the way!*

Das Rheingold, Scene Three

R. 3.1

Alberich has made himself a magic ring, and he forces other black elves (or dwarves) to make treasures for him. He compels his brother, Mime, to make him the 'Tarnhelm', a helmet which can make him invisible or allow him to take on any shape he pleases (*Ring*, 951–72).

[In *Der Nibelungen-Mythus* Wagner introduces Alberich's brother with the names Reigin (Mime = Eugel); see p. 119 above.]

Reginn the smith is known from the eddic poems *Reginsmál* and *Fáfnismál*, the Prose Edda and *Vǫlsunga saga*; in all these cases he is Fáfnir's brother and Sigurðr's foster-father. In *Þiðreks saga*, the brother of Mímir the smith is called Reginn, who changes himself into a dragon and is slain by Sigurðr (163 (268); 166 (271)). In Fouqué's play *Sigurd der Schlangentödter* (1808), this character is called Reigen.

Mímir (sometimes Mímr) as a wise giant appears in both the Poetic and the Prose Edda (*Vǫluspá* 28, 46; *Sigrdrífumál* 14; *SnE* G15, 51). In *Þiðreks saga* (57 (84), 163 (268)–168 (273)), on the other hand, he is a famous smith, and Sigurðr's foster-father, but not a dwarf. In *Heimskringla*, *Ynglinga saga* ch. 4, Mímir is a hostage of great wisdom, sent by the Æsir to live among the Vanir after the war between these two races of gods. His head is cut off and sent to Óðinn, who casts a spell on it so that the head acquires prophetic powers, and Óðinn carries this with him. In *Das Lied vom Hürnen Seyfrid*, Eugel (Eugeleyne) is the king of the dwarves, oppressed by the giant King Kuperan. Neither Mime nor any equivalent character occurs in *Das Nibelungenlied*.

Gradually the name Mime came to be preferred by Wagner; this can also mean an actor in German.

R. 3.2

Alberich (to Loge and Wotan; *Ring*, 1152–54, 1200–01):

Den Lichtalben	*So Loge now smiles*
lacht jezt Loge,	*on the light-elves,*
der list'ge Schelm:	*cunning rogue that he is?*
. . .	
Den Schwarz-Alben	*You eternal free-livers*
verachtet ihr ewigen Schwelger: –	*scorn the black elf: –*

The Prose Edda says of Álfheimr, the world of elves (*SnE* G17):

> *Þar byggvir folk þat er ljósálfar heita, en døkkálfar búa niðri í jǫrðu, ok eru þeir ólíkir þeim sýnum en myklu ólíkari reyndum. Ljósálfar eru fegri en sól sýnum, en døkkálfar eru svartari en bik.*
>
> *(There live the folk called light-elves, but dark-elves live down in the ground, and they are unlike them in appearance, and even more unlike them in nature. Light-elves are fairer than the sun to look at, but dark-elves are blacker than pitch.)*

Wagner, however, seems to use Lichtalben to mean gods and Schwarz-Alben as another name for dwarfs.

R. 3.3

Concerning the magic helmet, Alberich says (*Ring*, 1245–59):

Den hehlenden Helm	*The masking helmet*
ersann ich mir selbst;	*I thought up myself;*
der sorglichste Schmiedt,	*but Mime – most heedful of smiths –*
Mime, mußt' ihn mir schmieden:	*had to forge it for me:*
schnell mich zu wandeln,	*to transform me swiftly*
nach meinem Wunsch,	*and change my shape*
die Gestalt mir zu tauschen,	*to whatever I want*
taugt der Helm;	*the helmet serves;*
Niemand sieht mich,	*no one sees me,*
wenn er mich sucht;	*though he may seek me;*
doch überall bin ich,	*yet I am everywhere,*
geborgen dem Blick.	*hidden from sight.*

So, ohne Sorge	*And so, free from care,*
bin ich selbst sicher vor dir,	*I'm safe from you, too,*
du fromm sorgender Freund!	*my fondly caring friend!*

The Poetic and Prose Eddas and *Vǫlsunga saga* all mention an *ægishjálmr* ('helmet of terror') which had belonged to Hreiðmarr, and was stolen from him by Fáfnir. Though feared by all, it is not said to confer invisibility (*Fáfnismál* 16–17; *Reginsmál*, prose after stanza 14; *SnE* S40; *Vǫlsunga saga* chs 18, 20).

In *Das Nibelungenlied* Sîfrit forces Albrîch to give him a cloak of invisibility (*NL* 97, *Av.* 3; 431, *Av.* 7; 653 and 661, *Av.* 10). This makes Sîfrit invisible, but there is no mention of shape-changing. From the cloak of invisibility and the terror helmet, Wagner creates the Tarnhelm.

R. 3.4

Loge dares Alberich to change himself into a toad, and then he and Wotan succeed in seizing and manacling him (*Ring*, 1296–1317):

Loge's cunning in getting the better of Alberich is reminiscent of Loki's journey to the land of the (black) elves for gold, to save Óðinn and himself from mortal danger (*Vǫlsunga saga* ch. 14; cf. *SnE* S39):

> *'Einn dvergr hét Andvari,' segir Reginn. 'Hann var jafnan í forsinum, er Andvarafors heitir, í geddu líki . . . Þá sendu þeir Loka at afla gullsins. Hann kom til Ránar ok fekk net hennar, fór þá til Andvarafors ok kastaði netinu fyrir gedduna, en hon hljóp í netit.'*
>
> (*'There was a dwarf whose name was Andvari,' said Reginn. 'He was always in a waterfall known as the Andvari Falls in the semblance of a pike . . . So they sent Loki to get the gold. He went to Ran, got her net, and then went to the Andvari Falls, cast the net in front of the pike, and it ran into the net.'*)

Das Rheingold, Scene Four

R. 4.1

Wotan and Loge force Alberich to give up all the gold and the Tarnhelm, but he does his best to retain the magic ring (*Ring*, 1356–60):

Alberich (aside):

Doch behalt' ich mir nur den Ring,	*But if I can keep the ring for myself,*
des Hortes entrath' ich dann leicht:	*I can easily manage without the hoard:*
den von neuem gewonnen	*for it's soon replenished*

und wonnig genährt	*and splendidly fattened*
ist er bald durch des Ringes Gebot.	*by means of the ring's command.*

The corresponding account in the Prose Edda is (*SnE* S39):

> *Þá sendi Óðinn Loka í Svartálfaheim ok kom hann til dvergs þess er heitir Andvari. Hann var fiskr í vatni, ok tók Loki hann hǫndum ok lagði á hann fjǫrlausn alt gull þat er hann átti í steini sínum. Ok er þeir koma í steininn, þá bar dvergrinn fram alt gull þat er hann átti, ok var þat allmikit fé. Þá svipti dvergrinn undir hǫnd sér einum litlum gullbaug. Þá sá Loki ok bað hann fram láta bauginn. Dvergrinn bað hann taka eigi bauginn af sér ok lézk mega œxla sér fé af bauginum ef hann heldi.*
>
> *(Then Odin sent Loki into the world of black-elves and he came across a dwarf called Andvari. He was a fish in a lake, and Loki captured him and imposed on him as a ransom all the gold he had in his cave. And when they came into the cave the dwarf brought out all the gold he had, and that was a substantial amount of wealth. Then the dwarf slipped under his arm one small gold ring. But Loki saw and told him to hand over the ring. The dwarf asked him not to take the ring from him, saying he could multiply wealth for himself from the ring if he kept it.)*

Finally Wotan forcibly seizes the ring from Alberich, and places it on his finger.

Alberich lays a curse on the ring (*Ring*, 1486–1503, 1514–19):

Wie durch Fluch er mir gerieth,	*Just as it came to me through a curse,*
verflucht sei dieser Ring!	*so shall this ring be accursed in turn!*
Gab sein Gold	*Just as its gold once endowed me*
mir – Macht ohne Maaß,	*with might beyond measure,*
nun zeug' sein Zauber	*so shall its spell now deal*
Tod dem – der ihn trägt!	*death to whoever shall wear it!*
Kein Froher soll	*No joyful man*
seiner sich freu'n,	*shall ever have joy of it;*
keinem Glücklichen lache	*on no happy man*
sein lichter Glanz;	*shall its bright gleam smile;*
wer ihn besitzt,	*may he who owns it*
den sehre die Sorge,	*be wracked by care,*
und wer ihn nicht hat,	*and he who does not*
den nage der Neid!	*be ravaged by greed!*
Jeder giere	*Each man shall covet*
nach seinem Gut,	*its acquisition,*
doch keiner genieße	*but none shall enjoy*
mit Nutzen sein'.	*it to lasting gain.*
. . .	
So – segnet	*And so in direst need*

in höchster Noth	*the Nibelung*
der Nibelung seinen Ring. –	*blesses his ring. –*
Behalt' ihn nun,	*Keep it now*
hüte ihn wohl:	*and guard it well:*
meinem Fluch fliehest du nicht!	*you'll not escape from my curse!*

In the Prose Edda, the story of Loki and the dwarf Andvari continues as follows (*SnE* S39):

> *Loki kvað hann eigi skyldu hafa einn penning eptir ok tók bauginn af honum ok gekk út, en dvergrinn mælti at sá baugr skyldi vera hverjum hǫfuðsbani er átti.*
>
> *(Loki said the dwarf was not going to keep one penny and took the ring from him and went out, and the dwarf pronounced that this ring should be the deadly destruction of whoever possessed it.)*

In the eddic poem *Reginsmál* 5 the dwarf says, as he vanishes into the rock:

Þat skal gull	*That gold,*
er Gustr átti	*which Gust owned,*
brœðrum tveim	*shall cause the death*
at bana verða,	*of two brothers,*
ok ǫðlingum	*and for eight rulers*
átta at rógi;	*be cause of strife;*
mun míns fjár	*from my wealth*
mangi njóta.	*no one shall benefit.*

In *Das Nibelungenlied*, there is no particular curse upon the ring, which in time becomes one of the proofs that Sîfrit has lain with Prünhilt (*NL* 679, *Av.* 10; 847–48, *Av.* 14). There the ring is simply a splendid piece of jewellery, with no magic powers. The same applies to Brynhildr's finger-ring in *Þiðreks saga* 343 (388).

R. 4.2

When they return to the scene, the giants demand enough gold to hide Freia's body entirely (*Ring*, 1560–68):

Fasolt:

Das Weib zu missen,	*To lose the woman,*
wisse, gemuthet mich weh:	*you know, grieves me deeply:*
soll aus dem Sinn sie mir schwinden,	*if she's to fade from my thoughts,*
des Geschmeides Hort	*then heap up*
häufet denn so,	*the hoard of trinkets*
daß meinem Blick	*so that it hides*
die Blühende ganz er verdeck'!	*the radiant child from my sight!*

Wotan:

So stellt das Maaß	*Then set the measure*
nach Freia's Gestalt.	*to Freia's form.*

The giants' demand that Freia be hidden with gold has a clear prototype in the tale of the 'otter-ransom', though the objects are quite different: a goddess of love on the one hand, and a predator on the other. This motif occurs in the Prose Edda and *Vǫlsunga saga*; in the eddic poem *Reginsmál* (prose introduction), Reginn says:

> *Óðinn ok Hœnir ok Loki hǫfðu komit til Andvarafors . . . 'Otr hét bróðir várr,' kvað Reginn, 'er opt fór í forsinn í otrs líki. Hann hafði tekit einn lax ok sat á árbakkanum ok át blundandi. Loki laust hann með steini til bana. Þóttusk Æsir mjǫk hepnir verið hafa ok flógu belg af otrinum. Þat sama kveld sóttu þeir gisting til Hreiðmars ok sýndu veiði sína. Þá tóku vér þá hǫndum ok lǫgðum þeim fjǫrlausn at fylla otrbelginn með gulli ok hylja útan ok með rauðu gulli.'*
>
> *(Odin, Hænir and Loki had come to Andvari's falls . . . 'Our brother was called Otter,' said Regin, 'who often went in the falls in the form of an otter. He had caught a salmon and was sitting on the river bank, eating it in a doze. Loki struck him with a stone and killed him. The Æsir thought they had been very lucky and flayed off the otter's hide. The same evening they went to lodge with Hreidmar and showed what they had caught. Then we seized them and laid down as the ransom for their lives that they must fill the otter's hide with gold and cover it on the outside with red gold.')*

R. 4.3

After Freia has been covered with gold, the giants seek to catch a glimpse of her through the chinks (*Ring*, 1608–13, 1620–27, 1634–36, 1652–58):

Fafner:

Noch schimmert mir Holda's Haar:	*Holda's hair still glints through the gold:*
dort das Gewirk	*that trinket yonder*
wirf auf den Hort!	*add to the hoard!*

Loge:

Wie? auch den Helm?	*What? The helmet as well?*

Fafner:

Hurtig, her mit ihm!	*Be quick, give it here!*

Wotan:

Lass' ihn denn fahren!	*All right, let it go!*
. . .	

Fasolt:

Weh! noch blitzt	*Alas! Her glance*

ihr Blick zu mir her;	*still gleams on me here;*
des Auges Stern	*her starry eye*
strahlt mich noch an:	*still shines upon me:*
durch eine Spalte	*I cannot but see it*
muß ich's erspäh'n! –	*through the crack! –*
Seh' ich dieß wonnige Auge,	*While I still see this lovely eye,*
von dem Weibe lass' ich nicht ab.	*I'll not give up the woman.*
. . .	
Fafner:	
An Wotan's Finger	*On Wotan's finger*
glänzt von Gold noch ein Ring:	*a ring of gold still glints:*
den gebt, die Ritze zu füllen!	*give that to fill the cranny!*
. . .	
Wotan:	
Fordert frech was ihr wollt:	*Brazenly ask for whatever you want,*
alles gewähr' ich;	*everything will I grant you;*
um alle Welt doch	*but not for the world*
nicht fahren lass' ich den Ring!	*shall I give up the ring!*
Fasolt:	
Aus dann ist's!	*Then it's all off!*
beim Alten bleibt's:	*We're back where we started:*
nun folgt uns Freia für immer!	*Freia will follow us now for ever.*

Behind this dramatic scene lies the ancient story of how the gold was stolen from the dwarf Andvari, and how the gods strove to cover the otter-skin bag with gold (*SnE* G39):

Fór hann [Loki] í braut til Hreiðmars ok sýndi Óðni gullit. En er hann sá bauginn þá sýndisk honum fagr ok tók hann af fénu, en greiddi Hreiðmari gullit. Þá fyldi hann otrbelginn sem mest mátti hann ok setti upp er fullr var. Gekk þá Óðinn til ok skyldi hylja belginn með gullinu, ok þá mælir hann við Hreiðmar at hann skal sjá hvárt belgrinn er þá allr hulðr. En Hreiðmarr leit til ok hugði at vandliga ok sá eitt granahár ok bað þat hylja, en at ǫðrum kosti væri lokit sætt þeira. Þá dró Óðinn fram bauginn ok hulði granahárit.

(He [Loki] went off back to Hreidmar's and showed Odin the gold. And when Odin saw the ring he found it beautiful and removed it from the treasure, and started paying Hreidmar the gold. The latter then filled the otter-skin as tightly as he could and stood it up when it was full. Then Odin went up to it and began covering the skin with the gold. Then he told Hreidmar to see whether the skin was now fully covered, and Hreidmar looked and examined closely and saw one whisker and said it must be covered, otherwise it was the end of any agreement between them. Then Odin took out the ring and covered the whisker.)

R. 4.4

The seeress Erda rises up from the earth and speaks to Wotan (*Ring*, 1672–78, 1688–91, 1695–96):

Wie alles war, weiß ich;	*How all things were – I know;*
Wie alles wird,	*how all things are,*
Wie alles sein wird,	*how all things will be,*
seh' ich auch:	*I see as well:*
der ew'gen Welt	*the endless earth's*
Ur-Wala,	*primeval vala,*
Erda mahnt deinen Muth.	*Erda, bids you beware.*
. . .	
Alles was ist, endet!	*All things that are – end.*
Ein düst'rer Tag	*A day of darkness*
dämmert den Göttern:	*dawns for the gods:*
dir rath' ich, meide den Ring!	*I counsel you: shun the ring!*
. . .	
Ich warnte dich –	*I've warned you –*
du weißt genug.	*you know enough.*

Some of these words of Erda's seem to echo lines of the eddic poem *Vǫluspá* (28, 44, 57):

Ein sat hon úti,	*Alone sat she outside,*
þá er inn aldni kom	*when the old one came,*
yggjungr Ása,	*the fearful one of the Æsir,*
ok í augu leit:	*and looked in her eyes:*
'Hvers fregnið mik,	*'What are you asking me?*
Hví freistið mín?'	*Why do you try me?'*
. . .	
Fjǫlð veit hon frœða,	*Much knowledge she has,*
fram sé ek lengra	*I see further ahead*
um ragna rǫk	*beyond the doom of the powers,*
rǫmm, sigtýva.	*mighty, of the victory-gods.*
. . .	
Sól tér sortna,	*The sun begins to go black,*
sígr fold í mar,	*earth sinks into sea,*
hverfa af himni	*vanish from the sky*
heiðar stjǫrnur.	*bright stars.*

And her final words are especially reminiscent of the famous warning with which several stanzas of the poem end (28, 33, 35, 39, 41, 48, 62, 63):

Vituð ér enn, eða hvat?	*Do you see yet, or what?*

The word *vala* (spelled *Wala* in the *Ring*) is a back-formation from Icelandic *vǫlu-*, genitive of *vǫlva*, 'prophetess' (found in the name of the eddic poem *Vǫluspá*). It first appears in the seventeenth century, when it was sometimes taken to be the name of the prophetess in that poem.

R. 4.5

Thus warned, Wotan gives in to the giants' demand (*Ring*, 1711–15):

Wotan:

Zu mir, Freia!	*To me, Freia!*
Du bist befreit:	*You are freed:*
wieder gekauft	*now it's bought back,*
kehr' uns die Jugend zurück! –	*may our youth return! –*
Ihr Riesen, nehmt euren Ring!	*You giants, take your ring!*
Er wirft den Ring auf den Hort.	*(He throws the ring on to the hoard.)*

This episode of the Prose Edda narrative ends with these words (*SnE* G39):

Þá dró Óðinn fram bauginn ok hulði granahárit ok sagði at þá váru þeir lausir frá otrgjǫldunum. En er Óðinn hafði tekit geir sinn en Loki skúa sína ok þurftu þá ekki at óttask, þá mælti Loki at þat skyldi haldask er Andvari hafði mælt, at sá baugr ok þat gull skyldi verða þess bani er átti, ok þat helzk síðan.

(Then Odin took out the ring and covered the whisker and declared that they were now quit of the otter-payment. And when Odin had taken his spear and Loki his shoes and they had no need to have any more fear, then Loki pronounced that it should remain valid, what Andvari had pronounced, that the ring and the gold should be the death of him who possessed it, and this was subsequently fulfilled.)

R. 4.6

The giants quarrel, and fight over the ring and how the gold is to be shared between them (*Ring*, 1716–21, 1726–28, 1737–38):

Fasolt:

Halt, du Gieriger!	*Don't be so greedy!*
gönne mir auch 'was!	*Grant me some, too!*
Redliche Theilung	*Equal shares*
taugt uns beiden.	*befit us both.*

Fafner:

Mehr an der Maid als am Gold	*You set greater store by the maid*
lag dir verliebtem Geck:	*than you did by the gold, you lovesick loon!*
. . .	
theil' ich den Hort,	*If I now share the hoard,*
billig behalt' ich	*it's fair that I keep*
die größte Hälfte für mich.	*the biggest half for myself.*
. . .	

Fasolt:

Mein ist der Ring;	*The ring is mine:*
mir blieb er für Freia's Blick.	*I got it for Freia's glance.*

. . .

As they fight over the ring, Fafner slays Fasolt, and grabs the ring (*Ring*, 1743–44):

Nun blinz'le nach Freia's Blick:	*Now gaze your fill on Freia's glance:*
an den Reif rühr'st du nicht mehr!	*never again will you touch the ring!*

The Prose Edda continues the story (*SnE* S40):

Hreiðmarr tók þá gullit at sonargjǫldum, en Fáfnir ok Reginn beiddusk af nokkvors í bróðurgjǫld. Hreiðmarr unni þeim enskis pennings af gullinu. Þat varð óráð þeira brœðra at þeir drápu fǫður sinn til gullsins. Þá beiddisk Reginn at Fáfnir skyldi skipta gullinu í helminga með þeim. Fáfnir svarar svá at lítil ván var at hann mundi miðla gullit við bróður sinn er hann drap fǫður sinn til gullsins ok bað Regin fara braut, en at ǫðrum kosti mundi hann fara sem Hreiðmarr.

(Hreidmar then took the gold as atonement for his son, and Fafnir and Regin demanded something of it for themselves in atonement for their brother. Hreidmar would not let them have a single penny of the gold. The brothers then undertook this terrible course of action that they killed their father for the gold. Then Regin demanded that Fafnir should divide the gold equally between them. Fafnir replied that there was little likelihood of his sharing his gold with his brother when he had killed his father for the gold, and told Regin to be off, otherwise he would meet the same fate as Hreidmar.)

R. 4. 7

When Fafner has left, Donner and Froh create a walkway to Walhall (*Ring*, 1789–93):

Von ihren Füßen aus zieht sich mit blendendem Leuchten eine Regenbogen-Brücke über das Tal hinüber bis zur Burg . . .

(From their feet a rainbow bridge of blinding radiance stretches out across the valley to the castle . . .)

Froh:

Zur Burg führt die Brücke,	*The bridge leads to the stronghold,*
leicht, doch fest eurem Fuß:	*light yet firm to the foot:*
beschreitet kühn	*tread undaunted*
ihren schrecklosen Pfad!	*its terrorless path!*

The idea of the rainbow bridge is clearly from the Prose Edda, where the rainbow bridge *Bifrǫst* ('shivering way') is often mentioned, most clearly in the following (*SnE* G13):

Þá mælir Gangleri: 'Hver er leið til himins af jǫrðu?' Þá svarar Hár ok hló við: 'Eigi er nú fróðliga spurt. Er þér eigi sagt þat at guðin gerðu brú til himins ok heitir Bifrǫst? Hana muntu sét hafa, kann vera at þat kallir þú regnboga. Hon er með þrim litum ok mjǫk sterk ok ger með list ok kunnáttu meiri en aðrar smíðir.

(Then spoke Gangleri: 'What way is there to heaven from earth?' Then High replied, laughing: 'That is not an intelligent question. Has no one ever told you that the gods built a bridge to heaven from earth called Bifrost? You must have seen it, maybe it is what you call the rainbow. It has three colours and great strength and is built with art and skill to a greater extent than other constructions.)

R. 4.8

Before leading the gods over the bridge, Wotan gives a name to the castle (*Ring*, 1810–13):

Wotan:

Folge mir, Frau:	*Follow me, wife:*
in Walhall wohne mit mir!	*in Valhalla dwell with me!*

Fricka:

Was deutet der Name?	*What meaning lies in the name?*
Nie, dünkt mich, hört' ich ihn nennen.	*Never, I think, have I heard it before.*

The name Walhall is not used in the *Ring* until this point. The gods' hall *Valhǫll* ('hall of the slain') is mentioned in many eddic poems, but the most detailed descriptions are in the Prose Edda (*SnE* G40) and in the eddic poem *Grímnismál* 23:

Fimm hundruð dura	*Five hundred doors*
ok um fjórum tøgum,	*and forty more,*
svá hygg ek at Valhǫllu vera;	*these I think there are in Val-hall;*
átta hundruð einherja	*eight hundred lone fighters*
ganga ór einum durum	*will go through each doorway*
þá er þeir fara at vitni at vega.	*when they go to attack the wolf.*

DAS RHINEGOLD: SURVEY OF MOTIFS

The Ring	Eddic poems	Prose Edda	Vǫlsunga saga	Þiðreks saga	Nibelungenlied	Hürnen Seyfrid
Rheintöchter		Ránardœtr		sjókonur	merewîp	
Rheingold	gold in Rhine	gold in Rhine	gold in Rhine		gold in Rhine	gold in Rhine
Goldglanz		lýsigull				
Subterranean people	dvergar (dwarfs)	svartálfar, døkkálfar (dark-elves)	dvergr	dvergr	strong dwarf	king of dwarfs
Alberich	Andvari	Andvari	Andvari	Álfrekr	Albrîch	
Alberich's ring	ring	dwarf's ring	dwarf's ring	dwarf's ring	ring	
Power of the ring		multiply wealth Draupnir				
Riesen (giants)	jǫtnar (giants)	jǫtnar			huge men	giants
Burg		borg				
Giants desire Freia		giants demand Freyja				giants steal kings'daughter
Wotan's friendship with Loge	*Lokasenna Þrymskviða*	Óðinn's friendship with Loki				
Fafner	Fáfnir	Fáfnir	Fáfnir			
Fasolt				Fasold		
Freia's apples		Iðunn's apples				
eternal youth		eternal youth				

The Ring	Eddic poems	Prose Edda	Vǫlsunga saga	Þiðreks saga	Nibelungenlied	Hürnen Seyfrid
Tarnhelm	œgishjálmr	œgishjálmr	œgishjálmr		magic cape	magic cape
Wotan and Loge betray Alberich	Loki betrays dwarfs	Loki betrays Andvari				
Alberich's curse	dwarf's curse	dwarf's curse	dwarf's curse			
Freia covered with gold	otterskin covered with gold	otterskin covered with gold	otterskin covered with gold			
Erda's wisdom	Vǫlva in *Vǫluspá*					
Du weißt genug!	*Vitið þér enn?*					
Fafner kills Fasolt	Fáfnir kills Hreiðmarr	Fáfnir and Reginn kill Hreiðmarr	Fáfnir kills Hreiðmarr			
Rainbow bridge	Bifrǫst, rainbow	Bifrǫst, rainbow				
Walhall	Valhǫll	Valhǫll				

DIE VALKÜRE

Characters	Icelandic equivalents*
Humans	
Siegmund	Sigmundr
Sieglinde	Signý
Hunding	Siggeirr, Hundingr
Gods	
Wotan	Óðinn
Fricka	Frigg
Valkyries	
Brünnhilde	Brynhildr
Gerhilde	[Geirhildr]
Grimgerde	[Grímgerðr]
Helmwige	[Hjálmweig]
Ortlinde	[Oddlinda]
Rossweisse	[Jófríðr]
Schwertleite	[Hjǫrdís]
Siegrune	[Sigrún]
Waltraute	[Valþrúðr]

*The names in brackets are those used in the surtitles for the production of the *Ring* in Reykjavik in 1994, which were presented in an Icelandic version by Þorsteinn Gylfason. They are not found as names of Valkyries in early Icelandic texts.

Die Walküre

The idea of the valkyries derives from the Eddas and other early poetry. The German word *Walküre* is a nineteenth-century Germanisation of the Icelandic *valkyrja* ('chooser of the slain'). The Prose Edda says (*SnE* G36):

> *Enn eru þær aðrar er þjóna skulu í Valhǫll, bera drykkju ok gæta borðbúnaðar ok ǫlgagna . . . Þessar heita valkyrjur. Þær sendir Óðinn til hverrar orrostu. Þær kjósa feigð á menn ok ráða sigri.*
>
> *(There are still others, whose function it is to wait in Val-hall, serve drink and look after the tableware and drinking vessels . . . These are called valkyries. Odin sends them to every battle. They allot death to men and govern victory.)*

Most of the names of the valkyries were women's names found by Wagner in early German poems and tales, or adaptations of these; there are, however, no valkyries in that literature. On the role of valkyries as conductors of the dead to Walhall, which is not evident in Old Icelandic sources, see J. Grimm, *Deutsche Mythologie* 1854, 393; cf. Ettmüller 1830, 1, 56.

Die Walküre, Act One, Scene One

W. I.1.1

[Before line 1861 of *Der Ring*, there is an extended description of the ash-tree printed in *GSD* (1907) IV, 2. This is not in Wagner's full score, but it is printed in Huber 1988, and the translation is in *Wagner's Ring* 1993 in note 3 on p. 365):

Das Innere eines Wohnraumes. In der Mitte steht der Stamm einer mächtigen Esche, dessen stark erhabene Wurzeln sich weithin in den Erdboden verlieren; von seinem Wipfel ist der Baum durch ein gezimmertes Dach geschieden, welches so durchschnitten ist, daß der Stamm und die nach allen Seiten hin sich ausstreckenden Äste durch genau entsprechende Öffnungen hindurch gehen; von dem belaubten Wipfel wird angenommen, daß er sich über dieses Dach ausbreite.

(The interior of a dwelling. In the middle stands the trunk of a huge ash, whose prominently raised roots extend a considerable distance before disappearing into the ground. The top of the tree is cut off by a timber roof with holes let into it in such a way that the bole of the tree and the boughs which branch out from it pass through the holes, which fit them exactly. We are to imagine that the leafy top of the tree spreads out above this roof.)

Vǫlsunga saga says (ch. 2):

> *Svá er sagt at Vǫlsungr konungr lét gera hǫll eina ágæta, ok með þeim hætti at ein eik mikil stóð í hǫllinni, ok limar trésins með fǫgrum blómum stóðu út um ræfr hallarinnar, en leggrinn stóð niðr í hǫllina.*
>
> *(The tale goes that King Volsung had a magnificent hall built, and in such a way that there was a great oak standing inside, its branches with their colourful flowers spreading out through the roof, while its trunk stretched down into the hall.)*]

Die Walküre, Act One, Scene Two

W. I.2.1

Hunding comes home and finds a stranger (Siegmund) with his wife Sieglinde (*Ring*, 1943–45):

Heilig ist mein Herd: –	*Sacred is my hearth: –*
heilig sei dir mein Haus!	*may my house be sacred to you!*
Rüst' uns Männern das Mahl!	*Prepare a meal for us men!*

The name Hundingr appears in some eddic poems and in *Vǫlsunga saga*. In the introduction to *Helgakviða Hundingsbana II*, Sigmundr and Hundingr are said to be enemies, and in *Vǫlsunga saga* Sigmundr is slain by the sons of Hundingr (chs 11–12).

W. I.2.2

Hunding notices the resemblance between Siegmund and Sieglinde (*Ring*, 1946–48):

Hunding misst scharf und verwundert Siegmund's Züge, die er mit denen seiner Frau vergleicht.

(Hunding examines Siegmund's features closely and with surprise, comparing them with those of his wife.)

Hunding:

Wie gleicht er dem Weibe!	*How like the woman he looks!*
Der gleißende Wurm	*The selfsame glittering serpent*
glänzt auch ihm aus dem Auge.	*is glinting in his eye, too.*

Here the prototype is in *Ragnars saga loðbrókar* (ch. 9; *Fornaldar sögur Norðurlanda* I 244–46). Ragnarr's young wife, Kráka, maintains that she is not the daughter of a peasant, but of a king:

> *Nú spyrr hann, hverr faðir hennar var, ef hún væri eigi dóttir þess ins fátæka karls, er á Spangarheiði var. Hún segir, at hún var dóttir Sigurðar Fáfnisbana ok Brynhildar Buðladóttur . . . ok nú segir hún ok hefr þar upp sǫgu, sem þau hittust á fjallinu Sigurðr ok Brynhildr ok hún var byrjuð. 'Ok er Brynhildr varð léttari, var mér nafn gefit, ok var ek kǫlluð Áslaug.' . . . Þá svarar Ragnarr: 'Þessum mun ek við bregða Áslaugar órunum, er þú mælir.' Hún svarar: 'Þú veizt, at ek em eigi heill maðr, ok mun þat vera sveinbarn, er ek geng með, en á þeim sveini mun vera þat mark, at svá mun þykkja sem ormr liggi um auga sveininum . . . En ek vil, at sjá sveinn sé heitinn eftir feðr mínum, ef í hans auga er þetta frægðarmark, sem ek ætla, at vera muni.' . . . sá inn ungi maðr var borinn í hǫllina ok lagðr í skikkjuskaut Ragnars. En er hann sér sveininn, var hann spurðr, hvat heita skyldi. Hann kvað vísu:*
>
> *(Now he asks who her father was, if she was not the daughter of the poor man who lived on Spangarheath. She said she was the daughter of Sigurd, killer of Fafnir, and Brynhild, daughter of Budli . . . and now she tells him and begins the story where Sigurd and Brynhild met on the mountain, and she was begotten. 'And when Brynhild was delivered I was named and I was called Aslaug.' . . . Then Ragnar answers, 'I am amazed at this fantasy*

about Aslaug that you speak of.' She answers, 'You know that I am now with child, and it will be a boy that I am carrying, and on the boy will be this sign that it will seem that a snake lies round the boy's eye . . . But I desire that this boy be named after my father if that glorious symbol is in his eye, as I think will be the case.' . . . this young person was carried into the hall and laid in the lap of Ragnar's cloak. And when he sees the boy, they asked him what he should be called. He spoke a verse:)

Sigurðr mun sveinn of heitinn,	*Sigurd shall the boy be called;*
sá mun orrostur heyja,	*he will wage battles,*
mjǫk líkr vera móður	*be very like his mother,*
ok mǫgr fǫður kallaðr;	*and be called his father's son;*
sá mun Óðins ættar	*he shall be said to be*
yfirbátr vera heitinn,	*the most outstanding of Odin's line.*
þeim er ormr í auga,	*He has a snake in his eye*
er annan lét svelta.	*who had the other killed.*
. . .	
Sá ek engum sveini	*I have seen in no boy*
nema Sigurði einum	*except in Sigurd*
í brúnsteinum brúna	*laid in the stones of his brows [eyes]*
barðhjarls tauma lagða;	*brown [shining?] field-bands [snakes];*
sjá hefir dagrýrir dýja,	*this keen diminisher of water's shine [of gold, i.e. generous person]*
– dælt er hann at því kenna –	*– he is easy to recognise from it –*
hvass í hvarmatúni	*has in eyelid-field [eye]*
hring myrkviðar fengit.	*got dark-wood's ring [snake].*

Ragnars saga was available in German in Friedrich von der Hagen's *Altnordische Sagen und Lieder* (1814), and would very likely have been in Wagner's uncle Adolf's library (see p. 97 above).

W. I.2.3 (*Ring*, 1948–49)

Er [Hunding] birgt sein Befremden, und wendet sich wie unbefangen zu Siegmund.

(He [Hunding] conceals his dismay and turns to Siegmund as though quite naturally.)

Hunding's character resembles that of King Siggeirr, the husband of Sigmundr's twin sister, Signý, in *Vǫlsunga saga*. When Sigmundr contemptuously refuses to sell him the good sword which he has drawn from the tree (cf. W.I.3.3), the saga says (ch. 3):

> *Siggeirr konungr reiddisk við þessi orð, ok þótti sér háðuliga svarat vera. En fyrir því at honum var svá varit at hann var undirhyggjumaðr mikill, þá lætr hann nú sem hann hirði ekki um þetta mál, en þat sama kveld hugði hann laun fyrir þetta, þau er síðar kómu fram.*

(King Siggeir grew angry at these words, and considered that he had been given an insolent answer, but since he was a great dissembler, he now made as if he didn't mind about this matter, yet that very evening he thought of how he could pay him back, and that is what later came about.)

W. I.2.4

Siegmund conceals his real name, but relates his adventures with his father (*Ring*, 1982–86, 2007–15):

Wolfe, der war mein Vater;	*Wolfe was my father;*
zu zwei kam ich zur Welt,	*as one of twain I came into the world,*
eine Zwillingsschwester und ich.	*a twin-born sister and I.*
Früh schwanden mir	*Mother and maid*
Mutter und Maid.	*soon disappeared.*
. . .	
Geächtet floh	*Outlawed, the old man*
der Alte mit mir;	*fled with me;*
lange Jahre	*deep in the wildwood*
lebte der Junge	*the youngster lived*
mit Wolfe im wilden Wald:	*with Wolfe for many a year:*
manche Jagd	*many's the time*
ward auf sie gemacht;	*they were hunted down;*
doch muthig wehrte	*but wolf and whelp*
das Wolfspaar sich.	*would put up a stout defence.*

His story is reminiscent of the account in *Vǫlsunga saga* ch. 8 of the life of Sigmundr and his son Sinfjǫtli in the woods, in the shape of wolves (cf. also W. II.1.3):

Þat er nú at segja at Sigmundi þykkir Sinfjǫtli of ungr til hefnda með sér ok vill nú fyrst venja hann með nǫkkut harðræði. Fara nú um sumrum víða um skóga ok drepa menn til fjár sér. Sigmundi þykkir hann mjǫk í ætt Vǫlsunga, ok þó hyggr hann at hann sé sonr Siggeirs konungs . . . Nú er þat eitthvert sinn at þeir fara enn á skóginn at afla sér fjár, en þeir finna eitt hús ok tvá menn sofandi í húsinu með digrum gullhringum. Þeir hǫfðu orðit fyrir óskǫpum því at úlfahamir hengu í húsinu yfir þeim. It tíunda hvert dœgr máttu þeir komask ór hǫmunum. Þeir váru konungasynir. Þeir Sigmundr fóru í hamina ok máttu eigi ór komask, ok fylgði sú náttúra sem áðr var, létu ok vargsrǫddu.

(The story now tells how Sigmund thought Sinfjotli too young to go with him in search of vengeance, and decided he would first gain him experience in something that called for grit and determination. For some summers they roved far and wide through the forest and killed people for plunder. Sigmund thought that he took after the Volsungs, and markedly so, but he

believed him to be King Siggeir's son . . . Now one day they went again to the forest in order to find themselves riches, and they came to a cabin, and in the cabin were two men asleep, wearing heavy gold rings. An evil fate had overtaken them, for there were wolf skins hanging above them in the cabin. They could shed the skins once every ten days. They were princes. Sigmund and Sinfjotli got into the skins, and could not get out of them again—the strange power was there, just as before, and they even howled like wolves.)

W. I.2.5

Hunding becomes convinced that Siegmund is of a hostile family, but he decides not to kill the unarmed man until the following morning (*Ring*, 2116–21):

Mein Haus hütet,	*My house, Wölfing,*
Wölfing, dich heut';	*protects you today;*
für die Nacht nahm ich dich auf:	*for the night I have taken you in:*
mit starker Waffe	*but with sturdy weapon*
doch wehre dich morgen;	*defend yourself in the morning;*
zum Kampfe kies' ich den Tag.	*I choose the day for the fight.*

'A manslaughter during the night was considered a murder,' says Jakob Grimm in his *Deutsche Rechtsaltertümer* (1854), 87 n., without citing any source. This motif, however, appears in a few Icelandic sagas. The best-known case is in *Egils saga* ch. 59, when King Eiríkr Blood-Axe and Queen Gunnhildr plan to execute Egill in York. Then their mutual friend, the chieftain Arinbjǫrn, says:

'Eigi mun konungr . . . láta Egil drepa í nótt, því at náttvíg eru morðvíg.' Konungr segir: 'Svá skal vera, Arinbjǫrn, sem þú biðr, at Egill skal lifa í nótt; hafðu hann heim með þér ok fœr mér hann á morgin.'

('He [the king] will not have Egil killed tonight because night-killings are murders.' The king said: 'It shall be as you ask, Arinbjorn, Egil shall live tonight. Take him home with you and bring him to me in the morning.')

This chapter of *Egils saga* existed in German translation in an anthology from 1816, and a copy of this book was in Wagner's own library (see p. 106 above and Westernhagen 1966, 102).

Die Walküre, Act One, Scene Three

W. I.3.1

Left alone for the night, Siegmund ponders his situation; but Sieglinde soon comes to offer him help (*Ring*, 2131–34, 2192–2239):

Siegmund:

Ein Schwert verhieß mir der Vater,	*My father promised me a sword:*
ich fänd' es in höchster Noth. –	*I'd find it in direst need. –*
Waffenlos fiel ich	*Unarmed I chanced*
in Feindes Haus.	*on my enemy's house.*
. . .	

Sieglinde:

Eine Waffe lass' mich dir weisen – :	*Let me show you a weapon:*
O wenn du sie gewänn'st!	*if only you could win it!*
Den hehr'sten Helden	*As the noblest of heroes*
dürft' ich dich heißen:	*might I hail you:*
dem Stärk'sten allein	*the strongest alone*
ward sie bestimmt. –	*was destined to gain it. –*
O merke wohl, was ich dir melde! –	*Heed well what I have to tell you. –*
Der Männer Sippe	*The men from his clan*
saß hier im Saal,	*sat here in the hall,*
von Hunding zur Hochzeit geladen:	*as guests at Hunding's wedding:*
er frei'te ein Weib,	*he was wooing a woman*
das ungefragt	*whom villains, unasked,*
Schächer ihm schenkten zur Frau.	*had given him as his wife.*
Traurig saß ich	*Sadly I sat there*
während sie tranken:	*while they were drinking:*
ein Fremder trat da herein –	*a stranger then came in –*
ein Greis in grauem Gewand;	*an old man dressed in grey;*
tief hing ihm der Hut,	*his hat hung so low*
der deckt' ihm der Augen eines;	*that one of his eyes was hidden,*
doch des and'ren Strahl,	*but the flash of its fellow*
Angst schuf er allen,	*struck fear all around,*
traf die Männer	*as its lowering stare*
sein mächtiges Dräu'n:	*transfixed the men:*
mir allein	*in me alone*
weckte das Auge	*his eye awakened*
süß sehnenden Harm,	*sweetly yearning sorrow,*
Thränen und Trost zugleich.	*mingled with tears and solace.*
Auf mich blickt' er,	*He gazed at me*
und blitzte auf Jene,	*and glared at them*
als ein Schwert in Händen er schwang;	*as he brandished a sword in his hands;*
das stieß er nun	*he then drove it deep*
in der Esche Stamm,	*in the ash-tree's trunk;*
bis zum Heft haftet' es drin: –	*it was buried up to the hilt: –*
dem sollte der Stahl geziemen,	*the steel would rightly belong to him*
der aus dem Stamm' es zög'.	*who could draw it forth from the trunk.*
Der Männer Alle,	*Of all the menfolk,*
so kühn sie sich müh'ten,	*much as they struggled,*

die Wehr sich keiner gewann;
Gäste kamen
und Gäste gingen,
die stärk'sten zogen am Stahl –
keinen Zoll eintwich er dem Stamm':
dort haftet schweigend das Schwert. –
Da wußt' ich, wer der war,
der mich gramvolle gegrüßt:
ich weiß auch,
wem allein
im Stamm' das Schwert er bestimmt.

none could win the weapon;
guests would come
and guests would go,
the strongest tugged at the steel –
not an inch did it stir in the trunk:
in silence the sword still cleaves there. –
I knew then who he was
who greeted me in my grief:
I also knew
for whom alone
he destined the sword in the tree.

In *Vǫlsunga saga* the corresponding account is as follows (ch. 3):

Svá er sagt at þar váru miklir eldar gerðir eptir endilangri hǫllinni, en nú stendr sjá inn mikli apaldr í miðri hǫllinni, sem fyrr var nefndr. Nú er þess við getit, at þá er menn sátu við eldana um kveldit, at maðr einn gekk inn í hǫllina. Sá maðr er mǫnnum ókunnr at sýn. Sjá maðr hefir þess háttar búning, at hann hefir heklu flekkótta yfir sér. Sá maðr var berfœttr ok hafði knýtt línbrókum at beini. Sá maðr hafði sverð í hendi ok gengr at barnstokkinum, ok hǫtt síðan á hǫfði. Hann var hárr mjǫk ok eldiligr ok einsýnn. Hann bregðr sverðinu ok stingr því í stokkinn, svá at sverðit søkkr at hjǫltum upp. Ǫllum mǫnnum fellusk kveðjur við þennan mann. Þá tekr hann til orða ok mælti: 'Sá er þessu sverði bregðr ór stokkinum, þá skal sá þat þiggja at mér at gjǫf, ok skal hann þat sjálfr sanna at aldri bar hann betra sverð sér í hendi en þetta er.' Eptir þetta gengr sjá inn gamli maðr út ór hǫllinni, ok veit engi hverr hann er eða hvert hann gengr. Nú standa þeir upp ok metask ekki við at taka sverðit. Þykkisk sá bezt hafa er fyrst náir. Síðan gengu til inir gǫfgustu menn fyrst, en þá hverr at ǫðrum. Engi kemr sá til er nái, því at engan veg bifask er þeir taka til.

(It is said that big fires were lighted down the length of the hall, and as was mentioned before, the great apple-tree stood there in the middle of the hall. Now the story goes that, while the men were sitting round the fires in the evening, a man came into the hall. It was a man whose appearance was unfamiliar. This is how he was dressed: he had on a mottled cape, he was bare-footed and had bound his linen breeches round the leg. The man held a sword in his hand and went up to Barnstock [the tree in the centre of the hall] and had a low hood over his head; he was very grey, venerable and had but one eye. He drew back the sword and plunged it into the trunk, so that the sword sank in up to the hilt. No one was able to utter a word of welcome to the man. Then he started to speak, and these were his words: 'The man to pull out this sword from the trunk shall receive it from me as a gift, and he will find out for himself that he never bore in hand a better sword than this.' After that the old man went out of the hall, and no one knew who he was or where he was going. They

now got up, and no one hung back in taking hold of the sword. He counted himself best off who got it out first. Then the most notable among them went up first, and afterwards the others, one by one. And not one who went up succeeded, for when they took hold, the sword would not budge.)

W. I.3.2

Wagner definitely hints in the music that Wälse, the father of the twins, was in fact Wotan himself in disguise. [In the *Nibelungen-Mythus* of 1848 (p. 120 above) this is explained in the following way:

> *But not yet is the rightful hero born, in whom his self-reliant strength shall reach full consciousness, enabling him with the free-willed penalty of death before his eyes to call his boldest deed his own. In the race of the Wälsungen this hero at last shall come to birth: a barren union is fertilised by Wotan through one of Holda's apples, which he gives the wedded pair to eat: twins,* Siegmund *and* Sieglinde *(brother and sister), spring from the marriage.*]

In the final version, Wagner did not use this story about the impregnating apple. The story was, however, derived from *Vǫlsunga saga*, where it relates to the royal grandparents of Sigmundr, who in their old age pray to the gods to give them a child (chs 1–2):

> *Þat er nú sagt at Frigg heyrir bœn þeira, ok segir Óðni hvers þau biðja. Hann verðr eigi ǫrþrifaráða ok tekr óskmey sína, dóttir Hrímnis jǫtuns, ok fær í hǫnd henni eitt epli ok biðr hana fœra konungi. Hon tók við eplinu ok brá á sik krákuham ok flýgr til þess er hon kemr þar sem konungrinn er, ok sat á haugi. Hon lét falla eplit í kné konunginum. Hann tók þat epli ok þóttisk vita hverju gegna mundi; gengr nú heim af hauginum ok til sinna manna, ok kom á fund dróttningar ok etr þat epli sumt. Þat er nú at segja at dróttning finnr þat brátt at hon mundi vera með barni . . . Þat var sveinbarn . . . Þessum er nú nafn gefit ok er kallaðr Vǫlsungr.*
>
> *(And we are next told how Frigg heard their prayer and spoke to Odin about their request. He was not at a loss what to do and fetched an adoptive daughter ['wish-maiden', i.e. valkyrie] of his, the daughter of Hrimnir the Giant, put an apple in her hand and told her to take it to the king. She seized the apple, assumed the form of a crow, and flew until she came to where the king was sitting on a howe. She dropped the apple into the king's lap. He picked the apple up and guessed what it was all about. Then he left the howe and went back to his men, had a talk with the queen, and [she] ate part of the apple. You must now hear how the queen soon found that she was going to have a child . . . It was a boy . . . A name was now given to him and he was called Volsung.)*

W. I.3.3

Siegmund reveals his real name and that of his father (*Ring*, 2406–19):

Sieglinde:

Doch nanntest du Wolfe den Vater?	*But Wolfe, you said, was your father?*

Siegmund:

Ein Wolf war er feigen Füchsen!	*A wolf to fearful foxes!*
Doch dem so stolz	*But he whose eye*
strahlte das Auge,	*once flashed as proudly*
wie, Herrliche, hehr dir es strahlt,	*as yours, fair woman, flashes now –*
der war – Wälse genannt.	*Wälse was his name.*

Sieglinde:

War Wälse dein Vater,	*If Wälse's your father*
und bist du ein Wälsung,	*and if you're a Wälsung;*
stieß er für dich	*if he thrust the sword*
sein Schwert in den Stamm –	*in the tree for you –*
so lass' mich dich heißen	*then let me name you*
wie ich dich liebe:	*as I love you:*
Siegmund –	*Siegmund –*
so nenn' ich dich!	*thus do I call you!*

In *Vǫlsunga saga*, Sigmundr and Signý are twin children of King Vǫlsungr (ch. 2):

> *Nú þá er hann var alroskinn at aldri, þá sendir Hrímnir honum Hljóð, dóttur sína . . . Þau áttu tíu sonu ok eina dóttur. Inn elzti sonr þeira hét Sigmundr, en Signý dóttir. Þau váru tvíburar, ok váru þau fremst ok vænst um alla hluti barna Vǫlsungs konungs.*
>
> *(Now when he reached manhood Hrimnir sent his daughter, Hliod, to him . . . They had ten sons and one daughter; their eldest son was called Sigmund, and their daughter Signy. They were twins and in every way the best looking and the most remarkable of King Volsung's children.)*

The names Wälse and Wälsungen do not appear in medieval German; they are simply a Germanisation of the Icelandic names Vǫlsungr (which might have been understood to mean 'descendant of Vǫlsi') and Vǫlsungar, which are known from the Eddas and *Vǫlsunga saga*.

W. I.3.4 (*Ring*, before 2419 and 2441)

Siegmund springt auf . . . Er zieht mit einem gewaltigen Zuck das Schwert aus dem Stamme, und zeigt es der vor Staunen und Entzücken erfassten Sieglinde.

(Siegmund leaps up . . . With a violent effort he draws the sword from the tree and shows it to Sieglinde, who is seized by astonishment and ecstasy.)

Vǫlsunga saga (ch. 3):

> *Nú kom til Sigmundr, sonr Vǫlsungs konungs, ok tók til ok brá sverðinu ór stokkinum, ok var sem laust lægi fyrir honum.*
>
> *(Then Sigmund, the son of King Volsung, came up, gripped the sword and pulled it out of the trunk as if he found it quite loose.)*

W. I.3.5

Siegmund acknowledges his identity, and Sieglinde reveals herself as his sister (*Ring*, 2441–42, 2455–63):

Siegmund:

Siegmund, den Wälsung	*Siegmund the Wälsung*
sieh'st du, Weib!	*you see here, wife!*
...	

Sieglinde:

Bist du Siegmund,	*If you are Siegmund*
den ich hier sehe –	*whom I see here –*
Sieglinde bin ich,	*Sieglinde am I,*
die dich ersehnt:	*who has longed for you:*
die eig'ne Schwester	*your own true sister*
gewann'st du zueins mit dem Schwert!	*you've won for yourself with the sword!*

Siegmund:

Braut und Schwester	*Bride and sister*
bist du dem Bruder –	*you are to your brother –*
so blühe denn Wälsungen-Blut!	*so let the blood of the Wälsungs blossom!*

[The *Nibelungen-Mythus* of 1848 also says (p. 120 above):

> *To beget a genuine Wälsung, brother and sister wed each other.*]

The union of the twins is clearly derived from *Vǫlsunga saga*, which says that Signý wants to have a brave son in order to avenge her father, King Vǫlsungr. After two failed attempts, she disguises herself with the help of a sorceress, and visits her twin brother, Sigmundr, in his hiding place (ch. 7):

> *Nú er þat frá Signýju at segja at hon ferr til jarðhúss bróður síns ok biðr hann veita sér herbergi um nóttina,— 'því at ek hefi villzk á skóginum úti, ok veit ek eigi hvar ek fer.' Hann mælti at hon skyldi þar vera, ok vildi eigi synja henni vistar, einni konu, ok þóttisk vita at eigi mundi hon svá launa honum góðan beina at segja til hans. Nú ferr hon í herbergi til hans, ok setjask til matar. Honum varð opt litit til hennar ok lízk konan væn ok fríð. En er þau eru mett, þá segir hann henni at hann vill at þau hafi eina rekkju um nóttina, en hon brýzk ekki við því, ok leggr hann hana hjá sér þrjár nætr samt. Eptir þat ferr hon heim . . . Ok er fram liðu stundir, fœðir*

Signý sveinbarn. Sá sveinn var Sinfjǫtli kallaðr. Ok er hann vex upp, er hann bæði mikill ok sterkr ok vænn at áliti ok mjǫk í ætt Vǫlsunga.

(Signy, we are now told, went to her brother's retreat and asked him to give her shelter for the night — 'For I am lost here in the forest, and I don't know where I'm going.' He said she could stay there, and that he would not refuse her shelter, all alone as she was, and he felt that she would not repay his hospitality by giving him away. So she joined him in the shelter and they sat down to a meal. He often glanced at her, and she appeared to be a good-looking and attractive woman. And when they were satisfied, he told her that he wanted them to sleep together that night. She made no objection and for three nights in succession he laid her next to him. Afterwards she went back . . . And after some time had passed, Signy gave birth to a son. The boy was called Sinfjotli, and when he grew older he was tall, strong and handsome, and took after the Volsung family very markedly.)

Die Walküre, Act Two, Scene One

W. II.1.1

Wotan and Brünnhilde are revealed as battle deities (*Ring*, 2464–72):

Wotan, kriegerisch gewaffnet mit dem Speer: vor ihm Brünnhilde, als Walküre, ebenfalls in voller Waffenrüstung.

(Wotan, armed for battle, with his spear; before him Brünnhilde, as a valkyrie, likewise fully armed.)

Wotan:

Nun zäume dein Roß,	*Now harness your horse,*
reisige Maid!	*warrior maid!*
Bald entbrennt	*A furious fight*
brünstiger Streit.	*will soon flare up:*
Brünnhilde stürme zum Kampf,	*let Brünnhilde fly to the fray;*
dem Wälsung kiese sie Sieg!	*for the Wälsung let her choose victory!*
Hunding wähle sich	*Hunding may choose*
wem er gehört:	*to whom he belongs:*
nach Walhall taugt er mir nicht.	*he's no use to me in Valhalla.*

Historically, Brunhilda is known as a princess and later as a queen of the Visigoths around AD 600. In legends and poems about the Volsungs and Nibelungs, one of the main characters always carries some variant of her name. Only in the Icelandic version is she said to be a valkyrie.

W. II.1.2

Fricka enters and demands that Siegmund be punished for adultery and incest (*Ring*, 2509–16):

Ich vernahm Hunding's Noth,	*Hunding's distress I heard;*
um Rache rief er mich an:	*he called on me for vengeance:*
der Ehe Hüterin	*wedlock's guardian*
hörte ihn,	*gave him ear*
verhieß streng	*and promised to punish*
zu strafen die That	*severely the deed*
des frech frevelnden Paar's,	*of that brazenly impious pair*
das kühn den Gatten gekränkt.	*that dared to wrong a husband.*

As guardian of wedlock, Fricka here has more in common with the Greek Hera and the Roman Juno than the Norse Frigg. The real guardian of marriage in Norse mythology is called Vár, and there is another goddess called Lofn, who helps lovers. The Prose Edda says of the qualities of these goddesses (*SnE* G35):

Átta Lofn: hon er svá mild ok góð til áheita at hon fær leyfi af Alfǫðr eða Frigg til manna samgangs, kvenna ok karla, þótt áðr sé bannat eða þvertekit . . . Níunda Vár: hon hlýðir á eiða manna ok einkamál er veita sín á milli konur ok karlar . . . Hon hefnir ok þeim er brigða.

(Eighth Lofn: she is so kind and good to pray to that she gets leave from All-father or Frigg for people's union, between women and men, even if before it was forbidden or refused . . . Ninth Var: she listens to people's oaths and private agreements that women and men make between each other . . . She also punishes those who break them.)

W. II.1.3
Fricka accuses Wotan, as Wälse, of wandering wolf-like in the forest (according to *Ring*, 2037–40, he wore a wolf-skin) and of himself begetting the Wälsungs (*Ring*, 2560–2608). She denies that Siegmund is independent of Wotan, since Wotan has given him the sword (*Ring*, 2636–76). Wotan submits (*Ring*, 2725). Compare the parallels from *Vǫlsunga saga* in W. I.2.4 and W. I.3.1–5.

Die Walküre, Act Two, Scene Two

W. II.2.1
Once Fricka has left, Wotan meditates on the events that have led him to his present situation. He tells Brünnhilde how, after the cursing of the Ring, he sought more knowledge from Erda (*Ring*, 2805–13):

Wotan:

Da verlor ich den leichten Muth;	*Then I lost all lightness of heart;*
zu wissen begehrt' es den Gott:	*the god desired knowledge:*

in den Schooß der Welt
schwang ich mich hinab,
mit Liebes-Zauber
zwang ich die Wala,
stört' ihres Wissens Stolz,
daß sie Rede nun mir stand.
Kunde empfing ich von ihr.

into the womb of the world
I descended,
mastered the vala
with love's magic spell
and broke her wisdom's pride,
that she gave account of herself.
Knowledge I gained from her.

The Prose Edda account (*SnE* G58) of Bǫlverkr (Óðinn) visiting Gunnlǫð in order to get the mead of poetry is an obvious model for this scene:

Fór Bǫlverkr þar til sem Gunnlǫð var ok lá hjá henni þrjár nætr, ok þá lofaði hon honum at drekka af miðinum þrjá drykki.

(Bolverk went to where Gunnlod was and lay with her for three nights and then she let him drink three draughts of the mead.)

W. II.2.2

The valkyries, Wotan reveals, were the fruit of his union with Erda (*Ring*, 2815–22):

Wotan:

Der Welt weisestes Weib
gebar mir, Brünnhilde, dich.
Mit acht Schwestern
zog ich dich auf:
durch euch Walküren
wollt' ich wenden,
was mir die Wala
zu fürchten schuf.

The world's wisest woman
bore to me, Brünnhilde, you.
With eight sisters
I brought you up:
through you valkyries
I hoped to avert
the fate that the vala
had made me fear.

It was Wagner's own idea to make Brünnhilde the daughter of Wotan (in the Poetic Edda she is his adoptive daughter, *óskmær*), but the number of the valkyries is taken from the Eddas. The mothers of Heimdallr and the daughters of Ægir and Rán are both also said to number nine. In the eddic poem *Helgakviða Hjǫrvarðssonar* (prose before stanza 6) it says:

Hann sat á haugi; hann sá ríða valkyjur níu, ok var ein gǫfugligust.

(He was sitting on a burial-mound; he saw nine valkyries riding by, and one was the most imposing.)

W. II.2.3

The function of the valkyries is now explained (*Ring*, 2824–26, 2835–40):

Wotan:

Daß stark zum Streit
uns fände der Feind,

That our foe might find us
stalwart in strife

hieß ich euch Helden mir schaffen:	*I bade you bring me heroes:*
. . .	
die solltet zu Sturm	*you'd to spur them on*
und Streite ihr nun stacheln,	*to onslaught and strife,*
ihre Kraft reizen	*honing their strength*
zu rauhem Krieg,	*for hot-blooded battle,*
daß kühner Kämpfer Schaaren	*so that hosts of valiant warriors*
ich samm'le in Walhall's Saal.	*I'd gather in Valhalla's hall.*

Einherjar ('lone fighters'), the slain warriors in Valhǫll, are well known from the Eddas. In the Prose Edda, the pastime of these favourites of Óðinn is described thus (*SnE* G20, G41):

> *Óðinn heitir Alfǫðr, því at hann er faðir allra goða. Hann heitir ok Valfǫðr, þvíat hans óskasynir eru allir þeir er í val falla. Þeim skipar hann Valhǫll ok Vingólf, ok heita þeir þá einherjar . . . Hvern dag þá er þeir hafa klæzk þá hervæða þeir sik ok ganga út í garðinn ok berjask ok fellr hverr á annan. Þat er leikr þeira. Ok er líðr at dǫgurðarmáli þá ríða þeir heim til Valhallar ok setjask til drykkju.*
>
> *(Odin is called All-father, for he is father of all gods. He is also called Val-father [father of the slain], since all those who fall in battle are his adopted sons. He assigns them places in Val-hall and Vingolf, and they are then known as Einherjar . . . Each day after they have got dressed they put on war-gear and go out into the courtyard and fight each other and they fall each upon the other. This is their sport. And when dinner-time approaches they ride back to Val-hall and sit down to drink.)*

W. II.2.4

Wotan fears that Alberich may gain control of the magic ring and the gold guarded by Fafner (*Ring*, 2848–49, 2855–57, 2876–81, 2968–77):

Durch Alberich's Heer	*Through Alberich's host*
droht uns das Ende:	*our end now threatens.*
. . .	
Nur wenn je den Ring	*Only were he*
zurück er gewänne –	*to win back the ring*
dann wäre Walhall verloren:	*would Valhalla then be lost.*
. . .	
Fafner hütet den Hort,	*Fafner broods on the hoard*
um den er den Bruder gefällt.	*for which he killed his brother.*
Ihm müßt' ich den Reif entringen,	*From him I must wrest the ring,*
den selbst als Zoll ich ihm zahlte:	*which I paid him once as tribute:*
doch mit den ich vertrug,	*having treated with him,*
ihn darf ich nicht treffen.	*I cannot meet him.*
. . .	

Vom Niblung jüngst	*Of the Niblung I lately*
vernahm ich die Mär',	*heard it told*
daß ein Weib der Zwerg bewältigt,	*that the dwarf had had his way with a woman*
dess' Gunst Gold ihm erzwang.	*whose favours gold had gained him.*
Des Hasses Frucht	*A woman harbours*
hegt eine Frau;	*the seed of hate;*
des Neides Kraft	*the force of envy*
kreiß't ihr im Schooß;	*stirs in her womb:*
das Wunder gelang	*this wonder befell*
dem Liebelosen.	*the loveless dwarf.*

A model for Alberich's fathering a child is to be found in the conception of Hǫgni in *Þiðreks saga* (169 (274)):

> *Ok þat bar at eitt sinn, at hún var víndrukkin, þá er konungr var eigi heima í sinu ríki, ok var sofnuð í einum grasgarði úti, ok til hennar kom einn maðr ok liggr hjá henni . . . Ok er nú þaðan líðr nokkur stund, er dróttning ólétt, ok áðr hún fœði barn, þá berr þat at, þá er hún er ein saman stǫdd, at til hennar kemr inn sami maðr . . . En hann lézt vera einn álfr. 'En ef þat barn mætti upp vaxa, þá seg því sitt faðerni, en leyn hvern mann annarra. Nú er þat sveinbarn, sem mik varir,' segir hann, 'ok sá mun vera mikill fyrir sér, ok oftliga mun hann vera í nauðum staddr, ok hvert sinn, er hann er svá staddr, at eigi fær hann sik sjálfr leyst, þá skal hann kalla á sinn fǫður, ok mun hann þar vera, þá er hann þarf.' Ok nú hverfr þessi álfr svá sem skuggi.*
>
> *(It happened on one occasion that she was drunk with wine when the king was not at home in his kingdom, and she had fallen asleep in a grassy garden outdoors and to her came a man and lay with her . . . When some time has passed, the queen is pregnant and before she gives birth, it happens when she is alone that the same man comes to her . . . And he said that he was an elf. 'And if that child should manage to grow up, then tell it about its paternity, but keep it secret from everyone else. If it is a boy, as I expect,' he says, 'then he will be a great man, and will often be in great danger and every time he is in such a position that he cannot free himself, he shall call on his father, and he will be there when he is needed.' And now this elf disappears like a shadow.)*

For further comparison, see some of the aspects of Hagen in *Götterdämmerung*, especially G. I.2 and G. II.1 (*Ring*, 7158–69 and 7736–45).

W. II.2.5

Brünnhilde calls Wotan *Siegvater* (*Ring*, 3041). The equivalent name *Sigfaðir*/*Sigfǫðr* (Father of Victory or of Battle) is found as a name for Óðinn in *Vǫluspá* 55, *Grímnismál* 48 and *SnE* G20.

Die Walküre, Act Two, Scene Three

Flight of Sieglinde and Siegmund (*Ring*, 3051–3159). No prototypes exist in the Icelandic or German texts.

Die Walküre, Act Two, Scene Four

W. II.4.1
In compliance with the instructions that Fricka has compelled Wotan to give her, Brünnhilde appears to Siegmund in her role as a herald of death (*Ring*, 3160–63, 3166–95):

Brünnhilde:	
Siegmund! –	*Siegmund! –*
Sieh' auf mich!	*Look on me!*
Ich – bin's,	*I am she*
der bald du folg'st	*whom you'll follow soon.*
. . .	
Nur Todgeweihten	*The death-doomed alone*
taugt mein Anblick:	*are destined to look on me:*
wer mich erschaut,	*he who beholds me*
der scheidet vom Lebens-Licht.	*goes hence from life's light.*
Auf der Walstatt allein	*In battle alone*
erschein' ich Edlen;	*I appear before heroes:*
wer mich gewahrt,	*him who perceives me*
zur Wal kor ich ihn mir.	*I've chosen as one of the slain.*
Siegmund:	
Der dir nun folgt,	*The hero who follows you –*
wohin führ'st du den Helden?	*where will you lead him?*
Brünnhilde:	
Zu Walvater,	*The Lord of the Slain*
der dich gewählt,	*has chosen you –*
führ' ich dich:	*to him do I lead you now:*
nach Walhall folg'st du mir.	*you'll follow me to Valhalla.*
Siegmund:	
In Walhall's Saal	*In Valhalla's hall*
Walvater find' ich allein?	*shall I find the Lord of the Slain alone?*
Brünnhilde:	
Gefall'ner Helden	*The noble host*
hehrer Schaar	*of fallen heroes*
umfängt dich hold	*welcomes you fondly*
mit hoch-heiligem Gruß.	*with greeting most holy.*

Siegmund:

Fänd' ich in Walhall	*Might I find my own father,*
Wälse, den eig'nen Vater?	*Wälse, in Valhalla?*

Brünnhilde:

Den Vater findet	*The Wälsung will find*
der Wälsung dort!	*his father there.*

Siegmund:

Grüßt mich in Walhall	*Will a woman greet me*
froh eine Frau?	*gladly in Valhalla?*

Brünnhilde:

Wunschmädchen	*There Wish-Maidens*
walten dort hehr:	*hold sublime sway:*
Wotan's Tochter	*Wotan's daughter*
reicht dir traulich den Trank!	*will lovingly hand you your drink.*

Wagner's *Walvater* ('Lord of the Slain') is the equivalent of *Valfǫðr*, which is known as a name for Óðinn in Icelandic, e.g. in *Vǫluspá* 1, 27–28 and *Grímnismál* 48. The Prose Edda says of Óðinn (*SnE* G20):

> *Hann heitir ok Valfǫðr, þvíat hans óskasynir eru allir þeir er í val falla.*
>
> *(He is also called Val-father, since all those who fall in battle are his adopted sons.)*

The eddic poem *Oddrúnargrátur* (16) calls Brynhildr *óskmær* (wish-maiden, i.e. adoptive or chosen maiden). *Grímnismál* (36) says of the valkyries:

Þær bera einherjum ǫl.	*These serve ale to the Einheriar.*

Brünnhilde's role as a herald of death is strongly reminiscent of that of the valkyries in the poem *Hákonarmál* by the tenth-century Norwegian poet Eyvindr skáldaspillir, quoted in *Heimskringla* at the end of *Hákonar saga góða* (ch. 31). Here Óðinn sends two valkyries, Gǫndul and Skǫgul, to fetch the strong and victorious king to Valhǫll:

Gǫndul ok Skǫgul	*Gautatyr [Odin] sent*
sendi Gautatýr	*Gondul and Skogul*
at kjósa of konunga,	*to choose from the kings*
hverr Yngva ættar	*which ones of Yngvi's line*
skyldi með Óðni fara	*should go to be with Odin*
ok í Valhǫllu vesa.	*and be in Val-hall.*
. . .	
Gǫndul þat mælti,	*Gondul spoke this,*
studdisk geirskapti:	*she leaned on her spear-shaft:*
'Vex nú gengi goða,	*'The gods' following is growing*

er Hákoni hafa	*since the powers have summoned*
með her mikinn	*Hakon to their home*
heim bǫnd of boðit.'	*with a great host.'*
Vísi þat heyrði,	*The ruler heard this,*
hvat valkyrjur mæltu	*what the battle-maids were saying,*
mærar af mars baki.	*glorious, on horseback.*
Hyggiliga létu	*They spoke wisely*
ok hjalmaðar sátu	*and they sat, helmeted,*
ok hǫfðusk hlífar fyrir.	*and held their shields before them.*

Hákon feels the valkyrie's arrangement is unfair, and is reluctant, and Skǫgul answers him.

'Hví þú svá gunni,' kvað Hákon,	*'Why do you thus, Skogul,' said Hákon,*
'skiptir, Geir-Skǫgul?	*'ordain the battle?*
Várum þó verðir gagns frá goðum.'	*We deserved victory from the gods.'*
'Vér því vǫldum,' kvað Skǫgul,	*'We arranged it,' said Skogul,*
es þú velli helt,	*'that you held the field*
en þínir fíandr flugu.'	*and your foes fled.'*
'Ríða vit skulum,'	*'We two shall ride,'*
kvað en ríkja Skǫgul,	*said the mighty Skogul,*
'grœna heima goða	*to the gods' green homes*
Óðni at segja,	*to tell Odin*
at nú mun allvaldr koma	*that the most powerful ruler*
á hann sjálfan at séa.'	*is coming to see him in person.'*

Óðinn orders his followers to greet the king with honour:

'Hermóðr ok Bragi,'	*'Hermod and Bragi,'*
kvað Hroptatýr,	*said Hroptatyr [Odin],*
'gangið í gǫgn grami,	*'go forth to meet the ruler,*
þvít konungr ferr,	*for a king is coming*
sás kappi þykkir.	*who seems to be a hero*
til hallar hinig.'	*here to this hall.'*
. . .	
'Einherja grið	*'Safe-conduct shall you have*
skalt þú allra hafa.	*of all the Einheriar* (W. II. 2.3).
Þigg þú at Ásum ǫl.	*Take ale with the Æsir [gods].*
Jarla bági,	*Opponent of earls,*
þú átt inni hér	*you have in here*
átta brœðr,' kvað Bragi.	*eight of your brothers,' said Bragi.*

W. II.4.2

Siegmund refuses to accompany Brünnhilde to Walhall, unless he can take Sieglinde with him (*Ring*, 3199–14):

Doch Eines sag' mir, du Ew'ge!
Begleitet den Bruder
die bräutliche Schwester?
Umfängt Siegmund
Sieglinde dort?

But tell me one thing, immortal!
Will the sister-bride
go with her brother?
Will Siegmund embrace
Sieglinde there?

Brünnhilde:

Erdenluft
muß sie doch athmen:
Sieglinde
sieht Siegmund dort nicht!

Earthly air
she must breathe awhile:
Siegmund
will not see Sieglinde there!

Siegmund:

So grüße mir Walhall,
grüße mir Wotan,
grüße mir Wälse
und alle Helden –
grüß' auch die holden
Wunches-Mädchen: –
zu ihnen folg' ich dir nicht.

Then greet for me Valhalla,
greet for me Wotan,
greet for me Wälse
and all the heroes –
greet, too, Wotan's
gracious daughters: –
to them I follow you not.

In *Hákonarmál* the king is wary of Óðinn:

Ræsir þat mælti,
vas frá rómu kominn,
stóð allr í dreyra drifinn:
'Illúðigr mjǫk
þykkir oss Óðinn vesa.
Séumk vér hans of hugi.'
. . .
'Gerðir órar,'
kvað enn góði konungr,
'viljum vér sjalfir hafa.
Hjalm ok brynju
skal hirða vel.
Gótt es til gǫrs at taka.'

The ruler said this,
he was come from battle,
he stood all covered in blood:
'Very evilly disposed
looks Odin to us.
We fear his purpose.'
. . .
'Our armour,'
said the good king,
'shall we ourselves keep.
Helmet and mail-coat
must be guarded well.
It is good to have them to hand.'

The principal difference of content is that in Wagner, Siegmund's actions are attributable solely to love, while King Hákon's reluctance is due to his distrust of Óðinn and his desire to live longer.

This poem was one of the first skaldic poems to be printed and translated, and was widely available in Wagner's time, for instance in Thomas Percy's *Five Pieces of Runic Poetry* (1763) and in a number of German translations. Wagner also had two different translations of the relevant section of *Heimskringla* in his library in Dresden. Much the same themes also appear in *Eiríksmál* in *Fagrskinna*, but that poem is unlikely to have been known to Wagner.

W. II. 4.3

Siegmund says he will kill himself and Sieglinde rather than be parted from her. Brünnhilde finally decides to defy Wotan and spare Siegmund, while letting Hunding die (*Ring*, 3313–20):

Halt' ein, Wälsung!	*Stay your hand, Wälsung!*
Höre mein Wort!	*Hark to my word!*
Sieglinde lebe –	*Sieglind' shall live –*
und Siegmund lebe mit ihr!	*and Siegmund with her!*
Beschlossen ist's;	*My mind is made up;*
das Schlachtloos wend' ich:	*I'll change the course of the battle:*
dir, Siegmund,	*Siegmund, on you*
schaff' ich Segen und Sieg!	*both blessing and victory I bestow!*

The eddic poem *Sigrdrífumál* (prose between stanzas 4 and 5) and *Vǫlsunga saga* ch. 21 tell how a valkyrie, Sigrdrífa or Brynhildr, did not follow Óðinn's orders regarding who should die in a battle, Hjálm-Gunnarr or Agnarr (brother of Auði or Auða). The eddic poem *Helreið Brynhildar* 8 says:

Þá lét ek gamlan	*Then I made the old man*
á Goðþjóðu	*among the people of the gods [*or *Goths],*
Hjálm-Gunnar næst	*Hjalm-Gunnar next*
heljar ganga;	*go to the world of death;*
gaf ek ungum sigr	*I gave the victory to the young*
Auðu bróður;	*brother of Auða;*
þá var mér Óðinn	*Odin was very angry*
ofreiðr um þat.	*with me for that.*

Die Walküre, Act Two, Scene Five

W. II.5.1

When Siegmund eventually meets Hunding, the valkyrie gives him her encouragement in the fight, but Wotan appears and brings about Siegmund's death (*Ring*, 3384–88):

Brünnhilde:

Triff' ihn, Siegmund!	*Strike him, Siegmund!*
Traue dem Schwert!	*Trust in your sword!*

Als Sigmund so eben zu einem tödlichen Streiche auf Hunding ausholt, bricht von links her ein glühend röthlicher Schein durch das Gewölk aus, in welchem Wotan ersheint, über Hunding stehend und seinen Speer Siegmund quer entgegenhaltend.

(Siegmund is on the point of dealing Hunding a fatal blow when a bright red glow breaks through the clouds on the right; in it can be seen Wotan, standing over Hunding and holding his spear diagonally at Siegmund.)

Wotan:

Zurück vor dem Speer!	*Get back from the spear!*
In Stücken das Schwert!	*In splinters the sword!*

Brünnhilde weicht erschroken vor Wotan mit dem Schilde zurück: Siegmund's Schwert zerspringt an dem vorgehaltenen Speere.

(Still holding her shield, Brünnhilde recoils in terror before Wotan: Siegmund's sword shatters on the outstretched spear.)

In *Vǫlsunga saga* ch. 11 Sigmundr's sword shatters on Óðinn's spear, in spite of the protection of 'prophecy-women'. This is not a punishment, however: Sigmundr has grown old and his good fortune is exhausted.

> *Mart spjót var þar á lopti ok ǫrvar. En svá hlífðu honum hans spádísir at hann varð ekki sárr, ok engi kunni tǫl hversu margr maðr fell fyrir honum. Hann hafði báðar hendr blóðgar til axlar. Ok er orrosta hafði staðit um hríð, þá kom maðr í bardagann með síðan hǫtt ok heklu blá. Hann hafði eitt auga ok geir í hendi. Þessi maðr kom á mót Sigmundi konungi ok brá upp geirinum fyrir hann. Ok er Sigmundr konungr hjó fast, kom sverðit í geirinn ok brast í sundr í tvá hluti.*
>
> *(Numerous spears hurtled through the air, and arrows, too, but his norns (lit. 'prophecy-women') looked after him, so he remained unscathed, and no one kept count of the men who fell before him. Both his arms were bloody to the shoulders. Now when the battle had gone on for some time, a man who had on a dark cloak and a hat coming down low over his face entered the fray. He had but one eye and in his hand he held a spear. The man advanced towards King Sigmund, raising the spear to bar his way, and when King Sigmund struck fiercely, his sword hit against the spear and snapped in two.)*

Die Walküre, Act Three, Scene One

W. III.1.1

Eight valkyries gather at a mountain peak, some bearing across their saddles fallen heroes that they are bringing to Wotan (*Ring*, 3399–3453).

A gathering of valkyries has no prototype in the Poetic Edda, but *Vǫluspá* 30 contains an image of them riding together to Valhǫll, presumably after having chosen the fallen:

Sá hon valkyrjur,	*She saw valkyries*
vítt um komnar,	*come from afar,*
gǫrvar at ríða	*ready to ride*
til Goðþjóðar;	*to the people of the gods [*or *of men];*
Skuld helt skildi,	*Skuld held a shield,*
en Skǫgul ǫnnur,	*and Skogul another,*
Gunnr, Hildr, Gǫndul	*Gunnr, Hildr, Gǫndul*
ok Geirskǫgul;	*and Geirskǫgul;*
nú eru talðar	*now are numbered*
nǫnnur Herjans,	*Herjan's [Óðinn's] women,*
gǫrvar at ríða	*ready to ride*
grund, valkyrjur.	*the earth, valkyries.*

W. III.1.2

Brünnhilde arrives on horseback with Sieglinde, and asks the other valkyries where a hiding-place may be found for her (*Ring*, 3618–31):

Siegrune:

Nach Osten weithin	*Away to the east*
dehnt sich ein Wald:	*A forest stretches:*
der Nibelungen Hort	*there Fafner has taken*
entführte Fafner dorthin.	*the Nibelung hoard.*

Schwertleite:

Wurmes-Gestalt	*The savage assumed*
schuf sich der Wilde:	*the shape of a dragon*
in einer Höhle	*and in a cave*
hütet er Alberich's Reif!	*he guards Alberich's ring.*

Grimgerde:

Nich geheu'r ist's dort	*No place it is*
für ein hilflos Weib.	*for a helpless woman.*

Brünnhilde:

Und doch vor Wotan's Wuth	*And yet the forest*
schützt sie sicher der Wald:	*will surely shield her from Wotan's wrath:*
ihn scheut der Mächt'ge	*the mighty god shuns it*
und meidet den Ort.	*and shies from the spot.*

Here, for the first time in the *Ring*, Fafner is specifically stated to be in the form of a dragon (German *Wurm*, like Icelandic *ormr*, can mean both snake and dragon). This is consistent with the eddic poem *Reginsmál* (prose after stanza 14) and the Prose Edda (*SnE* S40), and *Vǫlsunga saga* (ch. 14) says:

> *'Síðan drap Fáfnir fǫður sinn,' segir Reginn, 'ok myrði hann, ok náða ek engu af fénu. Hann gerðisk svá illr at hann lagðisk út ok unni engum at njóta fjárins nema sér ok varð síðan at inum versta ormi og liggr nú á því fé.*

('Later on Fafnir killed his father,' said Regin, 'hiding his murdered body, and I didn't get any of the treasure. He grew so malevolent that he went off to live in the wilds and allowed none but himself to have any pleasure in the riches, and later on he turned into a terrible dragon and now he lies on the treasure.')

In *Þiðreks saga* (163 (268)) it is Reginn, Mímir's brother, who is changed into a dragon, but this dragon does not guard any hoard of gold. In *Das Nibelungenlied* (100, *Av.* 3) Sîfrit admittedly slays a dragon, bathes in his blood, and his skin grows 'horny' and invulnerable. But this dragon is not connected with any gold, either.

In *Das Lied vom Hürnen Seyfrid*, Seyfrid also kills a dragon and his skin becomes invulnerable (7–11), and he later kills another dragon to save a princess (127–49), but in this case the gold in the cave is irrelevant.

W. III.1.3

Brünnhilde tells Sieglinde that she is carrying Siegmund's child (*Ring*, 3591–95, 3644–48):

Lebe, o Weib, um der Liebe willen! Rette das Pfand das von ihm du empfing'st:	*O woman, live for the sake of love! Save the pledge you received from him:*
. . .	
Denn Eines wiss' und wahr' es immer: der hehrsten Helden der Welt heg'st du, o Weib, im schirmenden Schooß!	*Know this alone and ward it always: the world's noblest hero, O woman, you harbour within your sheltering womb!*

In *Vǫlsunga saga* (ch. 7) a son, Sinfjǫtli, is born to the twins, but Sigmundr later marries Hjǫrdís, daughter of Eylimi. She goes amidst the slain after Sigmundr's last battle and finds him mortally wounded. Sigmundr then informs Hjǫrdís that she is with child (ch. 12):

Þú ferr með sveinbarn ok fœð þat vel ok vandliga, ok mun sá sveinn ágætr ok fremstr af várri ætt.

(You are with child — a boy. Give him a good and careful upbringing — the boy shall be famous and the foremost of our house.)

W. III.1.4

Brünnhilde advises Sieglinde to flee eastward to the forest, near to Fafner's lair. She gives her the fragments of Siegmund's sword, which she gathered on the battlefield (*Ring*, 3659–66):

Verwahr' ihm die starken	*For him keep safe*
Schwertes-Stücken;	*the sword's stout fragments;*
seines Vaters Walstatt	*from his father's field*
entführt' ich sie glücklich:	*I haply took them:*
der neu gefügt	*let him who'll wield*
das Schwert einst schwingt,	*the newly forged sword*
den Namen nehm' er von mir –	*receive his name from me –*
'Siegfried' erfreu' sich des Sieg's!	*may 'Siegfried' joy in victory!*

In *Vǫlsunga saga* ch. 12 Sigmundr continues to give Hjǫrdís advice before his death. He says of the fragments of his sword:

> *Varðveit ok vel sverðsbrotin. Þar af má gera gott sverð er heita mun Gramr ok sonr okkarr mun bera ok þar mǫrg stórverk með vinna þau er aldri munu firnask, ok hans nafn mun uppi meðan verǫldin stendr.*
>
> *(Look after the pieces of the sword as well. A fine sword can be made from them — it will be called Gram, and our son will bear it and perform many great deeds with it, deeds which shall never be forgotten, and his name shall live as long as the world endures.)*

Die Walküre, Act Three, Scene Two

W. III.2.1

When Wotan arrives, he banishes Brünnhilde from him (*Ring*, 3770–73, 3797–3802, 3822–25):

Wunschmaid bist du nicht mehr;	*Wish-Maid you are no more;*
Walküre bist du gewesen: –	*valkyrie you have been: –*
nun sei fortan,	*now henceforth be*
was so du noch bist!	*what you are even now!*
. . .	
Hieher auf den Berg	*Here on the mountain*
banne ich dich;	*I'll lay you under a spell;*
in wehrlosen Schlaf	*in shelterless sleep*
schließ' ich dich fest;	*I'll shut you fast;*
der Mann dann fange die Maid,	*the maiden shall fall to the man*
der am Wege sie findet und weckt.	*who stumbles upon her and wakes her.*
. . .	
Dem herrischen Manne	*Henceforth she'll obey*
gehorcht sie fortan,	*the high-handed man;*
am Herde sitzt sie und spinnt,	*she'll sit by the hearth and spin,*
aller Spottenden Ziel und Spiel.	*the butt and plaything of all who despise her.*

Óðinn's punishment of a valkyrie for disobedience by putting her to sleep is mentioned in several eddic poems and in *Vǫlsunga saga* (ch.

21). The eddic poem *Sigrdrífumál* (prose between stanzas 4 and 5) contains a description of the self-willed valkyrie:

Hon nefndiz Sigrdrífa ok var valkyrja. Hon sagði, at tveir konungar bǫrðuz; hét annarr Hjálm-Gunnarr, hann var þá gamall ok inn mesti hermaðr, ok hafði Óðinn hánum sigri heitit; en

annarr hét Agnarr, Auðu bróðir,
er vætr engi vildi þiggja.

Sigrdrífa feldi Hjálm-Gunnar í orrostunni. En Óðinn stakk hana svefþorni í hefnd þess ok kvað hana aldri skyldu síðan sigr vega í orrostu ok kvað hana giptaz skyldu.

(She said her name was Sigrdrifa and she was a valkyrie. She said that there were two kings fighting each other; one was called Hjalm-Gunnar, he was now old and a very great warrior and Odin had promised him victory; but

the other was called Agnar, the brother of Auða,
whom no creature wished to accept.

Sigrdrifa slew Hjalm-Gunnar in the battle. And Odin pricked her with a sleep-thorn in revenge for this and said that she would never again win victory in battle and said that she should be married.)

Die Walküre, Act Three, Scene Three

W. III.3.1

Brünnhilde pleads with Wotan (*Ring*, 4061–78):

Dieß Eine	*This one thing*
mußt du erhöhren!	*you must allow me!*
Zerknicke dein Kind,	*Crush your child*
das dein Knie umfaßt;	*who clasps your knee,*
zertritt die Traute,	*trample your favourite underfoot,*
zertrümm're die Maid;	*and dash the maid to pieces;*
ihres Leibes Spur	*let your spear destroy*
zerstöre dein Speer:	*all trace of her body:*
doch gieb, Grausamer, nicht	*but, pitiless god, don't give her up*
der gräßlichsten Schmach sie Preis!	*to the shamefullest of fates!*
Auf dein Gebot	*At your behest*
entbrenne ein Feuer;	*let a fire flare up;*
den Felsen umglühe	*let its searing flames*
lodernde Gluth;	*encircle the fell;*
es leck' ihre Zung',	*its tongue shall lick,*
es fresse ihr Zahn	*its tooth consume*
den Zagen, der frech sich wagte,	*the coward who dares to draw near*
dem freislichen Felsen zu nah'n!	*to the fearsome rock in his rashness.*

In *Vǫlsunga saga* the valkyrie responds more curtly to Óðinn's plan to marry her off (ch. 21):

En ek strengða þess heit þar í mót at giptask engum þeim er hræðask kynni.

(And in return I made a solemn vow to marry no one who knew the meaning of fear.)

W. III.3.2

Wotan consents to Brünnhilde's request (*Ring*, 4095–4102, 4136–41):

Wotan:

Flammende Gluth	*Fiery flames shall*
umglühe den Fels;	*encircle the fell;*
mit zehrenden Schrecken	*with withering fears*
scheuch' es den Zagen;	*let them fright the faint-hearted;*
der Feige fliehe	*the coward shall flee*
Brünnhilde's Fels: –	*from Brünnhilde's fell: –*
denn Einer nur freie die Braut,	*for one man alone shall woo the bride,*
der freier als ich, der Gott!	*one freer than I, the god!*
. . .	
Herauf, wabernde Lohe,	*Arise, you flickering flame,*
umlod're mir feurig den Fels!	*enfold the fell with fire!*

Er stösst mit dem Folgenden dreimal mit dem Speer auf den Stein.

(During the following, he strikes the stone three times with his spear.)

Loge! Loge! Hieher!	*Loge! Loge! Come hither!*

Dem Stein entfährt ein Feuerstrahl, der zur allmählich immer helleren Flammengluth anschwillt . . . Hier bricht die lichte Flackerlohe aus . . . Lichte Brunst umgiebt Wotan mit wildem Flackern. Er weis't mit dem Speere gebieterisch dem Feuermeere den Umkreis des Felsenrandes zur Strömung an . . .

(A stream of fire springs from the rock, gradually increasing in intensity until it becomes a brilliant fiery glow . . . Bright flickering flames break out . . . Flickering wildly, tongues of lambent flame surround Wotan. With his spear, he directs the sea of fire to encircle the edge of the rock . . .)

Wer meines Speeres	*He who fears*
Spitze fürchtet,	*my spear-point*
durchschreite das Feuer nie!	*shall never pass through the fire!*

The fearless hero, who alone may wake the valkyrie, has a model in *Vǫlsunga saga* ch. 21 and in the eddic poem *Sigrdrífumál* (prose before stanza 5) and in the following passage from *Helreið Brynhildar* (9–10):

Lauk hann mik skjǫldum	*In shields he shut me*
í Skatalundi,	*in warrior-grove,*

rauðum ok hvítum,	*red and white,*
randir snurtu;	*rims touched;*
þann bað hann slíta	*him bade he break*
svefni mínum,	*my sleep*
er hvergi lands	*who in no land*
hræðaz kynni.	*could be afraid.*
Lét um sal minn	*He made round my hall*
sunnanverðan,	*in the south,*
hávan brenna	*blaze high*
her alls viðar;	*all wood's damager [fire];*
þar bað hann einn þegn	*there he bade one warrior*
yfir at ríða,	*ride across*
þanns mér færði gull,	*who brought me the gold*
þats und Fáfnir lá.	*which under Fafnir lay.*

The enchanted flames around Brynhildr's hall are also mentioned in the eddic poem *Fáfnismál* (42–43) and in the prose introduction to *Sigrdrífumál*, as well as in the Prose Edda (*SnE* S41) and *Vǫlsunga saga* (ch. 21), but not in *Das Nibelungenlied* or any other medieval German poem. The German word *Waberlohe* appears first in the nineteenth century (see Jakob and Wilhelm Grimm, *Deutsches Wörterbuch* 1854–1971, XIII 11), as a translation of the Old Icelandic *vafrlogi* (flickering flame).

It is worth considering whether the fearsome fire on a mountaintop may originally have been inspired by volcanic eruptions, which medieval Icelandic poets must often have seen, but which are unknown in central Europe. The red sky of morning or evening over mountaintops is more likely to inspire feelings other than fear.

DIE VALKYRIE: SURVEY OF MOTIFS

THE RING	EDDIC POEMS	PROSE EDDA	VǪLSUNGA SAGA	ÞIÐREKS SAGA	NIBELUNGENLIED
Impregnating apples			Impregnating apples		
Wurm im Auge			ormr í auga *[Ragnars saga]*		
Sanctuary for the night		Overnight truce *[Egils saga]*			
Wotan's sword in tree			Óðinn's sword in tree		
Union of twins		Child born of twins			
Brünnhilde	Brynhildr	Brynhildr	Brynhildr	Brynhildr	Prünhilt
Visit to Wala Wala's wisdom	Gunnlǫð	Gunnlǫð mead of poetry			
Walküren	valkyrjur	valkyrjur	*[Hákonarmál]*		
Announcement of death			*[Hákonarmál]*		
Brünnhilde protects Siegmund	Sigrdrífa protects Agnarr				
Wotan breaks Siegmund's sword			Óðinn breaks Sigmundr's sword		

The Ring	Eddic poems	Prose Edda	Vǫlsunga saga
Wotan's spear	Óðinn's spear	Óðinn's spear	Óðinn's spear
Brünnhilde foretells birth			Sigmundr foretells birth
Wotan punishes Brünnhilde	Óðinn punishes valkyrie		Óðinn punishes Brynhildr
Fearless hero shall awaken Brünnhilde	Fearless hero shall awaken Brynhildr		Fearless hero shall awaken Brynhildr
Brünnhilde's sleep	Brynhildr's sleep	Brynhildr's sleep	Brynhildr's sleep
Fire on the mountaintop	Fire on the mountaintop	Vafrlogi on the mountaintop	Vafrlogi on mountaintop

SIEGFRIED

CHARACTERS		ICELANDIC EQUIVALENTS
	Humans	
Siegfried		Sigurðr
	Gods	
The Wanderer		Gangráðr/Gangleri/Óðinn
	Valkyries	
Brünnhilde		Brynhildr
	Nibelungs	
Alberich		Andvari
Mime		Mímir
	Giant/dragon	
Fafner		Fáfnir
	Seeress	
Erda/Wala		Jǫrð/Vala
	Bird	
Waldvogel (woodbird)		Igður (nuthatches)

Siegfried, Act One, Scene One

S. I.1.1

Mime is in his cave, striving to make a sword for Siegfried, but Siegfried always breaks it. Mime has the fragments of Siegmund's sword, but cannot make a new sword from them. Yet he knows that only with that weapon can Siegfried defeat the dragon Fafner, who lies on the gold and the ring. Siegfried is very hostile towards his foster-father (*Ring*, 4162–75):

Mime:

Fafner, der wilde Wurm,	*Fafner, the grim-hearted dragon,*
lagert im finstern Wald;	*dwells in the gloomy wood;*
mit des furchtbaren Leibes Wucht	*with the weight of his fearsome bulk*
der Nibelungen Hort	*he watches over*
hütet er dort.	*the Nibelung hoard there.*

Siegfried's kindischer Kraft	*To Siegfried's childlike strength*
erläge wohl Fafner's Leib:	*Fafner would no doubt fall:*
des Nibelungen Ring	*the Nibelung's ring*
erränge er mir.	*he'd win for me.*
Nur ein Schwert taugt zu der That;	*One sword alone befits the deed*
nur Nothung nützt meinem Neid,	*and only Nothung serves my grudge,*
wenn Siegfried sehrend ihn schwingt: –	*if Siegfried wields it with fell intent: –*
und ich kann's nicht schweißen,	*yet I cannot forge it,*
Nothung das Schwert! –	*Nothung the sword! –*

Wagner's change of the name of the smith — Reigin–Mime — was discussed in connection with Scene III of *Das Rheingold* (R. 3.1). In *Þiðreks saga* (164 (269)) Mímir is Sigurðr's foster-father, but they soon become enemies, and Mímir never attempts to make a sword for him. In *Das Lied vom Hürnen Seyfrid* (5) the smith has no name. Seyfrid is only his apprentice. No sword is made. In *Das Nibelungenlied* there is no mention whatsoever of Sifrît's foster-father, or of the making of a sword. In the eddic poem *Reginsmál*, the Prose Edda (*SnE* S40) and *Vǫlsunga saga* (ch. 13), on the other hand, Reginn is a smith at the court of King Hjálprekr, father-in-law of Sigurðr's mother, Hjǫrdís. The prose introduction to *Reginsmál* says:

> *Þá var kominn Reginn til Hjálpreks, sonr Hreiðmars. Hann var hverjum manni hagari, ok dvergr of vǫxt; hann var vitr, grimmr ok fjǫlkunnigr. Reginn veitti Sigurði fóstr ok kenslu ok elskaði hann mjǫk.*
>
> *(Then Regin, the son of Hreidmar, had come to Hjalprek's; he was more skilled than anyone and a dwarf in stature; he was wise, fierce, and knowledgeable about magic. Regin fostered Sigurd and educated him, and loved him greatly.)*

S. I.1.2

Siegfried takes a sword and breaks it on the anvil, so the fragments fly about (*Ring*, 4226–31):

Den schwachen Stift	*This puny pin*
nenn'st du ein Schwert?	*you call a sword?*
Da hast du die Stücken,	*Here, take the pieces,*
schändlicher Stümper:	*you shameful bungler:*
hätt' ich am Schädel	*if only I'd smashed them*
dir sie zerschlagen!	*against your skull!*

[In the first draft of *Siegfried*, Mime makes two swords, which Siegfried breaks (see Strobel 1930, 66).]

In *Vǫlsunga saga*, the smith succeeds at his third attempt. At the second attempt, *Vǫlsunga saga* indicates some hostility on Sigurðr's part towards Reginn (ch. 15):

> *Reginn gerir nú eitt sverð ok fær í hǫnd Sigurði. Hann tók við sverðinu ok mælti, 'Þetta er þitt smíði, Reginn,' ok høggr í steðjann, ok brotnaði sverðit. Hann kastar brandinum ok bað hann smíða annat betra. Reginn gerir annat sverð ok fær Sigurði. Hann leit á. 'Þetta mun þér líka, en vant mun yðr at smíða.' Sigurðr reynir þetta sverð ok brýtr sem it fyrra. Þá mælti Sigurðr til Regins, 'Þú munt líkr vera inum fyrrum frændum þínum ok vera ótrúr.'*
>
> *(So Regin made a sword, and placed it in Sigurd's hands. He grasped the sword. 'This is what your work's like, Regin,' he said, striking the anvil — and the sword broke. He flung away the blade and told him to forge a second and better one. Regin made a second sword and brought it to Sigurd. He examined it. 'You'll be pleased with this one, though you're not an easy man to work metal for.' Sigurd tried out the sword, and broke it just like the first. Then Sigurd said to Regin: 'You're like your forebears — untrustworthy.')*

S. I.1.3

Siegfried knows nothing of his origins, and demands that Mime tell him who his parents are (*Ring*, 4445–47, 4463–72):

Heraus damit,	*Out with it,*
räudiger Kerl!	*scurvy wretch!*
Wer ist mir Vater und Mutter?	*Who are my father and mother?*
. . .	

Mime:

Einst lag wimmernd ein Weib	*Out there in the wildwood*
da draußen im wilden Wald:	*a woman once lay whimpering:*
zur Höhle half ich ihr her,	*I helped her into the cave*
am warmen Herd sie zu hüten.	*to ward her by the warming hearth.*
Ein Kind trug sie im Schooße;	*She bore a child within her womb:*
traurig gebar sie's hier;	*in sadness she gave it birth here;*
sie wand sich hin und her,	*back and forth she writhed,*
ich half, so gut ich konnt':	*I helped as best I could:*
groß var die Noth, sie starb –	*great was her travail; she died –*
doch Siegfried, der genas.	*but Siegfried, he survived.*

[The *Nibelungen-Mythus* of 1848 also says (p. 120 above):

> *After long gestation the outcast Sieglinde gives birth in the forest to* Siegfried.]

Siegfried's ignorance of his origins has a parallel in *Þiðreks saga* (162–64 (267–69), where the baby Sigurðr is washed ashore on a spit of land in a cask. He is found by a hind, who takes care of him until Mímir discovers him and takes him in. The wording of the *Nibelungen-Mythus* is reminiscent of the prolonged pregnancy of the mother of King Vǫlsungr (cf. W. I.3.2), the great-grandmother of Sigurðr in *Vǫlsunga saga* (ch. 2):

> *Nú ferr inu sama fram um vanheilsu dróttningar at hon fær eigi alit barnit, ok þessu ferr fram sex vetr at hon hefir þessa sótt. Nú finnr hon þat, at hon mun eigi lengi lifa, ok bað nú at hana skyldi særa til barnsins, ok svá var gert sem hon bað. Þat var sveinbarn, ok sá sveinn var mikill vexti þá er hann kom til, sem ván var at. Svá er sagt at sjá sveinn kyssti móður sína áðr hon dœi.*
>
> *(The queen's morbid condition, her inability to give birth to the child, remained unchanged, and after six years she was still not free of it. She then realised that she had not long to live and thereupon ordered that the child should be cut out of her, and what she ordered was done. It was a boy, and, as might be expected, the lad was a fair size when he was delivered. People say that the boy kissed his mother before she died.)*

S. I.1.4

Siegfried demands proof of his birth. Mime finally produces the fragments of the shattered sword (*Ring*, 4518–30, 4576–81):

Das gab mir deine Mutter:	*Your mother gave me this:*
für Mühe, Kost und Pflege	*for trouble, board and care*
ließ sie's als schwachen Lohn.	*she left it as paltry payment.*
Sieh' her, ein zerbroch'nes Schwert!	*See here, a shattered sword!*
Dein Vater, sagte sie, führt' es,	*Your father, she said, had borne it*
als im letzten Kampf er erlag.	*when he fell in his final fight.*
Siegfried:	
Und diese Stücken	*And these fragments*
sollst du mir schmieden:	*you shall forge for me:*
dann schwing' ich mein rechtes Schwert!	*then I'll wield my rightful sword!*
Auf! Eile dich, Mime,	*Come on now, Mime, bestir yourself*
mühe dich rasch;	*and be quick about it;*
kannst du 'was recht's,	*if there's aught you're good at,*
nun zeig' deine Kunst!	*then show me your art!*
. . .	
Mime:	
Wie füg' ich die Stücken	*How join the shards*
des tückischen Stahl's?	*of insidious steel?*
Keines Ofens Gluth	*No furnace's fire*
glüht mir die ächten;	*can fuse these sterling splinters,*

keines Zwergen Hammer	*nor any dwarf's hammer*
zwingt mir die harten.	*subdue their stubborn strength.*

In *Vǫlsunga saga* (ch. 15), Hjǫrdís, Sigurðr's mother, is still alive, and remarried, and it is she who gives him the fragments of the sword. When Reginn has twice failed in the attempt to make a good enough sword for him, Sigurðr goes to meet his mother:

> *Gekk nú til móður sinnar. Hon fagnar honum vel. Talask nú við ok drekka. Þá mælti Sigurðr, 'Hvárt hǫfum vér rétt til spurt at Sigmundr konungr seldi yðr sverðit Gram í tveim hlutum?' Hon svarar, 'Satt er þat.' Sigurðr mælti, 'Fá mér í hǫnd, ek vil hafa.' Hon kvað hann líkligan til frama ok fær honum sverðit. Sigurðr hittir nú Regin ok bað hann þar gera af sverð eptir efnum. Reginn reiddisk ok gekk til smiðju með sverðsbrotin ok þykkir Sigurðr framgjarn um smíðina.*

> *(He now went to his mother. She made him welcome, and they talked and drank together. 'Is what I've heard true?' said Sigurd then. 'Did King Sigmund entrust you with the sword Gram, in two pieces?' 'That is so,' she replied. 'Let me have them,' said Sigurd. 'I want them.' She said he seemed likely to win fame, and brought him the sword. Sigurd then sought out Regin and told him to fashion a sword from them to the best of his ability. Regin got angry and went to the smithy with the pieces of the sword, thinking that Sigurd was very exacting when it came to forging.)*

Siegfried, Act One, Scene Two

S. I.2.1
After Siegfried has left, the Wanderer (Wotan) visits Mime, saying that he is tired after a long journey (*Ring*, 4586–94):

Heil dir, weiser Schmied!	*Hail to you, wise smith!*
Dem wegmüden Gast,	*to a way-weary guest*
gönne hold	*you'll not begrudge*
des Hauses Herd!	*your house's hearth!*

Mime:

Wer ist's, der im wilden	*Who is it who seeks me out*
Walde mich sucht?	*in the wildwood?*
Wer verfolgt mich im öden Forst?	*Who tracks me through the desolate forest?*

Wanderer:

Wand'rer heißt mich die Welt:	*As Wanderer am I known to the world:*
weit wandert' ich schon.	*already I've wandered widely.*

Obligations towards guests, who must be offered shelter, warmth, food and drink, clothes, a warm welcome and conversation, are mentioned in the Poetic Edda (*Hávamál* 2–4) and the Prose Edda (*SnE* G2). The eddic poem *Vafþrúðnismál*, the principal model for this episode, includes the following (6–8):

[Óðinn:]	
Heill þú nú, Vafþrúðnir!	*Hail, Vafthrudnir!*
nú em ek í hǫll kominn,	*Now I am come into the hall*
á þik sjálfan sjá;	*to look on you yourself;*
hitt vil ek fyrst vita,	*this I want to know first,*
ef þú fróðr sér	*whether you are wise*
eða alsviðr, jǫtunn.	*or all-wise, giant.*
[Vafþrúðnir:]	
Hvat er þat manna,	*What person is this*
er í mínum sal	*who in my hall*
verpumk orðum á?	*is addressing words to me?*
Út þú né komir	*You shall not come out*
órum hǫllum frá,	*from our halls,*
nema þú inn snotrari sér.	*unless you are the wiser.*
[Óðinn:]	
Gagnráðr ek heiti;	*Gagnrad I am called;*
nú emk af gǫngu kominn	*now I have come from walking,*
þyrstr til þinna sala;	*thirsty to your halls;*
laðar þurfi	*in need of hospitality*
hefi ek lengi farit	*and welcome from you,*
ok þinna andfanga, jǫtunn.	*I have travelled long, giant.*

Óðinn often appears as a stranger in disguise in the Poetic and Prose Eddas. Some of his pseudonyms have the meaning of 'wanderer,' such as Gangleri ('walk-weary') in *Grímnismál* 46, and Vegtamr ('accustomed to the way') in *Baldrs draumar* 6 and 13.

S. I.2.2

Some of the lines of this scene appear to be direct borrowings from a frequently repeated passage in *Vafþrúðnismál* (*Ring*, 4607–10):

Wanderer:	
Viel erforscht' ich,	*Much I've fathomed,*
erkannte viel:	*much made out:*
wicht'ges konnt' ich	*matters of moment*
manchem künden.	*I've made known to many.*

Vafþrúðnismál 3, 44, 46, 48, 50, 52, 54:

[Óðinn:]	
Fjǫlð ek fór,	*Much I have travelled,*

fjǫlð ek freistaða,	*much have I put to the test,*
fjǫlð ek reynda regin.	*much have I tried the Powers.*

S. I.2.3

Wotan offers to stake his head in a contest of wisdom (*Ring*, 4633–40):

Hier sitz' ich am Herd,	*I sit by the hearth here*
und setze mein Haupt	*and stake my head*
der Wissens-Wette zum Pfand:	*as pledge in a wager of wits:*
mein Kopf ist dein,	*my head is yours*
du hast ihn erkies't,	*to treat as you choose,*
erfräg'st du mir nicht	*if you fail to ask*
was dir frommt,	*what you need to know*
lös' ich's mit Lehren nicht ein.	*and I don't redeem it with my lore.*

This scene is very similar in structure (and even in metre) to the equivalent section of *Vafþrúðnismál* (as well as, in structure, to that in *SnE* G2). Óðinn undertakes a contest of wisdom with the giant Vafþrúðnir, and wagers his life. There is, however, a great difference between the proud giant in his hall, who lays down the rules of the game, and the cowardly dwarf in his cave. Vafþrúðnir is instantly willing to compete, while Mime is evasive, and tries to get rid of this guest. In Wagner's version the contests are far from equal; in place of the 'all-knowing' giant of *Vafþrúðnismál* we have Wotan ironically terming his opponent a 'wise', 'knowledgeable' or 'honest' smith, dwarf or Nibelung.

S. I.2.4

The nature of the questions and their answers is also rather different in Wagner's version from what it is in *Vafþrúðnismál* (*Ring*, 4649–4822). These are, broadly speaking, concerned with various items of information that have already been given, for instance on the home of the Niblungs, black elves, giants, light elves, gods and heroes, and about the sword Nothung. The information is also added that the giants live in *Riesenheim* (*Ring*, 4675–77):

Wanderer:

Auf der Erde Rücken	*On the earth's broad back*
wuchtet der Riesen Geschlecht:	*weighs the race of giants:*
Riesenheim ist ihr land.	*Riesenheim is their land.*

[In both the older versions of *Siegfried* of the spring of 1851, the text is somewhat longer (Strobel 1930, 74, 121):

frost und hitze hat sie gezeugt	*Frost and heat begot them.*
frost zeugte sie	*Frost begot them,*
hitze gebar sie	*heat delivered them.*]

This idea appears to be borrowed directly from the Prose Edda, which tells of the frozen northern rivers, Élivágar, and sparks of fire from the south (*SnE* G5):

Ok þá er mœttisk hrímin ok blær hitans svá at bráðnaði ok draup, ok af þeim kvikudropum kviknaði með krapti þess er til sendi hitann, ok varð manns líkandi, ok var sá nefndr Ymir. En hrímþursar kalla hann Aurgelmi, ok eru þaðan komnar ættir hrímþursa.

(And when the rime and the blowing of the warmth met so that it thawed and dripped, there was a quickening from these flowing drops due to the power of the source of the heat, and it became the form of a man, and he was given the name Ymir. But the frost-giants call him Aurgelmir, and from him are descended the generations of frost-giants.)

The same idea is found in the eddic poem *Vafþrúðnismál* (31; this stanza is also quoted in the same chapter of *Gylfaginning* as was just quoted):

Ór Élivágum	*From Elivagar*
stukku eitrdropar,	*shot poison drops,*
svá óx, unz varð ór jǫtunn;	*and grew until from them came a giant;*
þar órar ættir	*in him our ancestries*
kómu allar saman;	*all converged;*
því er þat æ alt til atalt.	*thus ever too terrible is all this.*

S. I.2.5

The Wanderer poses his final question (*Ring*, 4819–22):

Sag' mir, du weiser	*Tell me, you wily*
Waffenschmied,	*weapon-smith,*
wer wird aus den starken Stücken	*who do you think will forge Nothung,*
Nothung das Schwert, wohl schweißen?	*the sword, out of these mighty fragments?*

This is, admittedly, a different question from that asked by Óðinn in *Vafþrúðnismál* 54, but it is of the same nature, in that it can only be answered by the person who asks the question:

Hvat mælti Óðinn,	*What said Odin*
áðr á bál stigi,	*before he mounted the pyre*
sjálfr í eyra syni?	*himself into his son's ear?*

Siegfried, Act One, Scene Three

S. I.3.1

The Wanderer leaves, having told Mime that Nothung can only be forged by a man who is totally fearless (cf. W. III.3.2). To that man he consigns the right to cut off Mime's head. When Siegfried enters it transpires that he does not know how to fear, and wishes to learn (*Ring*, 4939–41):

Ist's eine Kunst,
was kenn ich sie nicht? –
Heraus! Was ist's mit dem Fürchten?

If it's an art,
then why don't I know it? –
Out with it! What is this fear?

Vǫlsunga saga says of Sigurðr (ch. 23):

Eigi skorti hann hug, ok aldri varð hann hræddr.

(He never lacked courage and he was never afraid.)

Wagner soon observed the common ground between this motif and the Grimm's tale (no. 4) of the boy who went out into the world to learn fear, and he adds some features from the latter to his portrayal of the brave lad (see p. 114 above and S. III.3.1. below).

S. I.3.2

Mime tells Siegfried of the dragon Fafner, who will be able to teach him fear (*Ring*, 4975–85):

Folge mir nur,
ich führe dich wohl;
sinnend fand ich es aus.
Ich weiß einen schlimmen Wurm,
der würgt' und schlang schon viel:
Fafner lehrt dich das Fürchten,
folg'st du mir zu seinem Nest.

Just follow me
and I'll lead you there;
I've thought up a way of teaching you.
I know of an evil dragon
who's killed and devoured many:
Fafner will teach you fear
if you'll follow me to his lair.

Siegfried:

Wo liegt er im Nest?

Where does he lie in his lair?

Mime:

Neid-Höhle
wird es genannt:
im Ost, am ende des Wald's.

Neidhöhle
is it called:
to the east, at the edge of the wood.

[In the *Nibelungen-Mythus* of 1848 the giants have the gold guarded by an unnamed dragon on *Gnita-Haide* (cf. p. 119 above), and in the first version of *Siegfrieds Tod* (later *Götterdämmerung*) of 1848 (*SSD* II 219), Siegfried says that the dragon writhed on a 'barren heath.' When Wagner decided in 1851 to write a separate, lighter, opera on Siegfried's youth, he transferred the setting to a forest. This environment was, in fact, consistent with both *Þiðreks saga* (166 (271)) and *Das Lied vom Hürnen Seyfrid* (6–7), although in these cases the dragon guards no gold. In the first version of *Siegfried*, the dragon is already named Fafner, but is said to be found in a place named *Neidwald* (Strobel 1930, 66).]

The placename *Gnitaheiðr* occurs in several eddic poems, and the Prose Edda says (*SnE* S40):

> *Fáfnir fór upp á Gnitaheiði ok gerði sér þar ból ok brásk í orms líki ok lagðisk á gullit.*

> *Fafnir went up on to Gnita-heath and made himself a lair there and turned into the form of a serpent and lay down on the gold.*

The element *neid* (envy, hatred, calumny) admittedly has some similarity in sound to *gnit* in *Gnitaheiðr*, while the name is also a little reminiscent of Gnipahellir in the chilling refrain of the eddic poem *Vǫluspá* (44, 49, 58):

Geyr (nú) Garmr mjǫk	*Garmr (now) bays loud*
fyr Gnipahelli.	*in front of jutting cave.*

S. I.3.3

Siegfried begs Mime to make him a sword from the fragments of Siegmund's sword which, as mentioned earlier, the Wanderer had said could only be made by one who did not know fear. Siegfried soon determines to forge the sword himself (*Ring*, 4991–5001, 5009–11, 5278–79):

Siegfried:

Drum schnell! Schaffe das Schwert,	*Be quick then! Make me the sword,*
in der Welt will ich es schwingen.	*in the world I mean to wield it.*

Mime:

Das Schwert? O Noth!	*The sword? O woe!*

Siegfried:

Rasch in die Schmiede!	*Into the smithy with you!*
Weis' was du schuf'st!	*Show me what you've made.*

Mime:

Verfluchter Stahl!	*Accursèd steel!*
Zu flicken versteh' ich ihn nicht!	*I don't understand how to patch it up!*
Den zähen Zauber	*No dwarf's resources*
bezwingt keines Zwergen Kraft.	*can master the stubborn spell.*
Wer das Fürchten nicht kennt,	*He who's never known fear*

der fänd' wohl eher die Kunst.	*would sooner find the art.*
. . .	

Siegfried:

Des Vaters Stahl	*For me my father's blade*
fügt sich wohl mir:	*will doubtless fit together:*
Ich selbst schweiße das Schwert!	*I'll forge the sword myself!*
. . .	
Schau, Mime, du Schmied:	*See, Mime, you smith:*
so schneidet Siegfried's Schwert!	*thus severs Siegfried's sword!*

Er schlägt auf den Ambos, welchen er, von oben bis unten in zwei Stücken zerspaltet, so dass er unter grossem Gepolter auseinander fällt.

(He strikes the anvil, which splits from top to bottom and falls apart with a loud crash.)

In the Poetic and Prose Eddas and *Vǫlsunga saga*, Reginn makes the sword for Sigurðr from the fragments, and in all these cases he splits the smith's anvil with the sword. *Vǫlsunga saga* says (ch. 15):

> *Reginn gerir nú eitt sverð. Ok er hann bar ór aflinum, sýndisk smiðjusveinum sem eldar brynni ór eggjunum. Biðr nú Sigurð við taka sverðinu ok kvezk eigi kunna sverð at gera ef þetta bilar. Sigurðr hjó í steðjann ok klauf niðr í fótinn, ok brast eigi né brotnaði. Hann lofaði sverðit mjǫk ok fór til árinnar með ullarlagð ok kastar í gegn straumi, ok tók í sundr er hann brá við sverðinu.*
>
> *(Then Regin made a sword. And when he drew it from the furnace, it seemed to the lads working in the smithy as if the edges were all aflame. He next told Sigurd to take the sword, saying that if this one failed, then he didn't know how to make a sword. He struck at the anvil and cleft it right down to its base, and the sword neither shattered nor snapped. He praised the sword highly and went down to the river, taking along a tuft of wool which he threw in against the stream, and it was sliced through when he held the sword against it.)*

In *Þiðreks saga* 165 (270) and *Das Lied vom Hürnen Seyfrid* 5, no sword is made, and the young lad breaks the smith's anvil with a hammer. This incident in the smithy does not occur in *Das Nibelungenlied*. Wagner may have borrowed the idea of Sigurðr making his own sword from Ludwig Uhland's poem *Siegfrieds Schwert*, first published in 1812 (see *Uhlands Gedichte und Dramen* II, 1863, 218–19).

S. I.3.4

[The *Nibelungen-Mythus* of 1848 says (p. 120 above):

> *Then Mime prompts the lad to slay the Worm, in proof of his gratitude. Siegfried wishes first to avenge his father's murder: he fares out, falls upon Hunding, and kills him.*

Vengeance for his father is still one of the themes in the first version of *Siegfrieds Tod* of 1848, in this case directed against the sons of Hunding (Strobel 1930, 28; *SSD* II, 219).]

This episode in both early versions of the plot is derived from the Poetic Edda and *Vǫlsunga saga* (chs 15–17). It appears in its most concise form in the eddic poem *Grípisspá* 9:

Fyrst muntu, fylkir,	*First you will, ruler,*
fǫður um hefna	*avenge your father,*
ok Eylima	*and all Eylimi's*
alls harms reka;	*injuries repay;*
þú munt harða	*you will the tough*
Hundings sonu	*sons of Hunding,*
snjalla, fella;	*bold ones, slay;*
mundu sigr hafa.	*you'll have victory.*

In the first version of *Der junge Siegfried* in the spring of 1851, the theme of vengeance for the father has been omitted — indeed in the new version Siegfried does not even know who his father was. Once the libretto of *Die Walküre* was written in the autumn of 1852, Hunding was of course long dead, and without issue, by the time Siegfried had grown to manhood, and so there was no one on whom to wreak vengeance (see Strobel 1930, 77). The theme of father-vengeance is touched upon, however, in S. III.2 when Siegfried is confronted by Wotan, who declares that it was his spear that shattered Nothung. Delighted to have found his father's enemy, Siegfried attacks and defeats the god (*Ring*, 6453–67).

Siegfried, Act Two, Scene One

S. II.1.1

Alberich and the Wanderer (Wotan) speak together at Fafner's cave (*Ring*, 5280–5469).

This encounter is almost entirely Wagner's invention. The only slight similarity is with *Vǫlsunga saga* ch. 18, where an old man with a long beard (Óðinn) meets Sigurðr at Fáfnir's lair (see S. II.2.1 below).

Siegfried, Act Two, Scene Two

S. II.2.1

Mime and Siegfried come to Fafner's cave. Throughout Act One it was clear that Mime wanted Siegfried to slay the dragon, so that he could take the magic ring and the gold. After Siegfried had killed the dragon, Mime intended to kill him with poison (*Ring*, 5556–64, 5582–84):

Mime:

Ich lass' dich schon:	*I'll leave you now*
am Quell dort lagr' ich mich.	*and settle down by the spring.*
Steh' du nur hier;	*You just stay here;*
steigt dann die Sonne zur Höh',	*when the sun's at its highest*
merk' auf den Wurm,	*look out for the dragon,*
aus der Höhle wälzt er sich her:	*out of the cave it will crawl this way,*
hier vorbei	*then turn*
biegt er dann,	*off here*
am Brunnen sich zu tränken . . .	*in order to drink at the well . . .*
im Abgehen, für sich	*(to himself, as he goes)*
Fafner und Siegfried –	*Fafner and Siegfried –*
Siegfried und Fafner –	*Siegfried and Fafner –*
oh, brächten beide sich um!	*if only each might kill the other!*

In the prose introduction to *Fáfnismál*, Reginn goads Sigurðr on to kill Fáfnir, and then their journey is described thus:

Sigurðr ok Reginn fóru upp á Gnitaheiði ok hittu þar slóð Fáfnis, þá er hann skreið til vatns.

(Sigurd and Regin went up on Gnitaheid and found Fafnir's track there, where he crawled to water.)

The account in the Prose Edda (*SnE* S40) is nearly the same, but in *Vǫlsunga saga* ch. 18 it is somewhat more detailed. Here it is implied that Reginn plans that Fáfnir and Sigurðr should kill each other, for an old man with a long beard (Óðinn) appears, calls Reginn's instructions 'ill-advised' and suggests a better plan:

Reginn mælti, 'Ger grǫf eina ok sezk þar í. Ok þá er ormrinn skríðr til vatns, legg þá til hjarta honum ok vinn honum svá bana. Þar fyrir fær þú mikinn frama.' . . . Nú ríðr Sigurðr á heiðina, en Reginn hverfr í brott yfrit hræddr. Sigurðr gerði grǫf eina. Ok er hann er at þessu verki, kemr at honum einn gamall maðr með síðu skeggi ok spyrr hvat hann gerir þar. Hann segir. Þá svarar inn gamli maðr, 'Þetta er óráð. Ger fleiri grafar ok lát þar í renna sveitann, en þú sit í einni ok legg til hjartans orminum.' Þá hvarf sá maðr á brottu.

('Dig a pit,' said Regin, 'and sit in it, and when the dragon comes crawling to the water, stab him to the heart and so destroy him. Then you'll win great distinction.' . . . So Sigurd rode up to the moors and Regin went off in great fright. Sigurd dug a pit, and while he was about this an old man with a long beard came up to him and asked what he was doing there. He told him. 'That's ill-advised,' the old man then replied. 'Dig other pits and let the blood run into them — you are to sit in one and stab the dragon to the heart.' Then the old man vanished.)

In *Þiðreks saga* 166 (271) and *Das Lied vom Hürnen Seyfrid* 6–11 the youth is sent alone to the dragon's lair, and here he is clearly intended to be killed by the dragon. This dragon does not guard any gold, but Sigurðr/Seyfrid smears his body with the dragon's blood or fat, gaining an invulnerable 'horny' skin. *Das Nibelungenlied* (100, *Av.* 3; 899–902, *Av.* 15) mentions Sîfrit's youthful dragon-slaying only in passing, simply to explain his invulnerability.

Wagner does not mention Siegfried digging holes to hide in, and indeed this would not have been consistent with his concept of the fearless hero, who must of course face his enemy head-on.

S. II.2.2

Siegfried sits down beneath a lime tree, and considers what his parents may have looked like (*Ring*, 5606–13):

Aber – wie sah	*But – what must*
meine Mutter wohl aus?	*my mother have looked like? –*
Das – kann ich	*That I cannot*
nun gar nicht mir denken! –	*conceive of at all! –*
Die Rehhindin gleich	*Like those of the roe-deer,*
glänzten gewiß	*her bright-shining eyes*
ihr hell schimmernden Augen, –	*must surely have glistened –*
nur noch viel schöner! – –	*only far fairer! – –*

This could be a reference to the account in *Þiðreks saga* of how a hind cared for the baby Sigurðr, who after the death of his mother was carried down a river in a glass cask to the sea, and is finally cast ashore on a spit of land (160 (266), 162 (267)):

Nú hefir sveinninn nokkut vaxit, ok er kerit hrærir við eyrina, þá brotnar þat í sundr, ok grætr barnit. Nú kom þar at ein hind ok tekr barnit í munn sér ok berr heim til síns bœlis. Þar átti hún tvau bǫrn. Þar leggr hún sveininn niðr ok lætr sveininn drekka sik, ok þar fœðir hún hann sem sín bǫrn, ok er hann þar með hindinni tólf mánaði. Nú er hann svá sterkr ok mikill sem ǫnnur bǫrn fjǫgra vetra gǫmul.

> *(Now the boy has grown somewhat and when the vessel is thrown up against the sand-bank it breaks apart, and the child cries. A hind came along and takes the child in her mouth and carries him home to her lair. There she had two young. She puts the boy down and lets him drink from her, and she feeds him there like her own young and he is there with the hind for twelve months. Now he is as strong and big as other children at the age of four.)*

S. II.2.3

Soon Fafner appears in dragon form (*Ring*, 5701–06):

Er [Siegfried] zieht sein Schwert, springt Fafner an und bleibt herausfordernd stehen . . . Fafner wälzt sich weiter auf die Höhe herauf, und speit aus den Nüstern auf Siegfried . . . Siegfried weicht dem Geifer aus, springt näher zu, und stellt sich zur Seite . . . Fafner sucht ihn mit dem Schweife zu erreichen . . . Siegfried, welchen Fafner fast erreicht hat, springt mit einem Satze über diesen hinweg, und verwundet ihn in dem Schweife . . . Fafner brüllt, zieht den Schweif heftig zurück, und bäumt den Vorderleib, um mit dessen voller Wucht sich auf Siefried zu werfen; so bietet er diesem die Brust dar; Siegfried erspäht schnell die Stelle des Herzens, und stösst sein Schwert bis an das Heft hinein. Fafner bäumt sich vor Schmerz noch höher, und sinkt, als Siegfried das Schwert losgelassen und zur Seite gesprungen ist, auf die Wunde zusammen.

(He [Siegfried] draws his sword, leaps towards Fafner and stands there, challenging him. Fafner drags himself further up the slope and spits at Siegfried through his nostrils. Siegfried avoids the venom, jumps closer and stands to one side of the dragon. Fafner tries to reach him with his tail. Siegfried, whom Fafner has almost reached, jumps over him in a single bound and wounds him in the tail. Fafner roars, draws his tail back violently and raises the front half of his body in order to throw his full weight down on Siegfried; in doing so he exposes his breast to the latter; Siegfried quickly notes the position of the heart and thrusts in his sword as far as the hilt. Fafner rears up even higher in his pain and sinks down on the wound, as Siegfried releases the sword and leaps to one side.)

The slaying of the dragon is recounted in the eddic poem *Fáfnismál* and in the Prose Edda (*SnE* S40), but the most detailed account is in *Vǫlsunga saga* ch. 18:

> *Ok er ormrinn skreið til vatns, varð mikill landskjálfti, svá at ǫll jǫrð skalf í nánd. Hann fnýsti eitri alla leið fyrir sik fram, ok eigi hræddisk Sigurðr né óttask við þann gný. Ok er ormrinn skreið yfir grǫfina, þá leggr Sigurðr sverðinu undir bœxlit vinstra, svá at við hjǫltum nam. Þá hleypr Sigurðr upp ór grǫfinni ok kippir at sér sverðinu ok hefir allar hendr blóðgar upp til axlar. Ok er inn mikli ormr kenndi síns banasárs, þá laust hann hǫfðinu ok sporðinum svá at allt brast í sundr er fyrir varð.*

(And when the dragon crawled to the water, the earth tremors were so violent that all the land round about shook. He breathed out poison all over the path ahead, but Sigurd was neither frightened nor dismayed by the noise. And when the dragon crawled across the pit, Sigurd thrust in the sword under the left shoulder, and it sunk in up to the hilt. Then Sigurd leapt out of the pit, wrenching back the sword, and getting his arms bloody right up to the shoulders. And when the huge dragon felt its death wound, it lashed with its tail and head, shattering everything that got in its way.)

In *Þiðreks saga* 166 (271) Sigurðr kills the dragon, not with a sword, but with a wooden club. In *Das Lied vom Hürnen Seyfrid*, Seyfrid slays a dragon to save the princess Krimhilt (139–49). *Das Nibelungenlied* (100, *Av.* 3) says only that Sîfrit slew a dragon in his youth, and gives no further details.

S. II.2.4

Fafner and Siegfried have a conversation before the dragon dies (*Ring*, 5707–10, 5717–20):

Fafner:

Wer bist du, kühner Knabe, *der das Herz mir traf?* *Wer reizte des Kindes Muth* *zu der mordlichen That?*	*Who are you, valiant lad,* *who has wounded me to the heart?* *Who goaded the mettlesome child* *to commit this murderous deed?*
. . .	
Du helläugiger Knabe, *unkund deiner selbst,* *wen du gemordet,* *meld' ich dir.*	*You bright-eyed boy,* *unknown to yourself:* *I'll tell you* *whom you have murdered.*

The eddic poem *Fáfnismál* (1, 5) contains very similar material, though arranged rather differently:

Sveinn ok sveinn, *hverjum ertu sveini um borinn?* *Hverra ertu manna mǫgr,* *er þú á Fáfni rautt* *þinn inn frána mæki?* *Stǫndumk til hjarta hjǫrr.*	*Boy! and again, boy!* *to what boy were you born?* *Of what people are you son,* *that you should redden on Fafnir* *your shining sword?* *The blade stands in my heart.*
. . .	
Hverr þik hvatti, *hví hvetjaz lézt,* *mínu fjǫrvi at fara?* *Inn fráneygi sveinn,* *þú áttir fǫður bitran . . .*	*Who urged you,* *why did you let yourself be urged,* *to attack my life?* *Shining-eyed boy,* *you had a fierce father . . .*

S. II.2.5

Fafner tells Siegfried that Mime is plotting to kill him (*Ring*, 5731–34):

Blicke nun hell,	*See clearly now,*
blühender Knabe;	*you radiant youth;*
der dich Blinden reizte zur That,	*he who goaded you on in your blindness*
beräth jetzt des Blühenden Tod.	*is plotting the death of the radiant youth.*

In *Vǫlsunga saga* ch. 18 Fáfnir says:

Reginn, bróðir minn, veldr mínum dauða, ok þat hlœgir mik er hann veldr ok þínum dauða, ok ferr þá sem hann vildi.

(My brother Regin has brought about my death, and I am glad that he will bring about your death, too — that will be just what he wanted.)

S. II.2.6

Before Fafner dies, Siegfried asks the question uppermost in his mind (*Ring*, 5737–42):

Siegfried:

Woher ich stamme,	*Advise me yet*
rathe mir noch;	*on where I have come from;*
weise ja schein'st du	*wise you seem,*
Wilder im Sterben;	*wild beast, in dying;*
rath' es nach meinem Namen:	*divine it from my name:*
Siegfried bin ich genannt.	*Siegfried I am called.*

This corresponds to *Fáfnismál* 4:

Ætterni mitt	*My lineage,*
kveð ek þér ókunnigt vera	*I declare to be unknown to you,*
ok mik sjálfan it sama;	*and myself likewise;*
Sigurðr ek heiti,	*Sigurd I am called,*
Sigmundr hét minn faðir,	*Sigmund was my father,*
er hefk þik vápnum vegit.	*I who have slain you with weapons.*

S. II.2.7 (*Ring*, 5747–53)

Fafner hat sich im Sterben zur Seite gewälzt. Siegfried zieht ihm jetzt das Schwert aus der Brust; dabei wird seine Hand vom Blute benezt: er fährt heftig mit der Hand auf.

(Fafner, in dying, has rolled over on one side. Siegfried now draws his sword from his breast; as he does so, his hand comes into contact with the dragon's blood: he snatches his hand away.)

Siegfried:

Wie Feuer brennt das Blut!	*Its blood is burning like fire.*

Er führt unwillkürlich die Finger zum Munde, um das Blut von ihnen abzusaugen. Wie er sinnend vor sich hinblickt, wird seine Aufmerksamkeit immer mehr von dem Gesange der Waldvögel angezogen.

(Involuntarily, he raises his fingers to his mouth in order to suck the blood from them. As he gazes thoughtfully in front of him, his attention is caught increasingly by the song of the forest birds.)

Siegfried:

Ist mir doch fast –	*It's almost as though*
als sprächen die Vög'lein zu mir:	*the woodbirds were speaking to me:*
nützte mir das	*was this brought about*
des Blutes Genuß? –	*by the taste of the blood? –*
Das selt'ne Vög'lein hier –	*That strange little bird here –*
horch! was singt es mir?	*listen! what is it singing to me?*

The account of the dragon's blood on the tongue, and understanding of the speech of birds, occurs in the Prose Edda (*SnE* S40), *Vǫlsunga saga* chs 19–20, and in the following prose passage in the eddic poem *Fáfnismál* (between stanzas 31 and 32):

> *Sigurðr tók Fáfnis hjarta ok steikti á teini. Er hann hugði, at fullsteikt væri, ok freyddi sveitinn ór hjartanu, þá tók hann á fingri sínum ok skynjaði, hvárt fullsteikt væri. Hann brann ok brá fingrinum í munn sér. En er hjartblóð Fáfnis kom á tungu hánum, ok skilði hann fuglsrǫdd. Hann heyrði, at igður klǫkuðu á hrísinu.*
>
> *(Sigurðr took Fafnir's heart and roasted it on a spit. When he thought that it would be cooked, and the blood frothed out of the heart, he took his finger and tried whether it was cooked. He was burned and stuck his finger in his mouth. And when Fáfnir's heart-blood came on his tongue, then he understood the speech of birds. He heard that there were nuthatches twittering in the brushwood.)*

Wagner does not use the motif of roasting the heart. In *Þiðreks saga* Sigurðr does not taste the dragon's blood, but the broth from its meat, which he is cooking; the effect is the same.

S. II.2.8

The voice of a woodbird, now intelligible, is heard (*Ring*, 5754–61):

Hei! Siegfried gehört	*Hey! Siegfried now owns*
nun der Niblungen Hort:	*the Nibelung hoard:*
o, fänd' in der Höhle	*O might he now find*
den Hort er jetzt!	*the hoard in the cave!*
Wollt' er den Tarnhelm gewinnen	*If he wanted to win the Tarnhelm,*
der taugt' ihm zu wonniger That:	*it would serve him for wondrous deeds:*
doch wollt' er den Ring sich errathen,	*but could he acquire the ring,*

der macht' ihn zum Walter der Welt! *it would make him the lord of the world!*

[In the *Nibelungen-Mythus* of 1848 (p. 121 above) there seem to be many woodbirds; in the spring of 1851 a single nightingale, and later that summer just one woodbird (Strobel 1930, 83, 156).]

In the Prose Edda and in *Þiðreks saga* (166 (271)) there are two birds; their only advice to Sigurðr is to go home and kill Mímir, as he has just killed his brother, Reginn, and may expect him to seek vengeance. In the eddic poem *Fáfnismál* (32–38) there appear to be seven nuthatches, and six in *Vǫlsunga saga* (ch. 20). The fourth of these says:

> *Þá væri hann vitrari ef hann hefði þat sem þær hǫfðu ráðit honum, ok riði síðan til bóls Fáfnis ok tœki þat it mikla gull er þar er.*
>
> *(He would be wiser to do as they advised . . . and afterwards ride to Fafnir's lair, taking the great treasure that lies there.)*

On the Ring and its power (*Ring*, 5760–61), cf. R. 1.4.

S. II.2.9

Siegfried takes the woodbird's advice (*Ring*, 5762–64):

Siegfried:

Dank, liebes Vög'lein,	*My thanks for your counsel,*
für deinen Rath:	*you dear little bird:*
gern folg' ich dem Ruf.	*I'll gladly follow your call.*

Er wendet sich nach hinten, und steigt in die Höle hinab, wo er alsbald gänzlich verschwindet.

(He turns to the back of the stage and descends into the cave, where he soon disappears from sight.)

The prose at the end of the eddic poem *Fáfnismál* says (*Vǫlsunga saga* ch. 20 has an almost identical passage):

> *Sigurðr reið eptir slóð Fáfnis til bœlis hans ok fann þat opit, ok hurðir af járni ok gætti; af járni váru ok allir timbrstokkar í húsinu, en grafit í jǫrð niðr.*
>
> *(Sigurd rode along Fafnir's track to his lair and found it open and with doors and door-frames of iron; of iron too were all the beams in the house and it was dug into the ground.)*

Siegfried, Act Two, Scene Three

S. II.3.1

Over the body of the dragon, Alberich and Mime quarrel (*Ring*, 5765–5858).

This exchange has no parallel in medieval literature, either Icelandic or German, and is Wagner's invention.

S. II.3.2

Siegfried comes out of the cave with the Tarnhelm and the ring, leaving the gold behind (*Ring*, 5859–63):

Was ihr mir nützt,	*What use you are*
weiß ich nicht:	*I do not know:*
doch nahm ich euch	*but I took you*
aus des Hort's gehäuftem Gold,	*from the heaped-up gold of the hoard*
weil guter Rath mir es rieth.	*since goodly counsel counselled me to do so.*

The following is from the end of *Fáfnismál*:

> *Þar fann Sigurðr stórmikit gull ok fyldi þar tvær kistur. Þar tók hann œgishjálm ok gullbrynju ok sverðit Hrotta ok marga dýrgripi.*
>
> *(There Sigurd found a huge amount of gold and filled two chests with it. He took there a helmet of terror and a gold coat of mail and the sword Hrotti and many fine treasures.)*

In the Icelandic versions of the story the ring is not specifically mentioned as being in Sigurðr's possession until later, when he either gives the ring to Brynhildr (*SnE* S41), or takes it away from her (*Vǫlsunga saga* ch. 29).

S. II.3.3

The woodbird warns Siegfried against Mime (*Ring*, 5869–77):

Hei! Siegfried gehört	*Hey! Siegfried now owns*
nun der Helm und der Ring!	*the helm and the ring!*
O traute er Mime	*Oh let him not trust*
dem treulosen nicht!	*the treacherous Mime!*
Hörte Siegfried nur scharf	*Were Siegfried to listen keenly*
auf des Schelmen Heuchlergered':	*to the rogue's hypocritical words,*
wie sein Herz es meint	*he'd be able to understand*
kann er Mime versteh'n;	*what Mime means in his heart;*
so nützt' ihm des Blutes Genuß.	*thus the taste of the blood was of use to him.*

A similar warning occurs in *Vǫlsunga saga* ch. 20, and in the eddic poem *Fáfnismál* 33 (quoted *SnE* S40) the second nuthatch twitters:

Þar liggr Reginn,	*There lies Regin*
ræðr um við sik,	*planning with himself,*
vill tæla mǫg,	*intending to trick the boy*
þann er trúir hánum,	*who trusts him,*

berr af reiði	*in his wrath he composes*
rǫng orð saman.	*crooked speeches.*
Vill bǫlva smiðr	*The maker of mischiefs intends*
bróður hefna.	*to avenge his brother.*

S. II.3.4

Mime emerges from his hiding place and sees Siegfried deep in thought (*Ring*, 5878–84):

Er sinnt, und erwägt	*He ponders and broods on*
der Beute Werth: –	*the booty's worth: –*
weilte wohl hier	*has some wily Wand'rer*
ein weiser Wand'rer,	*been loitering here,*
schweifte umher,	*roaming around*
beschwatzte das Kind	*and beguiling the child*
mit list'ger Runen Rath?	*with his counsel of cunning runes?*

In this reference to the Wanderer (Wotan), who visited Mime in S. I.2 and who talked with Alberich on this very spot in S. II.1, we have yet another allusion to the old long-bearded man (Óðinn) who appears from time to time in *Vǫlsunga saga* to give Sigurðr and others advice (chs 13, 17, 18, cf. chs 3, 11 and 44).

S. II.3.5 (*Ring*, 5892–94)

Er tritt näher an Siegfried heran, und bewillkommet diesen mit schmeicheln-den Gebärden.

(He [Mime] comes closer to Siegfried and welcomes him with wheedling gestures.)

Willkommen, Siegfried!	*Welcome, Siegfried!*
Sag', du Kühner,	*Tell me, brave boy,*
hast du das Fürchten gelernt?	*have you learned the meaning of fear?*

In *Vǫlsunga saga* ch. 19 (and in similar terms in the eddic poem *Fáfnismál* 23), the corresponding meeting between Reginn and Sigurðr is recounted as follows:

> *Eptir þetta kom Reginn til Sigurðar ok mælti, 'Heill, herra minn; mikinn sigr hefir þú unnit er þú hefir drepit Fáfni, er engi varð fyrr svá djarfr at á hans gǫtu þorði sitja, ok þetta fremðarverk mun uppi meðan verǫldin stendr.'*
>
> *(After this Regin came to Sigurd and said: 'Greetings, my lord. You have won a great victory by killing Fafnir, when before no man was daring enough to lie in wait for him, and this great deed will live for as long as the world shall last.')*

S. II.3.6

Mime does his best to conceal the fact that he intends to kill Siegfried. But Siegfried, by tasting the blood of the dragon, has gained the ability to understand Mime's true intentions (*Ring*, 5903–16):

Siegfried:

Der mich ihn morden hieß,	*The man who bade me murder him*
den hass' ich mehr als den Wurm.	*I hate much more than the dragon.*

Mime:

Nur sachte! Nicht lange	*But soft! You'll not*
sieh'st du mich mehr:	*have to see me much longer.*
zum ew'gen Schlaf	*I'll soon lock*
schließ' ich dir die Augen bald!	*your eyes in lasting sleep!*
Wozu ich dich brauchte,	*You've done*
hast du vollbracht;	*what I needed you for;*
jetzt will ich nur noch	*all that I still want to do*
die Beute dir abgewinnen: –	*is to win from you the booty: –*
mich dünkt, das soll mir gelingen;	*I think that I ought to succeed in that;*
zu bethören bist du ja leicht!	*you're easy enough to fool after all!*

Siegfried:

So sinn'st du auf meinen Schaden?	*So you're planning to do me harm?*

Mime:

Wie sagt' ich denn das?	*What, did I say that?*

Wagner here makes use of the exchange between Reginn and Sigurðr and the twittering of the nuthatches in *Fáfnismál* (25, 33–38) and *Vǫlsunga saga* chs 19–20:

> *Nú stendr Reginn ok sér niðr í jǫrðina langa hríð. Ok þegar eptir þetta mælti hann af miklum móði, 'Bróður minn hefir þú drepit, ok varla má ek þessa verks saklauss vera.' Nú tekr Sigurðr sitt sverð, Gram, ok þerrir á grasinu ok mælti til Regins, 'Fjarri gekk þú þá, er ek vann þetta verk ok ek reynda þetta snarpa sverð með minni hendi, ok mínu afli atta ek við orms megin, meðan þú látt í einum lyngrunni, ok vissir þú eigi hvárt er var himinn eða jǫrð.' . . . [Sigurðr] heyrði at igður klǫkuðu á hrísinu hjá honum. 'Þar sitr Sigurðr ok steikir Fáfnis hjarta. Þat skyldi hann sjálfr eta. Þá mundi hann verða hverjum manni vitrari.' Ǫnnur segir, 'Þar liggr Reginn ok vill véla þann sem honum trúir.' Þá mælti in þriðja, 'Hǫggvi hann þá hǫfuð af honum, ok má hann þá ráða gullinu því inu mikla einn.' . . . Þá mælti in fimmta, 'Eigi er hann svá horskr sem ek ætla ef hann vægir honum, en drepit áðr bróður hans.' Þá mælti in sétta, ' Þat væri snjallræði ef hann dræpi hann ok réði einn fénu.'*
>
> *(Regin now stood looking down at the ground for a long time. And there-upon he said in great anger: 'You have killed my brother, but I can scarcely*

be free of blame for the deed.' Then Sigurd took up his sword Gram, wiped it on the grass and said to Regin: 'You went a good way off while I performed the deed, and I tried out this keen sword with my own hand, and with my own strength I strove against the might of the dragon — while you were lying in a heather bush, not knowing whether you were on your head or your heels!' . . . [Sigurd] heard some nuthatches twittering near him in the thicket. 'There sits Sigurd, roasting Fafnir's heart. He should eat it himself, and then he'd be wiser than any man.' 'There lies Regin meaning to play false the man who trusts him,' said a second. Then said a third: 'Let him srike off his head. Then he can have the great treasure all to himself.' . . . Then said a fifth: 'If he spares him, having previously killed his brother, he's not as wise as I imagine.' Then said the sixth: 'It would be a sound plan if he killed him and had the treasure all to himself.')

S. II.3.7 (*Ring*, 6003–06)

Siegfried *(holt mit sem Schwerte aus)*:	*(raising his sword)*:
Schmeck' du mein Schwert,	*Have a taste of my sword,*
ekliger Schwätzer!	*you loathsome babbler!*

Er führt . . . einen jähen Streich nach Mime; dieser stürzt sogleich todt zu Boden . . .

(He deals Mime a sudden blow; the latter immediately falls to the ground, dead . . .)

. . .

Siegfried:	
Neides-Zoll	*Nothung pays*
zahlt Nothung.	*the wages of spite.*

The killing of Reginn is told briefly in the eddic poem *Fáfnismál* (prose between stanzas 39 and 40) and the Prose Edda (*SnE* S40), and in *Vǫlsunga saga* ch. 20 the episode is as follows, after the birds have warned Sigurðr of Reginn's treachery:

Þá mælti Sigurðr, 'Eigi munu þau óskǫp at Reginn sé minn bani, ok heldr skulu þeir fara báðir brœðr einn veg.' Bregðr nú sverðinu Gram ok høggr hǫfuð af Regin.

'Death at Regin's hands is not my evil destiny,' said Sigurd then. 'Better instead for both brothers to go the same way.' Then he drew the sword Gram and struck off Regin's head.

The dragon's gold, his dying words, the tasting of the blood, understanding of the speech of birds and the slaying of the smith are, of course, not to be found in *Das Nibelungenlied* or in *Das Lied vom Hürnen Seyfrid*.

S. II.3.8

After having buried Fafner and Mime, Siegfried lies down again beneath the lime tree and sings of his loneliness (*Ring*, 6042–46):

Doch ich – bin so allein,	*But I am so alone,*
hab' nicht Brüder noch Schwestern:	*have no brothers or sisters;*
meine Mutter schwand,	*my mother died,*
mein Vater fiel:	*my father was slain:*
nie sah sie der Sohn! –	*their son never saw them! –*

This lament is strongly reminiscent of Sigurðr's words in *Fáfnismál* 2:

Gǫfugt dýr ek heiti,	*Noble animal I'm called,*
en ek gengit hefk	*but I have gone*
inn móðurlausi mǫgr;	*a motherless son;*
fǫður ek ákka,	*no father have I,*
sem fira synir,	*like sons of men,*
geng ek æ einn saman.	*always I go alone.*

S. II.3.9

The woodbird now tells Siegfried about Brünnhilde (*Ring*, 6065–73):

Hei! Siegfried erschlug	*Hey! Siegfried's now slain*
nun den schlimmen Zwerg!	*the evil dwarf!*
Jetzt wüßt ich ihm noch	*Now I know*
das herrlichste Weib.	*the most glorious wife for him.*
Auf hohem Felsen sie schläft,	*High on a fell she sleeps,*
Feuer umbrennt ihren Saal:	*fire burns round her hall:*
durchschritt' er die Brunst,	*if he passed through the blaze*
weckt' er die Braut,	*and awakened the bride,*
Brünnhilde wäre dann sein!	*Brünnhilde then would be his!*

The birds give similar advice in the eddic poem *Fáfnismál* (40, 42–44):

Mey veit ek eina,	*I know one maid,*
myklu fegrsta,	*by far the fairest,*
gulli gœdda,	*endowed with gold,*
ef þú geta mættir.	*if you might win her.*
. . .	
Salr er á há	*There is a hall on high*
Hindarfjalli,	*Hindarfell,*
allr er hann útan	*round the outside it is all*
eldi sveipinn;	*surrounded with fire;*
þann hafa horskir	*this have wise*
halir um gǫrvan	*heroes built*
ór ódøkkum	*of shining*
Ógnar ljóma.	*river's light [gold].*

Veit ek á fjalli	*I know on the mountain*
fólkvitr sofa,	*battle-maid sleeps,*
ok leikr yfir	*and plays over her*
lindar váði.	*lime-tree's destruction [fire].*
. . .	
Knáttu, mǫgr, sjá	*You shall, young man, see*
mey und hjálmi . . .	*maid under helmet . . .*

Siegfried, Act Three, Scene One

S. III.1.1

The Wanderer (Wotan) awakens the seeress Erda from her sleep (*Ring*, 6111–14, 6127–31):

Wache! Wala!	*Waken, vala!*
Wala, erwach'!	*Vala, awake!*
Aus langem Schlaf	*From lengthy sleep*
weck' ich dich schlummernde auf.	*I awake you, slumberer.*
. . .	
Allwissende!	*All-knowing!*
Urweltweise!	*Primevally wise!*
Erda! Erda!	*Erda! Erda!*
Ewiges Weib!	*Eternal woman!*
Wache, erwache,	*Waken, awaken,*
du Wala! erwache!	*you vala, awaken!*

On the name Wala, see R. 4.4. The context of the awakening of the seeress and Wotan's conversation with her have obvious models in the Poetic Edda, especially *Baldrs draumar, Vǫluspá* and *Grógaldr* which begins thus (1):

Vaki þú, Gróa!	*Wake thou, Gróa*
vaki þú, góð kona!	*wake thou, good woman!*
Vek ek þik dauðra dura.	*I awake thee at the doors of the dead.*

Although *Grógaldr* is not in the medieval collection of eddic poems, and is first found in manuscripts of the late seventeenth century, it was (like *Fjǫlsvinnsmál*, S. III.2.1) included by Simrock in his edda-translation of 1851 and would thus have been known to Wagner. Another possible model for him is the opening of *Hyndluljóð*, which, although it too is not in the main collection, is also in Simrock's translation:

Vaki, mær meyja,	*Awake, maid of maids,*
vaki, mín vina,	*awake, my friend,*
Hyndla systir,	*sister Hyndla,*
er í helli býr!	*who live in a cave!*

Nú er røkr røkra,	*Now is the twilight of twilights,*
ríða vit skulum	*ride we shall*
til Valhallar	*to Val-hall*
ok til vés heilags.	*and to the holy sanctuary.*

In the eddic poem *Baldrs draumar*, Óðinn calls himself *Vegtamr* ('accustomed to the way', lit. 'way-tame'), and his role here is reminiscent of Wagner's Wanderer. In this poem, he rides to Niflhel to seek knowledge of the fate of his son, Baldr, who has had ominous dreams (4):

Þá reið Óðinn	*Then rode Odin*
fyr austan dyrr,	*to the east of the doorway,*
þar er hann vissi	*where he knew*
vǫlu leiði;	*was the seeress's grave;*
nam hann vittugri	*he began for the wise one*
valgaldr kveða,	*a corpse-arousing spell to chant,*
unz nauðig reis,	*until perforce she rose,*
nás orð um kvað.	*spoke a corpse's words.*

S. III.1.2 (*Ring*, 6032–36)

Die Hölengruft erdämmert. Bläulicher Lichtschein: von ihm beleuchtet steigt mit dem Folgenden Erda sehr allmählich aus der Tiefe auf. Sie erscheint wie von Reif bedeckt; Haar und Gewand werfen einen glitzernden Schein von sich.

(The vaulted cave begins to glow with a bluish light, in which Erda is seen rising very slowly from the depths. She appears to be covered in hoarfrost; hair and garments give off a glittering sheen.)

Erda:

Stark ruft das Lied;	*Strong is the call of your lay;*
kräftig reizt der Zauber;	*mighty the lure of its magic spell;*
ich bin erwacht	*from knowing sleep*
aus wissendem Schlaf:	*am I roused:*
wer scheucht den Schlummer mir?	*who is it who drives my slumber away?*

In *Baldrs draumar* 5 the seeress says of herself:

Hvat er manna þat,	*Which of men is that*
mér ókunnra,	*unknown to me,*
er mér hefir aukit	*who has caused to me*
erfit sinni?	*this troublesome way?*
Var ek snivin snjóvi	*I was snowed on with snow,*
ok slegin regni	*and beaten with rain,*
ok drifin dǫggu;	*and driven with dew;*
dauð var ek lengi.	*long was I dead.*

S. III.1.3
The Wanderer gives Erda her answer (*Ring*, 6137–40, 6157–58):

Wanderer:

Der Weckrufer bin ich,	*Your awakener am I,*
und Weisen üb' ich,	*and strains I sing*
daß weithin wache	*that all may wake*
was fester Schlaf verschließt.	*whom heavy sleep enfolds.*
. . .	
Daß ich nun Kunde gewänne,	*That I may now gain knowledge,*
weck' ich dich aus dem Schlaf.	*I wake you from your sleep.*

Baldrs draumar (6):

Vegtamr ek heiti,	*Way-tame I am called,*
sonr em ek Valtams;	*I'm son of Slaughtered-tame;*
segðu mér ór helju –	*speak to me from the world of the dead –*
ek man ór heimi –	*I shall [speak to you] from [this] world –*

S. III.1.4
Erda avoids answering her interlocutor's questions, and asks him repeatedly to allow her to go back to sleep (*Ring*, 6222–23):

Lass' mich wieder hinab:	*Let me descend once more:*
Schlaf verschließe mein Wissen!	*let sleep enfold my knowledge!*

In *Baldrs draumar* the seeress says three times (7, 9, 11):

Nauðug sagðak,	*Under compulsion I told,*
nú mun ek þegja.	*now shall I be silent.*

S. III.1.5
Erda is appalled when the Wanderer tells her what he has done to Brünnhilde in punishment for her supposed disobedience (*Ring*, 6206–09, 6216–21):

Erda:

Wirr wird mir,	*I've grown confused*
seit ich erwacht:	*since I was wakened:*
wild und kraus	*wild and awry*
kreis't die Welt!	*the world revolves!*
. . .	
Der die That entzündet,	*Does he who urged the deed*
zürnt um die That?	*grow wroth when it is done?*
Der die Rechte wahrt,	*Does he who safeguards rights*
der die Eide hütet,	*and helps uphold sworn oaths*

wehret dem Recht,	*gainsay that right*
herrscht durch Meineid?	*and rule through perjured oath?*

This echoes the seeress's accounts of the moral degeneration of the world in *Vǫluspá*, especially stanzas 26 and 45:

Á genguz eiðar,	*The oaths were reneged on,*
orð ok sœri,	*words and vows,*
mál ǫll meginlig,	*all the mighty contracts*
er á meðal fóru.	*which had passed between them.*
. . .	
Brœðr munu berjaz	*Brothers will fight each other*
ok at bǫnum verðaz,	*and be each other's slayers,*
munu systrungar	*siblings will*
sifjum spilla.	*violate kinship.*

S. III.1.6

Finally they accuse each other of acting under false pretences (*Ring*, 6238–39, 6242–43):

Erda:

Du bist – nicht	*You are not*
was du dich nenn'st!	*what you say you are!*
. . .	

Wanderer:

Du bist – nicht,	*You are not*
was du dich wähn'st!	*what you think you are!*

In the next-to-last stanza of *Baldrs draumar* (13), the following exchange takes place.

'Ertattu Vegtamr,	*'You are not Way-tame,*
sem ek hugða,	*as I thought,*
heldr ertu Óðinn,	*rather are you Odin,*
aldinn gautr.'	*the ancient sacrificial victim.'*
'Ertattu vǫlva,	*'You are not a prophetess*
né vís kona,	*or a wise woman,*
heldr ertu þriggja	*rather are you mother*
þursa móðir.'	*of three giants.'*

The content of *Baldrs draumar* has little in common with the *Ring*, but the form and the course of events are similar.

Siegfried, Act Three, Scene Two

S. III.2.1

When the Wanderer/Wotan has dismissed Erda, Siegfried appears, on his way to the mountaintop. Wotan attempts by various means to hinder his progress and ascertain whether he really is the chosen one. Finally Siegfried breaks Wotan's spear with Siegmund's reforged sword, which Wotan had previously shattered with his spear. This is the ultimate proof of Siegfried's power. At this point Wotan gives up and disappears (*Ring*, 6291–466; cf. W. II.5.1; *Ring*, 3386–87).

The prolonged dispute between Wotan and Siegfried has no direct parallel in older literature, either German or Icelandic. But something similar takes place in the late eddic poem *Fjǫlsvinnsmál* (see S. III.1.1). Svipdagr comes in disguise to Menglǫð's castle, and is stopped by a guard. They exchange questions and answers for a long time until it is revealed that no one may sleep in Menglǫð's embrace but he whose name is Svipdagr. Only then will Fjǫlsviðr allow him inside.

S. III.2.2 (*Ring*, 6470–73)

Die wachsende Helle der immer tiefer sich senkenden Feuerwolken trifft Siegfried's Blick.

(Siegfried's attention is caught by the growing brightness of the clouds of fire that roll down the mountain towards him.)

Siegfried:

Ha, wonnige Gluth!	*Ha, rapturous glow!*
Leuchtender Glanz!	*Radiant gleam!*
Strahlend nun offen	*The pathway lies open,*
steht mir die Straße . . .	*Shining before me . . .*

Hellstes Leuchten der Flammen.

(The flames reach their brightest intensity.)

Compare this stanza in *Vǫlsunga saga* ch. 29, probably from a lost eddic poem:

Eldr nam at œsask	*The fire grew great,*
en jǫrð at skjálfa	*the ground did shake*
ok hár logi	*and tall flame*
við himni gnæfa.	*towered to the sky.*
Fár treystisk þar	*Few warrior kings*
fylkis rekka	*were willing to ride*
eld at ríða	*or fare onwards through*
né yfir stíga.	*the fire's rage.*

Once again, one may consider whether this could be a poetic description of a volcanic eruption (cf. W. III.3.2). Compare also *Vǫluspá* 57 (G. III.3.12).

Siegfried, Act Three, Scene Three

S. III.3.1
Having passed through the fire, Siegfried sees Brünnhilde asleep in her armour, lying beneath a shield (*Ring*, 6484–96, 6503–08):

Was strahlt mir dort entgegen? –	*What beam of light bedazzles my gaze? –*
Welch' glänzendes Stahl-geschmeid?	*What metalwork wrought in glittering steel?*
Blendet mir noch	*Is it the blaze*
die Lohe den Blick? –	*that still blinds my eye? –*
Helle Waffen? –	*Shining weapons! –*
Heb' ich sie auf?	*Shall I remove them?*

Er hebt den Schild ab, und erblickt Brünnhilde's Gestalt, während ihr Gesicht jedoch zum grossen Theil vom Helm verdeckt ist.

(He raises the shield and sees Brünnhilde's form, although her face remains largely concealed by her helmet.)

Ha! in Waffen ein Mann: –	*Ha! In weapons a man: –*
wie mahnt mich wonnig sein Bild! –	*how his likeness fills me with wonder! –*
Das hehre Haupt	*Does his helm perhaps*
drückt wohl der Helm?	*press on his noble head?*
Leichter würd' ihm,	*Lighter it were*
lös't' ich den Schmuck.	*if I loosened his headgear.*

Vorsichtig löst er den Helm, und hebt ihn der Schlafenden ab; langes lockiges Haar bricht hervor. Siegfried erschrickt.

(He carefully loosens the helmet and removes it from the sleeper; long curling hair breaks free. Siegfried starts:)

Ach! – wie schön! –	*Ah! – how fair! –*
. . .	
Von schwellendem Athem	*His breast is heaving*
schwingt sich die Brust: –	*with swelling breath: –*
brech' ich die engende Brünne?	*shall I break the trammelling breastplate open?*

Er versucht die Brünne zu lösen.

(He tries to loosen the byrnie.)

Komm', mein Schwert,	*Come my sword,*
Schneide das Eisen!	*and cut through the iron!*

Siegfried zieht sein Schwert, durchschneidet mit zarter Vorsicht die Panzerringe zu beiden Seiten der Rüstung, und hebt dann die Brünne und die Schienen ab, so dass nun Brünnhilde in einem weichen weiblichen Gewande vor ihm liegt . . . Er fährt erschreckt und staunend auf.

(Siegfried draws his sword and, with tender care, cuts through the rings of mail on both sides of the armour. He then lifts away the breastplate and greaves, so that Brünnhilde now lies before him in a woman's soft garment . . . He starts up in shock and astonishment.)

Das ist kein Mann! – –	*No man is this! – –*

The awakening of the valkyrie is described in the Poetic and Prose Eddas (*Sigrdrífumál*, introductory prose; *SnE* S41), and *Vǫlsunga saga* has the following (ch. 21):

> *En er hann kom at, stóð þar fyrir honum skjaldborg ok upp ór merki. Sigurðr gekk í skjaldborgina ok sá at þar svaf maðr ok lá með ǫllum hervápnum. Hann tók fyrst hjálminn af hǫfði honum ok sá at þat var kona. Hon var í brynju, ok var svá fǫst sem hon væri holdgróin. Þá reist hann ofan ór hǫfuðsmátt ok í gegnum niðr ok svá út í gegnum báðar ermar, ok beit sem klæði.*
>
> *(And when he got up to it there stood before him a shield rampart with a banner out on top. Sigurd went inside the shield rampart and saw a man there, asleep and lying fully armoured. First he removed the helmet from his head and saw that it was a woman. She had on a hauberk and it was as tight as if grown into the flesh. Then he sheared right down from the neck, then right along both sleeves, and the blade bit in as if cutting cloth.)*

Wagner depicts Siegfried acting far more carefully than Sigurðr in the saga, and watching the woman for longer. In the saga, Brynhildr cannot have been wearing much under her byrnie, since it was 'as though it had grown to her flesh.'

It is at this point in the *Ring* that Siegfried, gripped by sexual panic, learns what fear is (see p. 114 and S. I.3.1 above).

S. III.3.2

Overcoming his fear, Siegfried attempts to wake the sleeping woman (*Ring*, 6546–66):

Siegfried:

Erwache! erwache!	*Awake! Awake!*
heiliges Weib! – –	*Thrice-hallowed woman! – –*
Sie hört mich nicht. –	*She cannot hear me. –*
So saug' ich mir Leben	*So I suck life*
aus süßesten Lippen –	*from her sweetest of lips –*
sollt' ich auch sterbend vergeh'n!	*though I should perish and die!*

Er . . . heftet . . . seine Lippen auf ihren Mund . . . Brünnhilde schlägt die Augen auf. Siegfried fährt auf und bleibt vor ihr stehen . . .

(He . . . presses his lips on her mouth . . . Brünnhilde opens her eyes. Siegfried starts up and remains standing in front of her . . .)

Brünnhilde:

Heil dir, Sonne!	*Hail to you, sun!*
Heil dir, Licht!	*Hail to you, light!*
Heil dir, leuchtender Tag!	*Hail to you, light-bringing day!*
Lang' var mein Schlaf;	*Long was my sleep;*
ich bin erwacht:	*awakened am I:*
wer ist der Held,	*who is the hero*
der mich erweckt'?	*who woke me?*

Siegfried:

Durch das Feuer drang ich,	*I pressed through the fire*
das den Fels umbrann:	*that burned round the fell;*
ich erbrach dir den festen Helm:	*I broke open your tight-fitting helmet:*
Siegfried bin ich,	*Siegfried am I*
der dich erweckt.	*who woke you.*

Brünnhilde:

Heil euch, Götter!	*Hail to you, gods!*
Heil dir, Welt!	*Hail to you, world!*
Heil dir, prangende Erde!	*Hail to you, splendent earth!*

With the exception of the kisses, which are reminiscent of The Sleeping Beauty and other fairy-tales, the entire content and dialogue of this episode is found in the prose introduction and first four stanzas of the eddic poem *Sigrdrífumál*, though the order sometimes differs:

Þá tók hann brynju af henni; en hon vaknaði, ok settiz hon upp ok sá Sigurð ok mælti:

(Then he took the mailcoat off her, and she awoke, and she sat up and saw Sigurd, and said:)

'Hvat beit brynju?	*'What cut my mailcoat?*
Hví brá ek svefni?	*Why did I shake off my sleep?*
Hverr feldi af mér	*Who has taken off me*
fǫlvar nauðir?'	*my pale constraints?'*

Hann svaraði:	*He replied:*

'Sigmundar burr;	*'Sigmund's son;*
sleit fyr skǫmmu	*Sigurd's sword*
hrafns hrælundir	*tore just now*
hjǫrr Sigurðar.'	*raven's corpse-flesh.'*

'Lengi ek svaf,	*'Long I slept,*
lengi ek sofnuð var.	*long was I asleep.*
. . .	
Heill dagr!	*Hail day!*
Heilir dags synir!	*Hail sons of day!*
Heil nótt ok nipt!	*Hail night and her kin!*
. . .	
Heilir Æsir!	*Hail Æsir!*
Heilar Ásynjur!	*Hail goddesses!*
Heil sjá in fjǫlnýta fold!'	*Hail the most kindly earth!'*

The main difference here is that Wagner does not have Brünnhilde greeting the night, as she does the day. Perhaps he felt it was not fitting to mention darkness at this joyful moment. And of course he was not familiar with Iceland's bright summer nights.

S. III.3.3

Brünnhilde speaks of the prophetic love for Siegfried which motivated her apparent disobedience to Wotan (*Ring*, 6602–10):

Brünnhilde:

Was du nicht weißt,	*What* you *don't know*
weiß ich für dich:	*I know for you:*
doch wissend bin ich	*and yet I am knowing*
nur – weil ich dich liebe! –	*only because I love you! –*
O Siegfried! Siegfried!	*O Siegfried! Siegfried!*
Siegendes Licht!	*Conquering light!*
Dich liebt' ich immer:	*I loved you always:*
denn mir allein	*To me alone*
erdünkte Wotan's Gedanke.	*was Wotan's thought revealed.*

In the eddic poem *Fjǫlsvinnsmál* 49 (cf. S. III.1.1, S. III.2.1), Menglǫð says:

Lengi ek sat	*Long sat I*
Lyfjabergi á,	*on Lyfjaberg,*
beið ek þín dœgr ok daga;	*waited for you days and days;*
nú þat varð,	*now has come to be*
er ek vætt hefi,	*what I have waited for,*
at þú ert kominn, mǫgr! til minna sala.	*that you are come, young man! to my halls.*

S. III.3.4

[In the older versions of *Siegfried* of 1851, Brünnhilde tells the main story of *Die Walküre* at a similar point to that in which some references to it appear in the final version (*Ring*, 6608–25). Her narrative began as follows (Strobel 1930, 93, cf. 185):

> *Hilde hiess ich, wenn ich streif erregte, die brünne trug ich, wenn in kampf ich zog: Brünnhillde nannte mich Wodan.*
>
> *(I was called Hilde when I made war, I wore armour when I went into battle: Wodan named me Brünnhilde.)*

This account was, of course, made redundant as soon as the opera *Die Walküre* existed in its own right.]

It is reminiscent of the wording of the Prose Edda (*SnE* S41):

> *Þá vaknaði hon ok nefndisk Hildr. Hon er kǫlluð Brynhildr ok var valkyrja.*
>
> *(Then she awoke and said her name was Hild. She is known as Brynhild, and was a valkyrie.)*

Another parallel exists in the eddic poem *Helreið Brynhildar* (7):

Hétu mik allir	*All called me*
í Hlymdǫlum	*in Hlymdalir*
Hildi undir hjálmi,	*Hild under helmet,*
hverr er kunni.	*each who knew of me.*

S. III.3.5

A long courtship game commences. Siegfried is filled with passion, and longs for Brünnhilde. She is reluctant to submit to his will, feeling this is best for both of them. She refers to her armour, and to the horse Grane, as symbols of her untouchability as a valkyrie. Yet she admits she has longed for Siegfried all her life, and finally gives way (*Ring*, 6626–6898):

This episode has no direct prototype in the texts that describe the couple's first meeting on the mountaintop. In *Vǫlsunga saga*, on the other hand, the second meeting of Sigurðr and Brynhildr, in Brynhildr's hall, is described as follows (ch. 25):

> *Hann réttir í mót hǫndina kerinu ok tók hǫnd hennar með ok setti hana hjá sér. Hann tók um háls henni ok kyssti hana ok mælti, 'Engi kona hefir þér fegri fæzk.' Brynhildr mælti, 'Vitrligra ráð er þat at leggja eigi trúnað sinn á konu vald, því at þær rjúfa jafnan sín heit.' Hann mælti, 'Sá kœmi beztr dagr yfir oss at vér mættim njótask.' Brynhildr svarar, 'Eigi er þat skipat at vit búim saman. Ek em skjaldmær, ok á ek með herkonungum*

hjálm . . .' Sigurðr svarar, 'Þá frjóumsk vér mest ef vér búum saman . . . ok ekki lér mér tveggja huga um þetta, ok þess sver ek við guðin at ek skal þik eiga eða enga konu ella.' Hon mælti slíkt. Sigurðr þakkar henni þessi ummæli ok gaf henni gullhring, ok svǫrðu nú eiða af nýju.

(He reached for the cup and at the same time took her hand and drew her down beside him. Embracing her, he kissed her and said: 'No woman born is lovelier than you.' 'Wiser not to surrender your trust to a woman, for they always break their vows,' said Brynhild. 'The day we wed would be our happiest,' he said. 'We're not fated to share our lives together,' Brynhild replied. 'I am a shield-maiden, wearing a helmet along with warrior kings . . .' 'We shall prosper best if we share our lives together,' answered Sigurd . . . 'I'm not in two minds about this, and I swear by the gods that I either marry you or no one at all.' She spoke to the same effect. Sigurd thanked her for what she had said and gave her a gold ring. Then they again repeated their vows.)

SIEGFRIED: SURVEY OF MOTIFS

The Ring	Eddic poems	Prose Edda	Vǫlsunga saga	Þiðreks saga	Nibelungenlied	Hürnen Seyfrid
Long pregnancy			Long pregnancy			
Mime brings up and teaches Siegfried	Reginn fosters and teaches Sigurðr	Reginn fosters and teaches Sigurðr	Reginn fosters and teaches Sigurðr	Mime fosters and teaches Sigurðr		Seyfrid works for a smith
Siegfried's aversion to Mime				Sigurðr's aversion to Mímir		Seyfrid's aversion to smith
Serpent lies on gold	Serpent lies on gold	Serpent lies on gold	Serpent lies on gold	Serpent, but no gold	Dragon, but no gold	Gold kept by dragon
Wotan as Wanderer	Óðinn as Wanderer		Óðinn as Wanderer			
Wotan talks with Mime	Óðinn talks with dwarfs and giants					
Viel erforscht' ich, erkannte viel	*Fjǫlð ek fór, fjǫlð ek freistaða*					
Schwarzalben Lichtalben		døkkálfar, svart-álfar, ljósálfar				
Giants produced from frost and heat	Giants produced from frost and heat	Giants produced from frost and heat				
Sword from fragments three times	Sword from fragments	Sword from fragments	Sword from fragments three times			

The Ring	Eddic poems	Prose Edda	Vǫlsunga saga	Þiðreks saga	Nibelungenlied	Hürnen Seyfrid
Siegfried cleaves anvil with sword	Sigurðr cleaves anvil with sword	Sigurðr cleaves anvil with sword	Sigurðr cleaves anvil with sword	Sigurðr breaks anvil with hammer	[Grimm: boy breaks anvil]	Seyfrid breaks smith's anvil
Siegfried avenges father's death	Sigurðr avenges father's death		Sigurðr avenges father's death			
Mime incites Siegfried	Reginn incites Sigurðr	Reginn incites Sigurðr	Reginn incites Sigurðr			
Wanderer at Fafner's cave			One with long beard at Fáfnir's lair			
Serpent creeps to water	Serpent creeps to water	Serpent creeps to water	Serpent creeps to water			
Siegfried gives false name	Sigurðr hides his name		Sigurðr hides his name			
Helläugige Knabe	fráneygi sveinn		fráneygi sveinn			
Fafner in form of serpent	Fáfnir in form of serpent	Fáfnir turns into serpent shape	Fáfnir becomes a serpent	Reginn becomes a serpent		
Who incited you?	Who incited you?		Who incited you?			
Fafner warns Siegfried against inciter and hoard	Fáfnir warns Sigurðr against Reginn and gold		Fáfnir warns Sigurðr against Reginn and gold			
Killing of serpent	Killing of Fáfnir	Killing of Fáfnir	Killing of Fáfnir	Killing of serpent	Killing of dragon	Killing of dragon
Blood in mouth	Blood on tongue	Blood on tongue	Blood on tongue	Broth on tongue		

The Ring	Eddic poems	Prose Edda	Vǫlsunga saga	Þiðreks saga	Nibelungenlied	Hürnen Seyfrid
Bird's voice	Understanding of birds' speech	Understanding of birds' speech	Understanding of birds' speech	Understanding of birds' speech		
Bird's warning against Mime	Bird warns Sigurðr against Reginn	Bird warns Sigurðr against Reginn	Bird warns Sigurðr against Reginn	Bird warns Sigurðr against Mímir		
Siegfried kills Mime	Sigurðr kills Reginn	Sigurðr kills Reginn	Sigurðr kills Reginn	Sigurðr kills Mímir		
Siegfried takes little from cave	Sigurðr takes all the gold	Sigurðr takes all the gold	Sigurðr takes all the gold			
Bird suggests going to Brünnhilde	Birds direct to valkyrie		Birds direct to Brynhildr			
Felsenburg	Hindarfjall	fjall	Hindarfjall	borg		cave
Wotan speaks with Wala	Óðinn's talks with seeresses					
Siegfried cuts Brünnhilde's mailcoat	Sigurðr cuts Brynhildr's mailcoat	Sigurðr cuts Brynhildr's mailcoat	Sigurðr cuts Brynhildr's mailcoat			
Siegfried wakes Brünnhilde	Siegfried wakes Brynhildr	Siegfried wakes Brynhildr	Siegfried wakes Brynhildr			
Brünnhilde's hymn of praise	*Sigrdrífumál*					
Hilde hieß ich	*Hétu mik Hildi*	Names herself Hildr				

GÖTTERDÄMMERUNG

CHARACTERS	ICELANDIC EQUIVALENTS*
Humans	
Siegfried	Sigurðr
Gunther	Gunnarr
Gutrune	Guðrún
Hagen	Hǫgni
Mannen (vassals)	[Gjúkaþegnar]
Frauen (women)	
Supernatural beings	
The three Norns	Urðr, Verðandi, Skuld (*nornir*)
Brünnhilde	Brynhildr
Waltraute	[Valþrúðr]
Rheintöchter	Ránardœtr

*The names in brackets are those used in the surtitles for the production of the *Ring* in Reykjavik in 1994, which were presented in an Icelandic version by Þorsteinn Gylfason. They are not found in early Icelandic texts.

Götterdämmerung, title

The title for the last opera of the *Ring*, which literally means 'twilight (or dusk) of the gods', and replaced Wagner's earlier title (*Siegfrieds Tod*) for his draft of this opera, is a literal translation of the Old Icelandic word *Ragnarøkkr*, which is the one used in the Prose Edda and the eddic poem *Lokasenna* 39. The word found in other eddic poems including *Vǫluspá*, is *Ragnarǫk*, and means 'doom of the powers', and is presumably the earlier form. The word in the Prose Edda may be the result of 'folk-etymology'. Though Wagner did find out that his title was not the oldest term for the myth, he decided not to change it, thinking that it was a more poetic and suitable concept for what he had in mind.

Götterdämmerung, Prologue

G. P. 1
The three Norns, tall female figures in long, dark, veil-like garments, are seen at Brünnhilde's rock in the pre-dawn darkness (*Ring*, 6899, 6909–18):

First Norn:

An der Welt-Esche	*At the world-ash*
wob ich einst,	*once I wove*
da groß und stark	*when, tall and strong,*
dem Stamm entgrünte	*a forest of sacred branches*
weihlicher Äste Wald;	*blossomed from its bole;*
im kühlen Schatten	*in its cooling shade*
rauscht' ein Quell,	*there plashed a spring,*
Weisheit raunend	*whispering wisdom,*
rann sein Gewell';	*its ripples ran:*
da sang ich heil'gen Sinn.	*I sang then of sacred things.*

Three Fates, who spin the threads of men's lives, are familiar from Graeco-Roman mythology. In the Prose Edda, their Norse cousins, the Norns, the ash Yggdrasill and the well at its roots are introduced as follows (*SnE* G15):

Askrinn er allra tréa mestr ok beztr. Limar hans dreifask yfir heim allan ok standa yfir himni . . . Þar stendr salr einn fagr undir askinum við brunninn, ok ór þeim sal koma þrjár meyjar þær er svá heita: Urðr, Verðandi, Skuld. Þessar meyjar skapa mǫnnum aldr. Þær kǫllum vér nornir . . . Góðar nornir og vel ættaðar skapa góðan aldr, en þeir menn er fyrir óskǫpum verða, þá valda því illar nornir.

(The ash is of all trees the biggest and best. Its branches spread out over all the world and extend across the sky . . . There stands there one beautiful hall under the ash by the well, and out of this hall come three maidens whose names are Weird, Verdandi [becoming], Skuld [necessity]. These maidens shape men's lives. We call them norns. . . . Good norns, ones of noble parentage, shape good lives, but as for those people that become the victims of misfortune, it is evil norns that are responsible.)

G. P. 2

The Norns begin to speak of Wotan's role in the disaster that overcame the world-ash (*Ring*, 6919–22):

First Norn:

Ein kühner Gott	*A dauntless god*
trat zum Trunk an den Quell;	*came to drink at the spring;*
seiner Augen eines	*one of his eyes*
zahlt' er als ewigen Zoll.	*he paid as toll for all time.*

The Prose Edda says of the ash tree and Óðinn's eye (*SnE* G15):

En undir þeiri rót er til hrímþursa horfir, þar er Mímis brunnr, er spekð ok mannvit er í fólgit, ok heitir sá Mímir er á brunninn. Hann er fullr af vísindum fyrir því at hann drekkr ór brunninum af horninu Gjallarhorni.

Þar kom Alfǫðr ok beiddisk eins drykkjar af brunninum, en hann fekk eigi fyrr en hann lagði auga sitt at veði.

(But under the root that reaches towards the frost-giants, there is where Mimir's well is, which has wisdom and intelligence contained in it, and the master of the well is called Mimir. He is full of learning because he drinks of the well from the horn Gjallarhorn. All-father went there and asked for a single drink from the well, but he did not get one until he placed his eye as a pledge.)

The myth of Mímir's well and Óðinn's eye is also mentioned in the eddic poem *Vǫluspá* 28 (quoted in *SnE* G15):

Alt veit ek, Óðinn,	*I know it all, Odin,*
hvar þú auga falt,	*where you deposited your eye,*
í inum mæra	*in that renowned*
Mímis brunni.	*well of Mimir.*
Drekkr mjǫð Mímir	*Mimir drinks mead*
morgin hverjan	*every morning*
af veði Valfǫðrs –	*from Val-father's pledge.*
vituð ér enn, eða hvat?	*Know you yet, or what?*

G. P. 3

[Wagner wrote a draft of a prelude to *Götterdämmerung* as early as October 1848. At the beginning, the Norns mention three of the points of the compass (Strobel 1930, 56):

First Norn:

Im Osten knüpft ich das Seil.	*In the east I knot a thread.*

Second Norn:

Nach Westen winde ich es.	*To the west I turn it.*

Third Norn:

Nach Norden will ich's werfen.	*To the north I fling it.*

This is reminiscent of the beginning of *Helgakviða Hundingsbana I* (4), where the Norns twist the threads of destiny of the new-born hero:

Þær austr ok vestr	*They east and west*
enda fálu,	*secretly fastened its ends,*
þar átti lofðungr	*the ruler owned*
land á milli;	*the land in between;*
brá nipt Nera	*the kinswoman of Neri [a norn]*
á norðrvega	*towards the north*
einni festi,	*threw one cord;*
ey bað hon halda.	*she bade it hold for ever.*

The entire episode was reworked by Wagner in the final version, until little was left except a reference to Wotan and the fount of wisdom.]

G. P. 4

The Norns throw a rope from one to another, and exchange words. Five times they end with the following question, or a variation of it (*Ring*, 6941, 6962, 6991, 7002, 7024):

Weißt du, wie das wird?	*Do you know what will become of it?*

This is undeniably similar to the oft-repeated refrain in the eddic poem *Vǫluspá* (27, 28, 33, 35, 39, 41, 48, 62, 63):

Vituð ér enn, eða hvað?	*Know you yet, or what?*

G. P. 5

Finally, they say they have no more wisdom to tell the world, and say that they will return to the mother below (*Ring*, 7043–46):

Zu End' ewiges Wissen!	*An end to eternal wisdom!*
Der Welt melden	*Wise women no longer*
Weise nichts mehr.	*tell the world their tidings.*
Hinab! Zur Mutter! Hinab!	*Descend! To our mother! Descend!*

These words are equally reminiscent of the end of *Vǫluspá* (66):

Nú mun hon søkkvaz.	*Now will she sink down.*

G. P. 6

Siegfried and Brünnhilde, about to part, appear and reminisce about their love (*Ring*, 7055–58):

Brünnhilde:

Was Götter mich wiesen,	*What gods have taught me*
gab ich dir:	*I gave to you:*
heilige Runen	*a bountiful store*
reichen Hort.	*of hallowed runes.*

A long section of the eddic poem *Sigrdrífumál* (5–19) and the corresponding section of *Vǫlsunga saga* (ch. 21) list various runes that can be used for magical purposes. This is the part of the list in stanza 19:

Þat eru bókrúnar,	*These are book-runes,*
þat eru bjargrúnar,	*these are birth-helping runes,*
ok allar ǫlrúnar,	*and all ale-runes,*
ok mætar meginrúnar,	*and valuable power-runes,*
hveim er þær kná óviltar	*for any who can, unconfused*
ok óspiltar	*and uncorrupted,*
sér at heillum hafa;	*use them for their good;*
njóttu, ef þú namt,	*enjoy them, if you have learned them,*
unz rjúfaz regin.	*until the powers are destroyed.*

G. P. 7

Brünnhilde continues (*Ring*, 7059–62):

Doch meiner Stärke	*But the maidenly source*
magdlichen Stamm	*of all my strength*
nahm mir der Held,	*was taken away by the hero*
dem ich nun mich neige.	*to whom I now bow my head.*

Only in *Þiðreks saga* is Brynhildr's superhuman strength attributed to her virginity; she has denied her husband, Gunnarr, his conjugal rights, and he confides in his friend Sigurðr (228 (319)):

> *Ok nú svarar Sigurðr: 'Ek mun segja þér, hvat til berr, er á þessa lund ferr. Hún hefir þá náttúru, at á meðan hún fær haldit sínum meydómi, mun varliga fást sá karlmaðr, er afl hafi við henni, ok þegar er því er brugðit, þá er hún ekki sterkari en aðrar konur.'*
>
> *(And Sigurd replies: 'I shall tell you why it is that this happens. Her nature is such, that as long as she is able to keep her virginity, a man can hardly be found who is equal to her in strength, but when it is lost she will be no stronger than other women.')*

G. P. 8

The lovers speak of Siegfried's obligation (*Ring*, 7071–78, 7090–97):

Siegfried:

Mehr gab'st du, Wunderfrau,	*You gave me more, O wondrous woman,*
als ich zu wahren weiß:	*than I know how to cherish:*
nicht zürne, wenn dein Lehren	*chide me not if your teaching*
mich unbelehret ließ!	*has left me untaught!*
Ein Wissen doch wahr' ich wohl:	*One lore I cherish yet:*
daß mir Brünnhilde lebt;	*that Brünnhilde lives for me;*
eine Lehre lernt' ich leicht:	*one lesson I learned with ease:*
Brünnhilde's gedenken!	*to be ever mindful of Brünnhild'!*
. . .	

Brünnhilde:

Gedenk' der Eide,	*Recall the oaths*
die uns einen;	*that unite us;*
gedenk' der Treue,	*recall the trust*
die wir tragen;	*that we place in each other;*
gedenk' der Liebe,	*recall the love*
der wir leben:	*for which we live:*
Brünnhilde brennt dann ewig	*Brünnhilde then will burn for aye*
heilig dir in der Brust! –	*with holy fire in your breast! –*

Sigurðr's vows to Brynhildr are mentioned in the eddic poem *Grípisspá* (31), *Vǫlsunga saga* (ch. 22) and *Þiðreks saga* (227 (319)), but not, of course, in *Das Nibelungenlied*. In *Vǫlsunga saga*, Sigurðr's exchange with Brynhildr on this occasion ends as follows (ch. 22):

> *Sigurðr mælti, 'Engi finnsk þér vitrari maðr, ok þess sver ek at þik skal ek eiga, ok þú ert við mitt œði.' Hon svarar, 'Þik vil ek helzt eiga, þótt ek kjósa um alla menn.' Ok þetta bundu þau eiðum með sér.*
>
> *('No one is wiser than you,' said Sigurd, 'and I swear it is you I shall marry, and we are ideally suited.' 'I should wish to marry you,' she answered, 'even though I might have the choice of all the men there are.' And this they swore, each to the other.)*

In *Þiðreks saga* 227 (319) their vows are recalled after Sigurðr has married Grímhildr, when he accompanies Gunnarr to ask for Brynhildr's hand:

> *It fyrra sinn, er þau hǫfðu hitzt, þá hafði hann því heitit henni með eiðum, at hann skyldi engrar konu fá nema hennar, ok hún it sama at giftast engum manni ǫðrum.*
>
> *(The previous time they had met he had promised her with oaths that he would take no other wife than her, and she likewise that she would take no other husband.)*

G. P. 9

Siegfried gives Brünnhilde the Nibelung's ring as a pledge of fidelity (*Ring*, 7098–7107):

Siegfried:

Lass' ich, Liebste, dich hier	*If, my dearest, I leave you here*
in der Lohe heiliger Hut,	*in the fire's hallowed guard,*
zum Tausche deiner Runen	*in return for all your runes*
reich' ich dir diesen Ring.	*I hand this ring to you.*
Was der Thaten je ich schuf,	*Whatever deeds I have done,*
dess' Tugend schließt er ein;	*their virtue it enfolds;*
ich erschlug einen wilden Wurm,	*I slew a savage dragon*
der grimmig lang' ihn bewacht.	*that long had guarded it grimly.*
Nun wahre du seine Kraft	*Now keep its power safe*
als Weihe-Gruß meiner Treu'!	*in solemn token of my troth.*

In the Prose Edda, Sigurðr does not give Brynhildr the ring until they meet each other again, and he is then in the form of Gunnarr (*SnE* S41). In *Vǫlsunga saga* too, Sigurðr does not give her the gold ring until their second encounter (ch. 25), cf. S. III.3.5. In *Þiðreks saga* he exchanges rings with her (229 (319)) and in *Das Nibelungenlied* (679–

80, *Av.* 10) the hero does not give her a ring as a bed present, but takes a ring and a belt as well from her.

G. P. 10

Brünnhilde places the ring on her finger (*Ring*, 7108–09, 7118–22):

Ihn geiz' ich als einziges Gut:	*I covet it as my only wealth:*
für den Ring nimm nun auch mein Roß!	*for the ring now take my horse!*
. . .	
Doch wohin du ihn führ'st,	*But wherever you lead him*
– sei es durch's Feuer –	*– be it through fire –*
grauenlos folgt dir Grane;	*Grane will fearlessly follow;*
denn dir, o Helde,	*for you, O hero,*
soll er gehorchen!	*he shall obey!*

The name of the horse has appeared twice before (*Ring*, 3469 and 6648). In the prose introduction to the eddic poem *Reginsmál* and in *Vǫlsunga saga* ch. 13, Sigurðr chooses the horse from the stud of King Hjálprekr; in *Vǫlsunga saga* this is on Óðinn's advice, and Grani is there said to be descended from Sleipnir, Óðinn's eight-footed steed.

In *Þiðreks saga* (168 (273) the horse is Brynhildr's gift to Sigurðr. In this case her home is a castle, and not a mountaintop. Sigurðr comes to her after killing his foster-father, Mímir.

> *Hingat hefi ek ætlat mitt erendi, því at Mímir, minn fóstri, vísaði mér hingat til hests eins, er Grani heitir, er þú átt. Nú vilda ek hann þiggja, ef þú vill veitt hafa.' 'Þiggja máttu einn hest af mér, ef þú vill, ok þótt fleiri vilir þú.'*
>
> *('I decided to come here, because my foster-father Mimir directed me here for a horse of yours called Grani. Now I would accept it if you are willing for it to be mine.' 'You can have a horse from me, if you wish, and more than one, if you like.')*

The horse Grani is mentioned neither in *Das Nibelungenlied* nor in *Das Lied vom Hürnen Seyfrid.*

Götterdämmerung, Act One, Scene One

G. I.1.1

Gunther and Gutrune, who are brother and sister (children of Gibich and Grimhild), and their maternal half-brother Hagen, sit in their hall by the Rhine. Hagen is the illegitimate son of Alberich and Grimhild. He says it is a disgrace that both Gunther and Gutrune remain unmarried, and this will not contribute to their power or respect (*Ring*, 7154–79).

The name-forms Gunther and Hagen are from *Das Nibelungenlied* (*NL* 4, 9, *Av.* 1; in the form Hagene in this poem), where the two are quite unrelated, and Gunther's sister is called Kriemhilt (*NL* 2). There is also similarity and in most cases etymological connection between these names and those of the names of Gjúki and his wife Grímhildr, and their offspring Gunnarr, Hǫgni and Guðrún, in many of the eddic poems, the Prose Edda and *Vǫlsunga saga*. In these texts, Hǫgni is in no way inferior to Gunnarr. Guttormr/Gothormr is the name of Gjúki's stepson. In *Þiðreks saga*, Gunnarr's sister is named Grímhildr, corresponding to the Kriemhilt of *Das Nibelungenlied*, and Hǫgni is their half-brother, the son of an elf who impregnated their mother as she lay in drunken slumber in a garden (cf. W. II.2.4). Hǫgni is here a malevolent character.

G. I.1.2
Siegfried comes sailing down the Rhine to the Gibichungs' castle, with his horse aboard ship. The brothers decide to give him a warm reception (*Ring*, 7255–74).

In all earlier versions, German and Icelandic, the hero arrives on horseback (*NL* 71–72, *Av.* 3; *SnE* S41; *Vǫlsunga saga* ch. 28).

Götterdämmerung, Act One, Scene Two

G. I.2.1
When he enters, the hero behaves in a typically forthright way (*Ring*, 7277–80):

Siegfried (to Gunther):

Dich hört' ich rühmen	*I heard you praised*
weit am Rhein:	*far along the Rhine:*
nun ficht mit mir,	*now fight with me,*
oder sei mein Freund!	*or be my friend!*

This challenge to a duel appears to be derived from *Das Nibelungenlied*, where a prolonged exchange of insults takes place between Sîfrit and the Burgundian king before they make their peace (*NL* 104–28, *Av.* 3). The Poetic and Prose Eddas and *Vǫlsunga saga* ch. 28 do not mention any confrontation when Sigurðr comes to the Gjúkungs. On the contrary, he appears to receive an immediate welcome, and indeed his own behaviour is courteous (*Sigurðarkviða in skamma* 1–2).

G. I.2.2

On Hagen's instructions, Gutrune gives Siegfried a drink, prepared by Hagen, to make him forget the past (*Ring*, 7334–47):

Gutrune:

Willkommen, Gast,	*Welcome, guest,*
in Gibich's Haus!	*to Gibich's home!*
Seine Tochter reicht dir den Trank.	*His daughter brings you this drink.*

Siegfried:

Vergaß' ich alles	*Were all forgotten*
was du mir gab'st,	*that you gave me,*
von einer Lehre	*one lesson alone*
lass' ich doch nie: –	*I'll never neglect: –*
den ersten Trunk	*this first drink*
zu treuer Minne,	*to true remembrance,*
Brünnhilde, bring' ich dir!	*Brünnhild', I drink to you!*

Er setzt das Trinkhorn an und trinkt in einem langen Zuge . . . Er reicht das Horn an Gutrune zurück, welche, verschämt und verwirrt, die Augen vor ihm niederschlägt. Siegfried heftet den Blick mit schnell entbrannter Leidenschaft auf sie.

(He raises the horn to his lips and takes a long draught. He returns the horn to Gutrune who, ashamed and confused, stares at the ground. Siegfried fixes his gaze on her with suddenly inflamed passion.)

Die so mit dem Blitz	*You who sear my sight*
den Blick du mir seng'st,	*with your flashing glance,*
was senk'st du dein Auge vor mir?	*why lower your eyes before me?*
Ha, schönstes Weib!	*Ha, fairest of women!*

The actual potion of forgetfulness is derived from *Vǫlsunga saga* alone. In this case it is neither Hǫgni nor Guðrún herself who administers the drink to Sigurðr, but their mother, Grímhildr, who was a sorceress (ch. 28):

> *Þat finnr Grímhildr hvé mikit Sigurðr ann Brynhildi, ok hvé opt hann getr hennar; hugsar fyrir sér at þat væri meiri gipta at hann staðfestisk þar ok ætti dóttur Gjúka konungs . . . Eitt kveld er þeir sátu við drykk, ríss dróttning upp ok gekk fyrir Sigurð ok kvaddi hann og mælti, 'Fǫgnuðr er oss á þinni hérvist, ok allt gott viljum vér til yðar leggja. Tak hér við horni ok drekk . . . brœðr þínir [skulu vera] Gunnarr ok Hǫgni ok allir er eiða vinnið . . .' Sigurðr tók því vel, ok við þann drykk munði hann ekki til Brynhildar. Hann dvalðisk þar um hríð . . . Ok eitt kveld skenkir Guðrún. Sigurðr sér at hon er væn kona ok at ǫllu in kurteisasta.*
>
> *(Grimhild noticed how deeply Sigurd loved Brynhild, and how often he talked of her. She thought that it would be a good thing if he settled there and married King Gjuki's daughter . . . One evening as they sat drinking, the queen got up, went to Sigurd and addressing him said: 'We are delighted*

that you are here. We wish to give you all that's good. Take this horn and drink . . . Gunnar and Hogni, and all who take the oaths, shall be your brothers . . .' Sigurd took this well, and with that drink he lost all memory of Brynhild. He stayed there for a time . . . One evening Gudrun was serving wine. Sigurd saw tht she was a beautiful woman and most courtly in every way.)

Sigurðr's loss of memory and the wiles of Grímhildr are also mentioned in the eddic poem *Grípisspá* 31–35.

G. I.2.3

Gunther explains that he has a certain bride in mind (*Ring*, 7365–66, 7369, 7371, 7373, 7375–84):

Auf eine setzt' ich den Sinn, *die kein Rath mir je gewinnt.*	*On one have I set my mind* *whom no shift can ever win me.*
. . .	
Auf Felsen hoch ihr Sitz –	*High on a fell her home –*
. . .	
ein Feuer umbrennt den Saal. –	*a fire burns round the hall. –*
. . .	
Nur wer durch das Feuer bricht –	*Only he who breaks through the fire –*
. . .	
– darf Brünnhilde's Freier sein. *Nun darf ich den Fels nicht erklimmen;* *das Feuer verglimmt mir nie!*	*– may sue for Brünnhilde's love.* *Now I may not climb that fell;* *the fire will never die down for me!*
Siegfried: *Ich – fürchte kein Feuer:* *für dich frei' ich die Frau;* *denn dein Mann bin ich,* *und mein Muth ist dein –* *gewinn' ich mir Gutrun' zum Weib.*	 *I'm not afraid of any fire:* *for you I'll woo the woman;* *for your liegeman am I* *and my courage is yours, –* *if I can win Gutrun' as wife.*
Gunther: *Gutrune gönn' ich dir gerne.*	 *I grant you Gutrune gladly.*
Siegfried: *Brünnhilde bring' ich dir.*	 *I'll bring back Brünnhilde for you.*

The description of Brünnhilde's home and conduct is quite similar to that in the Prose Edda (*SnE* S41):

Hon sat á Hindafjalli ok var um sal hennar vafrlogi, en hon hafði þess heit strengt at eiga þann einn mann er þorði at ríða vafrlogann.

(She was living on Hindafell and around her hall was a flickering flame, and she had made a vow to wed only that man who dared to ride the flickering flame.)

A similar description of Brynhildr's situation is found in *Vǫlsunga saga* ch. 29, and the eddic poem *Grípisspá* (35) says of Sigurðr's proposition:

Þik mun Grímhildr	*Grimhild will*
gǫrva véla,	*completely trick you,*
mun hon Brynhildar	*she'll urge you to ask*
biðja fýsa	*for the hand of Brynhild*
Gunnari til handa,	*on Gunnar's behalf,*
Gotna dróttni;	*lord of Goths;*
heitr þú fljótliga fǫr	*at once you'll promise*
fylkis móður.	*the ruler's mother to go.*

G. I.2.4

Gunther wants to know how Siegfried can help him (*Ring*, 7385–87):

Gunther:

Wie willst du sie täuschen?	*How do you plan to deceive her?*

Siegfried:

Durch des Tarnhelm's Trug	*Through the Tarnhelm's disguise*
tausch' ich mir deine Gestalt.	*I'll change my shape with yours.*

The Prose Edda (*SnE* S41) and *Vǫlsunga saga* (ch. 29) say only that Sigurðr and Gunnarr 'exchanged forms/appearances' (and in the Prose Edda names), and there is no mention of a magical helmet. In *Vǫlsunga saga* Grímhildr is said to have enabled them to do this:

> *Gunnarr ríðr nú at eldinum, ok vill Grani eigi ganga. Gunnarr má nú eigi ríða þenna eld. Skipta nú litum, sem Grímhildr kenndi þeim Sigurði ok Gunnari.*
>
> *(Gunnar then rode at the fire, but Grani wouldn't go on. So Gunnar could not ride through the fire. Sigurd and Gunnar then exchanged appearances as Grimhild had taught them.)*

G. I.2.5

Siegfried and Gunther swear oaths of loyalty (*Ring*, 7388–7400):

Gunther:

So stelle Eide zum Schwur!	*Swear oaths, then, as a vow!*

Siegfried:

Blut-Brüderschaft	*Let an oath be sworn*
schwöre ein Eid!	*to blood-brotherhood.*

Hagen füllt ein Trinkhorn mit frischem Wein; dieses hält er dann Siegfried und Gunther hin, welche sich mit ihren Schwertern die Arme ritzen und diese kurze Zeit über die Öffnung des Trinkhorns halten.

(Hagen fills a drinking-horn with new wine and offers it to Siegfried and Gunther, who scratch their arms with their swords and hold them for a moment over the top of the horn. Both men place two fingers on the horn, which Hagen continues to hold between them.)

Siegfried:

Blühenden Lebens	*The freshening blood*
labendes Blut	*of flowering life*
träufelt' ich in den Trank.	*I let trickle into the drink.*

Gunther:

Bruder-brünstig	*Bravely blended*
muthig gemischt	*in brotherly love,*
blüh' im Trank unser Blut.	*may our lifeblood blossom in the drink!*

Both:

Treue trink' ich dem Freund:	*Faith I drink to my friend:*
froh und frei	*happy and free*
entblühe dem Bund	*may blood-brotherhood*
Blut-Brüderschaft heut'!	*spring from our bond today*!

The vows of Sigurðr, Gunnarr and Hǫgni are referred to repeatedly in the Prose Edda (*SnE* S41), *Vǫlsunga saga* (chs 28, 32) and the eddic poem *Grípisspá*; in the fragment of *Sigurðarkviða* (*Brot af Sigurðarkviðu* 17), the mixing of blood is also mentioned:

Mantattu, Gunnarr,	*You did not, Gunnar,*
til gǫrva þat,	*remember too clearly,*
er þit blóði í spor	*that you both let your blood*
báðir rendut.	*run into your footprints.*

Das Nibelungenlied tells only of the comradeship of Sîfrit and Gunther, and of Sîfrit's marriage to Gunther's sister (*NL* 126–32, *Av.* 3; 607–29, *Av.* 10), but not of any formal vows (except Gunther's vow that he would give Sîfrit Kriemhilt in marriage, *NL* 608, *Av.* 10).

G. I.2.6

Hagen has not taken part in the oath-swearing (*Ring*, 7409–17):

Siegfried (to Hagen):

Was nahm'st du am Eide nicht Theil?	*Why did you take no part in the oath?*

Hagen:

Mein Blut verdürb' euch den Trank!	*My blood would mar your drink!*
Nicht fließt mir's ächt	*It doesn't flow truly*
und edel wie euch;	*and nobly like yours;*
störrisch und kalt	*stubborn and cold*
stockt's in mir;	*it curdles within me,*

nicht will's die Wange mir röthen.	*refusing to redden my cheek.*
D'rum bleib' ich fern	*So I keep well away*
vom feurigen Bund.	*from your fiery bond.*

In no early narrative of the Nibelung/Niflung story does one of the brothers-in-law avoid participating in the oath, but in some cases their stepbrother Guttormr/Gothormr is not invited to be one of the oath-takers, and hence he may later kill Sigurðr (*Sigurðarkviða inn skamma* 20; *SnE* S41; *Vǫlsunga saga* ch. 32).

In *Gísla saga Súrssonar* ch. 6, on the other hand, Þorgrímr refuses to swear an oath of blood-brotherhood with Vésteinn, Gísli's brother-in-law; Gísli and his brother Þorkell were, in turn, Þorgrímr's brothers-in-law:

> *Ok nú vekja þeir sér blóð ok láta renna saman dreyra sinn í þeiri moldu, er upp var skorin undan jarðarmeninu, ok hræra saman allt, moldina ok blóðit; en síðan fellu þeir allir á kné ok sverja þann eið, at hverr skal annars hefna sem bróður síns, ok nefna ǫll goðin í vitni. Ok er þeir tókusk í hendr allir, þá mælti Þorgrímr: 'Œrinn vanda hefi ek, þótt ek gera þetta við þá báða, Þorkel ok Gísla, mága mína, en mik skyldir ekki við Véstein' — ok hnykkir hendi sinni. 'Svá munu vér þá fleiri gera,' segir Gísli ok hnykkir ok sinni hendi, — 'ok skal ek eigi binda mér vanda við þann mann, er eigi vill við Véstein, mág minn.'*
>
> *(And now they draw blood and let their blood run together in the earth which was scratched up under the sod, and mix it all together, earth and blood; and then they kneel and swear an oath, that each shall avenge the other as his brother, and they call all the gods to witness. But when they came to shake hands Thorgrim said: 'There is burden enough in this for me if I do it with these two, Thorkel and Gisli, my brothers-in-law; but I have no ties with Vestein' – and he draws back his hand. 'Then more of us will do the same,' says Gisli, and he too draws back his hand, 'for I will not bind myself to the man who will not bind himself to Vestein, my wife's brother.')*

Þorgrímr later murders Vésteinn, just as Hagen murders Siegfried. This episode from *Gísla saga* was included in the German selection from the sagas of Icelanders published in 1816. This book is known to have been in both Wagner's earlier and later libraries (i.e. before 1849 and later on; see pp. 106 and 117 above and Westernhagen 1966, 102).

Hagen's description of himself is very like the description of Hǫgni in *Þiðreks saga* (169 (274)):

> *Ok nú er hann fjǫgra vetra gamall, er hann gengr í leika með sveinum, ok er hann harðr ok sterkr ok illr viðreignar, ok nú er honum því brugðit, at*

> *hann er yfirlits sem troll, en eigi sem menn, ok eftir skapi sínu er hans ásjóna. Ok þessu reiðist hann mjǫk ok gengr til eins vatns ok sér sinn skugga, ok nú sér hann, at hans andlit er svá bleikt sem bast ok svá fǫlt sem aska ok þat er mikit ok hræðiligt ok grimmligt.*
>
> *(And now he is four years old, when he starts to play with boys, and he is tough and strong and difficult to deal with, and now he is accused of being like trolls in appearance and not like people, and of his face matching his temperament. He becomes very angry at this and goes to a pond and looks at his reflection, and now he sees that his face is as wan as bast and as pale as ashes and it is large and frightening and fierce.)*

G. I.2.7
Siegfried is eager to win Brünnhilde for Gunther (*Ring*, 7419–21, 7425–26, 7431–32):

Siegfried:

Frisch auf die Fahrt!	*Quick, let's be off!*
Dort liegt mein Schiff;	*There lies my boat;*
schnell führt es zum Felsen.	*to the fell it will bring us swiftly.*
. . .	

Gunther:

Rastest du nicht zuvor?	*Won't you rest beforehand?*

Siegfried:

Um die Rückkehr ist's mir jach.	*I'm longing to return.*
. . .	

Hagen (to Gutrune):

Sieh', wie's ihn treibt	*See how he hastens*
zum Weib dich zu gewinnen!	*to win you as wife!*

In all the Old Icelandic sources, the brothers-in-law and sworn brothers go on horseback to seek Brynhildr's hand for Gunnarr. Sigurðr has by this time long been married to Guðrún. In *Vǫlsunga saga* (ch. 28) he stays at least two and a half years with the Gjúkungs before they set off on the journey of courtship. In *Das Nibelungenlied*, on the other hand, they sail all the way to 'Islande,' where Prünhilt rules as queen (*NL* 325–528, *Av.* 6–8).

Götterdämmerung, Act One, Scene Three

G. I.3.1
The valkyrie Waltraute visits Brünnhilde on the mountaintop, and asks for the ring in order to save the gods from destruction, but Brünnhilde refuses to give up this token of Siegfried's love (*Ring*, 7452–7665).

[In the version of the *Siegfrieds Tod* of 1848, the whole troop of valkyries ride past Brünnhilde's rock, and exchange words with her (*SSD* II, 183–86).]

This episode is entirely Wagner's invention, and has no prototype.

G. I.3.2
Left alone again, Brünnhilde notices turbulence in the fire encircling the mountain below her rock (*Ring*, 7666–73):

Es ist Abend geworden. Aus der Tiefe leuchtet der Feuerschein allmählich heller auf . . .

(It is evening. From below, the glow of the fire gradually increases in brightness . . .)

Brünnhilde:

Abendlich Dämmern	*Evening twilight*
deckt den Himmel:	*shrouds the heavens:*
heller leuchtet	*more brightly shines*
die hütende Lohe herauf. –	*the sheltering blaze below. –*
Was leckt so wüthend	*Why does the blazing billow*
die lodernde Welle zum Wall?	*lick at the bulwark in such wild fury?*
Zur Felsenspitze	*The fiery tide is rolling*
wälzt sich der feurige Schwall.	*towards the top of the fell.*

Sigurðr's ride through the flames is described as follows in *Vǫlsunga saga* ch. 29):

Eldr nam at æsask	*The fire grew great,*
en jǫrð at skjálfa	*the ground did shake*
ok hár logi	*and tall flame*
við himni gnæfa.	*towered to the sky.*

The description is, once again, reminiscent of a view of a volcanic eruption and of *Vǫluspá* 57, cf. W. III.3.2 and S. III.2.2.

G. I.3.3
A man emerges from the flames (*Ring*, 7678–80, 7684–88, 7697–99):

Siegfried, auf dem Haupte den Tarnhelm, der ihm bis zur Hälfte das Gesicht verdeckt und nur die Augen frei läßt, erscheint in Gunthers Gestalt . . . Siegfried, im Hintergrunde auf dem Steine verweilend, betrachtet Brünnhilde, regungslos auf seinem Schild gelehnt.

(On his head Siegfried wears the Tarnhelm, which covers half his face, leaving only his eyes free. He appears in Gunther's form . . . Siegfried remains on the rock at the back, observing Brünnhilde and resting motionlessly on his shield.)

. . .

Brünnhilde:

Wer ist der Mann,	*Who is the man*
der das vermochte,	*who has done*
was dem stärksten nur bestimmt?	*what only the strongest was fated to do?*

Siegfried:

Ein Helde, der dich zahmt –	*A hero who'll tame you,*
bezwingt Gewalt dich nur.	*if force alone can constrain you.*
. . .	
Ein Gibichung bin ich,	*A Gibichung am I,*
und Gunther heißt der Held,	*and Gunther's the name of the hero*
dem, Frau, du folgen soll'st.	*whom, woman, you must follow.*

Vǫlsunga saga recounts the same events as follows (ch. 29):

> *Ok er Sigurðr kom inn um logann, fann hann þar eitt fagrt herbergi, ok þar sat í Brynhildr. Hon spyrr hverr sá maðr er. En hann nefndisk Gunnarr Gjúkason — 'Ertu ok ætluð mín kona með jáyrði feðr þíns, ef ek riða þinn vafrloga, ok fóstra þíns með yðru atkvæði.' 'Eigi veit ek gerla hversu ek skal þessu svara,' segir hon. Sigurðr stóð réttr á gólfinu ok studdisk á sverðshjǫltin ok mælti til Brynhildar . . . 'Mǫrg stórvirki hafi þér unnit, en minnizk nú á heit yður, ef þessi eldr væri riðinn, at þér mundið með þeim manni ganga er þetta gerði.'*
>
> *(And when Sigurd went in past the flames he found a fine dwelling, and Brynhild was sitting within. She asked who the man was. He said he was Gunnar, Gjuki's son. 'And you are to be my wife — your father consented if I rode through your leaping flames, as did your foster-father, if you so decided.' 'I hardly know how to answer,' she said. Sigurd stood erect on the floor, leaning on the hilt of his sword, and said to Brynhild . . . 'You have performed many great deeds . . . but now think of your oath, that if any one rode through the fire you would go with the man who did so.')*

In *Das Nibelungenlied* Gunther, King of the Burgundians in Worms, is finally accepted by Queen Prünhilt when he defeats her in a contest of arms; but it is Sîfrit, standing by his side wearing a cloak of invisibility, who performs the feats for him (*NL* 431–74, *Av.* 7).

G. I.3.4 (*Ring*, 7722–26)

[Siegfried] faßt sie bei der Hand und entzieht ihrem Finger den Ring . . .

([Siegfried] seizes her by the hand and tears the ring from her finger . . .)

Jetzt bist du mein!	*Now you are mine!*
Brünnhilde, Gunther's Braut –	*Brünnhilde, Gunther's bride,*
gönne mir nun dein Gemach!	*allow me to enter your chamber!*

Brünnhilde:

Was könntest du wehren,	*How could you stop him,*
elendes Weib!	*woman most wretched!*

These events are recounted in rather variable ways in all the probable sources. In *Vǫlsunga saga* there appears to be no violence, but in this version Sigurðr and Brynhildr have been together twice before (ch. 29):

> *Hann tók þá af henni hringinn Andvaranaut er hann gaf henni, en fekk henni nú annan hring af Fáfnis arfi.*
>
> *(Then he took from her the ring Andvaranaut [Andvari's gift] which he had given her, and gave her another from Fafnir's inheritance.)*

In the Prose Edda, the process is reversed, and Sigurðr gives her the ring – and in this version it appears to be a different Brynhildr whom he has never met before (*SnE* S41):

> *En at morni þá er hann stóð upp ok klæddi sik, þá gaf hann Brynhildi at línfé gullbauginn þann er Loki hafði tekit af Andvara, en tók af henni annan baug til minja.*
>
> *(And in the morning when he got up and dressed, he gave Brynhild as morning gift the gold ring that Loki had taken from Andvari, and received from her another ring as keepsake.)*

In *Þiðreks saga*, the exchange of rings takes place in Gunnarr's hall, after Sigurðr has, with Gunnarr's permission, lain with Brynhildr in the royal bedchamber (229 (319)):

> *Ok er morgnar, þá tekr hann af hennar hendi eitt fingrgull ok lætr á annat í staðinn.*
>
> *And in the morning he took from her hand a gold ring and put another on in its place.*

In *Das Nibelungenlied* the events are the same as in *Þiðreks saga*, except that Sîfrit gives her no ring in place of the one he takes from her (*NL* 679, *Av.* 10). He also takes her belt, which is mentioned again later as part of the evidence that Sîfrit had slept with her (*NL* 847–49, *Av.* 14). Neither in *Das Nibelungenlied* nor in *Þiðreks saga* does the ring have any supernatural power.

G. I.3.5

Siegfried drives her away with a gesture of command. He draws his sword (*Ring*, 7727–30):

Nun, Nothung, zeuge du,	*Now, Nothung, attest*
daß ich in Züchten warb:	*that I wooed her chastely:*

die Treue wahrend dem Bruder,	*keeping faith with my brother,*
trenne mich von seiner Braut!	*keep me apart from his bride!*

The naked sword in the bed between Siegfried and Brünnhilde has a direct prototype in the Prose Edda and the Poetic Edda, *Brot af Sigurðarkviðu* 18–19 and *Sigurðarkviða in skamma* 4, which reads as follows:

Seggr inn suðrœni	*The southern warrior*
lagði sverð nekkvið,	*laid a naked sword,*
mæki málfán,	*an inlaid blade,*
á meðal þeira;	*between them;*
né hann konu	*he did not*
kyssa gerði,	*kiss the woman,*
né húnskr konungr	*nor did the Hunnish king*
hefja sér at armi;	*raise her on his arm;*
mey frumunga	*the maid very young*
fal hann megi Gjúka.	*he kept for the son of Gjuki.*

Vǫlsunga saga has a rather more detailed account:

> *Þar dvelsk hann þrjár nætr, ok búa eina rekkju. Hann tekr sverðit Gram ok leggr í meðal þeira bert. Hon spyrr hví þat sætti. Hann kvað sér þat skipat at svá gerði hann brúðlaup til konu sinnar eða fengi ella bana.*
>
> *(He stayed there three nights, and they shared the same bed. He took the sword Gram and laid it naked between them. She asked the reason. He said it was ordained that he should marry his wife in this way, or else die.)*

This not very convincing explanation here presumably alludes to the fact that if he were to break faith with his sworn-brother he would be punished by death. The episode of the sword in the bed does not occur in *Þiðreks saga* or *Das Nibelungenlied* or *Das Lied vom Hürnen Seyfrid.*

Götterdämmerung, Act Two, Scene One

G. II.1.1

Alberich has a long conversation with Hagen, in which he reminds him of his filial duties (*Ring*, 7731–7829).

This episode has no prototype, and is Wagner's own invention.

Götterdämmerung, Act Two, Scene Two

G. II.2.1

Apparently thanks to the power of the Tarnhelm (cf. p. 122), Siegfried is instantly at the hall of the Gibichungs. He announces that Gunther and Brünnhilde are on their way, and that preparations should be made for their arrival (*Ring*, 7830–7906).

The sources make no mention of this quality of the magic helmet. The return of Sigurðr after visiting Brynhildr is recounted in similar terms in *Vǫlsunga saga* ch. 29 (though here they do not go direct to Gjuki's home) and the Prose Edda (*SnE* S41):

> *Sigurðr hljóp þá á hest sinn ok reið til félaga sinna. Skipta þeir Gunnarr þá aptr litum ok fóru aptr til Gjúka með Brynhildi.*
>
> *(Sigurd then leapt on his horse and rode to his companions. He and Gunnar then changed back their forms and they returned to Gjuki with Brynhild.)*

In *Das Nibelungenlied* Sîfrit is sent on ahead to Worms on horseback after a nine-day ocean voyage from 'Islande', to bring the joyful news that Gunther is on his way with Prünhilt, and to order the preparation of a feast (*NL* 529–62, *Av*. 9).

Götterdämmerung, Act Two, Scene Three

G. II.3.1
Hagen summons his followers to slaughter animals and prepare drinks for the wedding feast (*Ring*, 7907–94).

In *Das Nibelungenlied*, Gunther's brothers, sisters and mother immediately begin to invite guests to the feast (*NL* 563–66, *Av*. 9).

Götterdämmerung, Act Two, Scene Four

G. II.4.1
Gunther presents Brünnhilde to his followers, along with Siegfried and Gutrune. Siegfried does not remember Brünnhilde, but she recognises both him and the ring on his finger (*Ring*, 8021, 8027, 8031–45):

Brünnhilde:

Siegfried . . . hier . . ? Gutrune . . ?	*Siegfried . . . here? . . Gutrune . . ?*
. . .	
Siegfried . . . kennt mich nicht?. . .	*Siegfried . . . knows me not! . . .*
. . .	
Ha! – der Ring . . . *an seiner Hand!* *Er . . . Siegfried?*	*Ha! . . . the ring . . .* *upon his hand!* *He . . . Siegfried?*

Some vassals:

Was ist? Was ist?	*What is it? What is it?*

Hagen:	
Jetzt merket klug, *was die Frau euch klagt!*	*Mark closely now* *what the woman discloses!*
Brünnhilde (to Siegfried):	
Einen Ring sah ich *an deiner Hand; –* *nicht dir gehört er,* *ihn entriß mir*	*A ring I saw* *upon your hand: –* *it belongs not to you* *but was wrested from me*
auf Gunther deutend	*(pointing to Gunther)*
– dieser Mann! *Wie mochtest von ihm* *den Ring du empfah'n?*	*– by this man here!* *How could you have* *got the ring from him?*
Siegfried:	
Den Ring empfing ich *nicht von ihm.*	*I did not get* *the ring from him.*

In the Prose Edda (*SnE* S41) and *Vǫlsunga saga* (ch. 30) the fateful exchange of rings is not discovered until Brynhildr and Guðrún wade out into the Rhine to wash their hair, and begin to argue with each other about who has the braver husband and who took Brynhildr's virginity. This dramatic scene is not used by Wagner.

In *Þiðreks saga* the long dispute takes place in the hall of Gunnarr in the land of the Niflungs. When Brynhildr demands that Grímhildr give up her seat, because she has the nobler husband, Grímhildr says (343 (388)):

> *'Nú hefr þú upp þenna leik, er þú munt vilja, at vit talim fleira okkar á milli, hvat þér er til sœmdar eða ósœmdar. Seg nú mér fyrstu spurning, er ek spyr þik: Hverr tók þinn meydóm, eða hverr er þinn frumverr?' Þá svarar Brynhildr: 'Þar hefir þú mik spurt þess, er ek kann vel at segja ok mér er engi ósœmd í. Ríki konungr Gunnarr kom til minnar borgar . . . tók ek hann til manns, ok var ek honum gift með margs konar prýði . . . Ok þessu vil ek eigi þik leyna ok engi annan, ef eftir spyrr, at hann er minn frumverr.' Nú svarar Grímhildr: 'Nú lýgr þú þat, er ek spurða þik, sem mér var ván. Sá maðr, er þinn meydóm tók fyrsta sinn, heitir Sigurðr sveinn.' Nú svarar Brynhildr: 'Ek varð aldrigi Sigurðar kona ok aldri hann minn maðr.' Þá mælti Grímhildr: 'Þat skýt ek hér til þessa fingrgulls, er hann tók af þér, þá er hann hafði tekit þinn meydóm. Þetta sama gull tók hann af þinni hendi ok gaf mér.'*
>
> *('Now you are beginning a game such that you will want us to talk further together about what is to your honour and what is to your shame. Answer me now the first question I ask you: Who took your virginity and who was your first husband?' Then Brynhild replied: 'There you have asked me*

something I can easily tell you, and there is no shame to me in it. The powerful King Gunnar came to my castle . . . I took him as husband and I was then married to him with many kinds of splendour . . . And this I shall conceal neither from you nor from anyone else who enquires, that he is my first husband.' Now Grimhild replies: 'Now you are telling a lie about what I asked you, as I expected. The man who first took your virginity is called Boy Sigurd [Young Sigurd].' Now Brynhild replies: 'I never was Sigurd's wife and he was never my husband.' Then said Grimhild: 'I call to witness in this matter this gold ring, which he took from you when he had taken your virginity. This same gold he took from your hand and gave to me.')

In *Das Nibelungenlied* Kriemhilt and Prünhilt also quarrel over their husbands' heroic qualities, and who should take precedence when entering the cathedral. This is followed by Kriemhilt's revelation about the ring and belt (*NL* 814–50, *Av.* 14).

The fateful ring is, in all these versions, on the hand of one of the women when it is shown as a piece of evidence: Brynhildr, Guðrún, Grímhildr or Kriemhilt. Nowhere is it said to be on the hand of Sigurðr/Sîfrit. Wagner is alone in this.

G. II.4.2

The argument continues (*Ring*, 8046–56):

Brünnhilde (to Gunther):

Nahm'st du von mir den Ring,	*If you took from me the ring*
durch den ich dir vermählt,	*by which I was wed to you,*
so melde ihm dein Recht,	*then tell him of your right to it,*
ford're zurück das Pfand!	*demand the token back!*

Gunther:

Den Ring? – Ich gab ihm keinen: –	*The ring? – I gave him none: –*
doch kenn'st du ihn auch gut?	*but are you sure that it's the same?*

Brünnhilde:

Wo bärgest du den Ring,	*Where are you hiding the ring*
den du von mir erbeutet?	*that you carried off as your prize?*

Gunther schweigt . . . *(Gunther says nothing . . .)*

Brünnhilde:

Ha! – Dieser war es,	*Ha! He it was*
der mir den Ring entriß.	*who wrested the ring away from me:*
Siegfried, der trugvolle Dieb!	*Siegfried, the treacherous thief!*

In *Vǫlsunga saga*, after the revelation about the ring, Brynhildr takes to her bed and asks Gunnarr (ch. 31):

Hvat gerðir þú af hring þeim er ek selda þér, er Buðli konungr gaf mér at efsta skilnaði, er þér synir Gjúka konungs kómuð til hans ok hétuð at herja eða brenna, nema þér næðið mér?

(What did you do with the ring I gave you, King Budli's gift to me at our last parting, when you sons of King Gjuki came to him, swearing to harry and burn if you didn't get me?)

G. II.4.3

Brünnhilde maintains that Siegfried has lain with her (*Ring*, 8102–03, 8108–26):

Er zwang mir Lust und Liebe ab.	*He forced delight from me, and love.*
. . .	
Siegfried:	
Hört, ob ich Treue brach! Blutbrüderschaft hab' ich Gunther geschworen! Nothung, das werthe Schwert, wahrte die Treue Eid: mich trennte seine Schärfe von diesem traur'gen Weib.	*Listen whether I broke my faith! Blood-brotherhood have I sworn to Gunther. Nothung, my worthy sword defended the oath of loyalty; its sharp edge sundered me from this unhappy woman.*
Brünnhilde:	
Du listiger Held, sieh' wie du lüg'st, – wie auf dein Schwert du schlecht dich beruf'st! Wohl kenn' ich seine Schärfe, doch kenn' auch die Scheide, darin so wonnig ruht' an der Wand Nothung, der treue Freund, als die Traute sein Herr sich gewann.	*You cunning hero, look how you're lying, just as you're wrong to appeal to your sword! Well do I know its sharp-set edge, but I also know the scabbard in which your true friend, Nothung, rested serenely against the wall while its master won him his sweetheart.*
The vassals:	
Wie? Brach er die Treue? Trübte er Gunther's Ehre?	*What? Has he broken faith? Has he tarnished Gunther's honour?*

The question of whether Sigurðr had sexual relations with the betrothed wife of his sworn brother, Gunnarr, is handled in different ways in the early sources. In surviving eddic poetry, this interpretation is rejected. It is simply frustrated love for Sigurðr and jealousy of Guðrún that drive Brynhildr to vengeance. In *Sigurðarkviða in skamma* 28 Sigurðr says of Brynhildr on his deathbed:

Mér unni mær	*The girl loved me*
fyr mann hvern,	*beyond all men,*
en við Gunnar	*but against Gunnar*
grand ekki vannk;	*I committed no injury;*
þyrmða ek sifjum,	*I respected relationship,*
svǫrnum eiðum,	*sworn oaths,*
síðr værak heitinn	*lest I should be called*
hans kvánar vinr.	*his wife's lover.*

The eddic poem *Helreið Brynhildar* 12 is even more specific:

Sváfu við ok unðum	*We slept and were content*
í sæing einni,	*in one bed,*
sem hann minn bróðir	*as if he my brother*
um borinn væri;	*born were;*
hvártki knátti	*neither of us*
hǫnd yfir annat	*their arm over the other*
átta nóttum	*for eight nights*
okkart leggja.	*did lay.*

Das Nibelungenlied does not give a clear answer to the question. It says only that Sîfrit forced Prünhilt to submission with Gunther's consent; the latter did not, however, want Sîfrit to have sexual relations with her. It is not clear, on the other hand, how he succeeded in subjugating her (*NL* 651–55 and 666–80, *Av.* 10; 840–50, *Av.* 14).

The Prose Edda (*SnE* S41) and *Vǫlsunga saga* (chs 31–32) are also vague on the subject, though it emerges already in *Vǫlsunga saga* ch. 29 that Sigurðr and Brynhildr have a daughter, Áslaug (not said to be Brynhildr's in the Prose Edda). In *Vǫlsunga saga* Sigurðr and Brynhildr are also said to have met twice before. (The complexity of the various versions of the story of Brynhildr, of which different versions are combined in different ways in the various sources, is well treated in T. M. Andersson, *The Legend of Brynhild*, 1980 (Islandica XLIII).)

Þiðreks saga is the most unambiguous. After Brynhildr has refused her husband, Gunnarr, his conjugal rights, the latter says to Sigurðr (228–29 (319)):

> *'Fyrir sakar okkarrar vináttu ok mágsemdar þá trúi ek engum manni jafnvel sem þér, þó at þat mál sé, er mikit liggi við, at leynt sé, ok ek veit, at þú ert svá sterkr maðr, at þú mátt fá hennar meydóm, ef nokkurr maðr er sá í verǫldunni, ok helzt má ek þér til trúa, at þat skal aldrigi upp koma fyrir engan mann, þótt á þenna veg sé gert.' Nú svarar Sigurðr ok lézt svá gera vilja sem hann vill. Ok nú er þetta ráðit. Ok nú er kveld kemr ok Gunnarr skal fara til sinnar hvílu, ok er þat í fyrsta lagi, þá er svá til hagat, at Sigurðr sveinn ferr í rekkjuna, en Gunnarr ferr í braut með klæði Sigurðar,*

> *ok hyggja þat nú allir menn, at þar sé Sigurðr sveinn. Ok nú kastar Sigurðr klæðum á hǫfuð sér ok lætr allómáttuliga ok liggr svá þar til, er allir menn eru sofnaðir ok á braut farnir. Ok þá tekr hann til Brynhildar ok fær skjótt hennar meydóm.*
>
> *('For the sake of our friendship and relationship I trust no man as well as you, even in an affair which it is very important should be kept secret, and I know that you are so strong a man that you can take her virginity if there is any such man in the world, and I can trust you best to do it so that it will never become known to any man that it was done in this way.' Now Sigurd replies and says he will do as he wishes. And now this is arranged. And now when evening comes and Gunnar is to go to his bed, and this is at the first opportunity, then it is managed that Boy Sigurd gets into the bed, while Gunnar goes off with Sigurd's clothes on, and everyone thinks it is Boy Sigurd. And now Sigurd throws clothes over his head and behaves as if he has absolutely no strength and lies like that until everyone has gone to sleep and gone away. And then he takes hold of Brynhild and quickly takes her virginity.)*

The clear implication in *Þiðreks saga* is that Brynhildr herself was aware of the pretence from the start. Things only go wrong when Grímhildr discloses the secret in a rage. Brynhildr says to Gunnarr (344 (388)):

> *Sigurðr sveinn hefir rofit ykkur trúnaðarmál ok sagt sinni konu Grímhildi allt, hversu þú lagðir þinn trúnað undir hann, ok þá er þú fekkt eigi sjálfr mitt lag ok lézt Sigurð sveinn taka minn meydóm. Þat sama fœrði Grímhildr mér í brigzli í dag fyrir ǫllum mǫnnum.*
>
> *(Boy Sigurd has broken your confidence and told his wife Grimhild everything, how you placed your confidence in him and when you yourself could not obtain marital relations with me, you let Boy Sigurd take my virginity. Grimhild has now upbraided me with this today in front of everyone.')*

Wagner appears to decide that Siegfried and Brünnhilde should make love at their first encounter, but not at the second, when Siegfried had no memory of her and was in the form of Gunther.

G. II.4.4

Siegfried and Brünnhilde both swear on Hagen's spear that they are telling the truth (*Ring*, 8125–69).

In *Das Nibelungenlied* (*NL* 855–60, *Av.* 14) Sîfrit offers to swear at Gunther's request that he has not had sexual relations with Prünhilt. No such oath is mentioned in the Icelandic sources.

Götterdämmerung, Act Two, Scene Five

G.II.5.1

When Siegfried has left, Brünnhilde ponders her shame (*Ring*, 8204–22):

Brünnhilde:

Welches Unhold's List	*What demon's art*
liegt hier verhohlen?	*lies hidden here?*
Welches Zaubers Rath	*What store of magic*
regte dieß auf?	*stirred this up?*
Wo ist nun mein Wissen	*Where is now my wisdom*
gegen dieß Wirrsal?	*against this bewilderment?*
Wo sind meine Runen	*Where are my runes*
gegen dieß Räthsel?	*against this riddle?*
Ach Jammer! Jammer!	*Ah, sorrow! Sorrow!*
Weh'! ach Wehe!	*Woe, ah woe!*
All' mein Wissen	*All my wisdom*
wies ich ihm zu:	*I gave to him:*
in seiner Macht	*in his power*
hält er die Magd;	*he holds the maid;*
in seinen Banden	*in his bonds*
hält er die Beute,	*he holds the booty*
die, jammernd ob ihrer Schmach,	*which, sorrowing for her shame,*
jauchzend der reiche verschenkt! –	*the rich man exultantly gave away. –*

In *Vǫlsunga saga*, Brynhildr's laments and imprecations are even more prolonged and colourful, for example (ch. 32):

Eptir þetta gekk Brynhildr út ok settisk undir skemmuvegg sinn ok hafði margar harmtǫlur, kvað sér allt leitt, bæði land ok ríki, er hon átti eigi Sigurð.

(After this, Brynhild went out and sat beneath the wall of her private quarters, and gave vent to her grief. She said that everything was hateful to her, land and power, too, since Sigurd was not hers.)

Her fury and grief are also described in *Das Nibelungenlied* (*NL* 863–64, *Av.* 14) and *Þiðreks saga* (344 (388)).

G. II.5.2

Brünnhilde's thoughts now turn to vengeance (*Ring*, 8223–37):

Brünnhilde:

Wer bietet mir nun das Schwert,	*Who'll offer me now the sword*
mit dem ich die Bande zerschnitt'?	*with which to sever those bonds?*

Hagen:

Vertraue mir,	*Have trust in me,*
betrog'ne Frau!	*deserted wife!*

Wer dich verrieth,	*Whoever betrayed you,*
das räche ich.	*I shall avenge it.*
Brünnhilde:	
An wem?	*On whom?*
Hagen:	
An Siegfried, der dich betrog.	*On Siegfried, who deceived you.*
Brünnhilde:	
An Siegfried? . . du?	*On Siegfried? . . You?*
Ein einz'ger Blick	*A single glance*
seines blitzenden Auges,	*from his flashing eye –*
– das selbst durch die Lügengestalt	*which, even through his false disguise,*
leuchtend strahlte zu mir –	*brightly lighted upon me –*
deinen besten Muth	*would make*
machte er bangen!	*your greatest courage quail!*

The motif of Siegfried's keen gaze may be attributed to a very similar form of words in two places in *Vǫlsunga saga* (chs 23, 32):

> *Augu hans váru svá snǫr at fár einn þorði at líta undir hans brún . . . Augu Sigurðar váru svá snǫr at fár einn þorði gegn at sjá.*
>
> *His eyes were so piercing that few dared look him in the face . . . Sigurd's eyes were so piercing that few dared meet them.*

G. II.5.3

Brünnhilde has revealed that Siegfried is almost invulnerable (*Ring*, 8258–65):

Hagen:	
So kann keine Wehr ihm schaden?	*And so no weapon can harm him?*
Brünnhilde:	
Im Kampfe nicht: – doch –	*In battle, no! But –*
träf'st du im Rücken ihn.	*if you struck him in the back.*
Niemals – das wußt' ich –	*Never, I knew,*
wich' er dem Feind,	*would he yield to a foe,*
nie reicht' er fliehend ihm den Rücken:	*never, fleeing, present his back;*
an ihm d'rum spart' ich den Segen.	*so I spared it the spell's protection.*
Hagen:	
Und dort trifft ihn mein Speer!	*And there my spear shall strike him!*

In *Þiðreks saga*, Sigurðr bathes in the blood of the dragon, which makes his skin invulnerable, except for a place between his shoulder-blades where he could not reach to spread the blood (166 (271)). In *Das Nibelungenlied* he also bathes in the dragon's blood, with the same results, but the vulnerable place is due to a leaf which was stuck against his back. In this case Hagene tricks Kriemhilt into telling him of the vulnerable place (*NL* 100, *Av.* 3; 899–902, *Av.* 15). In *Das Lied vom Hürnen Seyfrid*, he spreads himself with the fat from the dragon's burned body, which gives him invulnerable 'horny' skin except between the shoulder-blades, where he could not reach (7–11).

Vǫlsunga saga and the Poetic and Prose Eddas do not mention Sigurðr being invulnerable. The only parallel is that Sigmundr is said to be immune to poisons, internally and externally, while his sons are only immune to poisons externally (*SnE* S42; cf. the prose passage *Frá dauða Sinfjǫtla* before the eddic poem *Grípisspá*):

> *Svá er sagt at Sigmundr Vǫlsungsson var svá máttugr at hann drakk eitr ok sakaði ekki, en Simfjǫtli, sonr hans, ok Sigurðr váru svá harðir á húðna at þá sakaði ekki eitr at útan kvæmi á þá bera.*
>
> *(They say that Sigmund Volsungsson was so tough that he could drink poison and not be harmed, while his son Sinfiotli and Sigurd had such hard skins that poison did not harm them if it got on to their bare flesh.)*

Wagner adds a new significance to Brynhildr's talk of magic runes in *Vǫlsunga saga* and the eddic poem *Sigrdrífumal*; not only is Brünnhilde supposed to have taught Siegfried wisdom at their first encounter, but also to have made his body largely invulnerable.

G. II.5.4

Brünnhilde now turns her anger against Gunther (*Ring*, 8276–84):

Brünnhilde (to Gunther):

O feiger Mann!	*O craven man!*
falscher Genoß!	*False companion!*
Hinter dem Helden	*Behind the hero*
hehltest du dich,	*you hid yourself,*
daß Preise des Ruhmes	*that the harvest of fame*
er dir erränge!	*he might reap for you!*
Tief wohl sank	*The much-loved race*
das theure Geschlecht,	*has sunk far indeed*
das solche Zagen gezeugt!	*that fathers such faint-hearts as you!*

Brynhildr's reproaches to Gunnarr appear in various places in eddic poems; the following example is from *Vǫlsunga saga* (ch. 31):

> *Ok þar kom at ek hétumsk þeim er riði hestinum Grana með Fáfnis arfi ok riði minn vafrloga ok dræpi þá menn er ek kvað á. Nú treystisk engi at ríða nema Sigurðr einn. Hann reið eldinn, því at hann skorti eigi hug til. Hann drap orminn ok Regin ok fimm konunga, en eigi þú, Gunnarr, er þú fǫlnaðir sem nár, ok ertu engi konungr né kappi.*

(And so I promised to marry the man who would ride the steed Grani with Fafnir's inheritance, and ride through my leaping flames, and kill the men I named. Now none dared the ride save Sigurd alone. He rode through the fire, for he did not lack the courage for the feat. He it was who killed the dragon, and Regin and five kings — and not you, Gunnar, for you turned pale as a corpse, and you're no king, nor a hero.)

G. II.5.5

Gunther feels the justice of her reproaches (*Ring*, 8285–86, 8298–99, 8305–13):

Gunther:

Betrüger ich – und betrogen!	*Deceiver I – and deceived!*
Verräther ich – und verrathen!	*Betrayer I – and betrayed!*
. . .	
Blutbrüderschaft	*Blood-brotherhood*
schwuren wir uns!	*we swore to one another!*
. . .	

Brünnhilde:

Dich verrieth er,	*You he betrayed,*
und mich verriethet ihr alle!	*and me have you all betrayed!*
Wär' ich gerecht,	*If I had my due,*
alles Blut der Welt	*all the blood in the world*
büßte mir nicht eure Schuld!	*could never make good your guilt!*
Doch des Einen Tod	*But one man's death*
taugt mir für alle:	*will serve for all:*
Siegfried falle –	*may Siegfried fall*
zur Sühne für sich und euch!	*to atone for himself and you!*

These lines are paralleled by the following section of *Vǫlsunga saga* (chs 31–32):

'Ek vil eigi lifa,' sagði Brynhildr, 'því at Sigurðr hefir mik vélt ok eigi síðr þik, þá er þú lézt hann fara í mína sæng. Nú vil ek eigi tvá menn eiga senn í einni hǫll, ok þetta skal vera bani Sigurðar eða þinn eða minn, því at hann hefir þat allt sagt Guðrúnu, en hon brigzlar mér.' . . . Ok enn kom Gunnarr til hennar. Þá mælti Brynhildr, 'Þú skalt láta bæði ríkit ok féit, lífit ok mik, ok skal ek fara heim til frænda minna ok sitja þar hrygg, nema þú drepir Sigurð ok son hans. Al eigi upp úlfhvelpinn.' Gunnarr varð nú mjǫk hugsjúkr ok þóttisk eigi vita hvat helzt lá til, alls hann var í eiðum við Sigurð, ok lét ýmist í hug, þótti þat þó mest svívirðing er konan gengi frá honum.

('I don't want to live,' said Brynhild, 'for Sigurd betrayed me, and he betrayed you no less when you let him sleep with me. Now I'll not have

two husbands at one and the same time in one hall, and this will mean Sigurd's death — or yours or mine, for he's told Gudrun everything, and she taunts me with it.' . . . And Gunnar came to her once more. Then Brynhild said: 'You'll lose both power and wealth, your life and me, and I shall go back to my family and live there sorrowfully, if you don't kill Sigurd and his son. Don't rear the wolf cub.' Gunnar now grew very distressed. He did not know, he thought, what had best be done, for he was bound to Sigurd by oath, and his mind toyed, now with this, now with that, but he thought it would be a terrible disgrace if his wife left him.)

G. II.5.6

Hagen too incites Gunther to seek Siegfried's death (*Ring*, 8314–17):

Hagen (to Gunther):

Er falle – dir zum Heil!	*May he fall – for your good!*
Ungeheure Macht wird dir,	*Tremendous power will then be yours*
gewinn'st von ihm du den Ring,	*if you win from him the ring*
den der Tod ihm wohl nur entreißt.	*that death alone would wrest from him.*

Das Nibelungenlied (*NL* 870, *Av.* 14) contains an equivalent stanza:

Sîn gevolgte niemen, niwan daz Hagene
riet in allen zîten Gunther dem degene,
ob Sîfrit niht enlebte, sô wurde im undertân
vil der künege lande. der helt dô trûren began.

(Yet none followed Ortwin's proposal, except that Hagen kept putting it to Gunther that if Siegfried were no more, Gunther would be lord of many kingdoms, at which Gunther grew very despondent.)

But in *Vǫlsunga saga* it is Gunnarr who explains the problem to Hǫgni (ch. 32):

Ok kallar til sín Hǫgna, bróður sinn, ok mælti, 'Fyrir mik er komit vandmæli mikit,' — segir at hann vill drepa Sigurð, kvað hann hafa vélt sik í tryggð, — 'Ráðum vit þá gullinu ok ǫllu ríkinu.' Hǫgni segir, 'Ekki samir okkr sœrin at rjúfa með ófriði. Er oss ok mikit traust at honum.' . . . Gunnarr svarar, 'Þetta skal fram fara, ok sé ek ráðit. Eggjum til Guttorm, bróður okkarn. Hann er ungr ok fás vitandi ok fyrir utan alla eiða.' . . . Gunnarr segir Sigurð deyja skulu, — 'Eða mun ek deyja ella.' Hann biðr Brynhildi upp standa ok vera káta. Hon stóð upp ok segir þó, at Gunnarr mun eigi koma fyrr í sama rekkju henni en þetta er fram komit. Nú rœðask þeir við brœðr. Gunnarr segir at þetta er gild banasǫk at hafa tekit meydóm Brynhildar.

(And he summoned his brother, Hogni. 'I am faced with a difficult problem,' he told him, and said he meant to kill Sigurd, who, he declared, had broken faith with him — 'Then the gold and all the power will be ours.' 'It would

not be right,' said Hogni, 'to break our oaths by a hostile act. And he's a great asset to us.' . . . 'It will have to be carried out,' said Gunnar, 'and I see a way. Let's urge on our brother Guttorm to do it. He is young and simple and free from any oath.' . . . Gunnar said that Sigurd must die — 'Or else I shall die.' He told Brynhild to get up and be gay. She got up but said that Gunnar would not share her bed until it was done. The brothers now talked it over. Gunnar said that to have robbed Brynhild of her virginity fully deserved death.)

G. II.5.7
Gunther has scruples about the killing (*Ring*, 8322–32):

Gunther:

Doch Gutrune, ach!	*But Gutrune, ah!*
der ich ihn gönnte:	*whom I didn't begrudge him:*
straften den Gatten wir so,	*if we punished her husband so,*
wie bestünden wir vor ihr?	*how would we stand in her sight?*

Brünnhilde:

Was rieth mir mein Wissen?	*What did my wisdom tell me?*
Was wiesen mich Runen?	*What did my runes have to teach me?*
Im hilflosen Elend	*In my helpless distress*
achtet mir's hell:	*it dawns upon me now:*
Gutrune heißt der Zauber,	*Gutrun's the name of the spell*
der den Gatten mir entzückt!	*that spirited away my husband!*
Angst treffe sie!	*May she be struck by dread!*

In the Icelandic sources there is no direct mention of Gunnarr's affection for his sister, but in *Das Nibelungenlied* Gunther is highly reluctant to take part in the plot (*NL* 866–68, *Av.* 14). Brynhildr/Prünhilt's hatred and jealousy of Sigurðr/Sîfrit's wife are mentioned, however, in all sources, for example in the eddic poem *Sigurðarkviða in skamma* 8:

Opt gengr hon innan,	*Often she left the house,*
ills um fyld,	*filled with bitterness,*
ísa ok jǫkla,	*on ice and glaciers,*
aptan hvern,	*every evening,*
er þau Guðrún	*when he and Gudrun*
ganga á beð	*go to bed*
ok hana Sigurðr	*and her Sigurd*
sveipr í ripti,	*wraps in bedclothes,*
konungr inn húnski,	*the Hunnish king*
kván friá sína.	*to caress his wife.*

G. II.5.8
Hagen suggests the means of killing Siegfried (*Ring*, 8333–38):

Muß sein Tod sie betrüben,	*Since his death is bound to afflict her,*
verhehlt sei ihr die That.	*then let the deed be hid from her.*
Auf munt're s Jagen	*Tomorrow let's merrily*
ziehen wir morgen;	*go a-hunting:*
der Edle braus't uns voran –	*the noble hero will rush on ahead –*
ein Eber bracht' ihn da um.	*a boar might bring him down.*

In *Þiðreks saga* (345–46 (390–91)) Hǫgni plans the hunting expedition, while in *Das Nibelungenlied* Gunther and Hagene conspire (*NL* 911–16, *Av.* 15–16). The hunting trip is not mentioned in the Poetic or Prose Edda or *Vǫlsunga saga*, and indeed hunting for game in forests was not part of the Icelandic social scene.

G. II.5.9

Finally, the killing is resolved upon (*Ring*, 8339–57):

Gunther:

So soll es sein!	*So shall it be!*
Siegfried falle:	*May Siegfried fall:*
sühn' er die Schmach,	*let him purge the shame*
die er mir schuf!	*that he caused me!*
Des Eides Treue	*The oath of loyalty*
hat er getrogen:	*he has betrayed:*
mit seinem Blut	*with his blood*
büß' er die Schuld!	*let him cleanse his guilt!*

Gunther's *volte-face* is described in *Das Nibelungenlied* (*NL* 874–76, *Av.* 14), and in *Þiðreks saga* (344 (388)) Gunnarr says to Brynhildr:

> *Frú, eigi skaltu gráta, ok þegi þú þegar í stað. Sigurðr sveinn mun eigi lengi vera várr herra ok mín systir Grímhildr mun eigi vera þín drottning.*
>
> *(Lady, you must not cry, be quiet immediately. Boy Sigurd will not long be our lord and my sister Grimhild will not be your queen.)*

Gunnarr's consent and planning of the murder are described in eddic poems, the Prose Edda and *Vǫlsunga saga*, at varying length. Gunnarr says in *Brot af Sigurðarkviðu* 2:

Mér hefir Sigurðr	*To me Sigurd*
selda eiða,	*gave oaths,*
eiða selda,	*oaths gave,*
alla logna;	*all false;*
þá vélti hann mik,	*then he deceived me*
er hann vera skyldi	*when he should have been*
allra eiða	*of every oath*
einn fulltrúi.	*sole guarantor.*

Götterdämmerung, Act Three, Scene One

G. III.1.1
The three Rhine Maidens meet Siegfried on the banks of Rhine. They want the ring, but after some banter Siegfried refuses to give it up (*Ring*, 8391–8557).

Possible prototypes for the Rhine Maidens are discussed in connection with *Das Rheingold* (R. 1.1). This episode, with Siegfried as the protagonist, is otherwise entirely Wagner's invention. Nevertheless it corresponds in various ways to Hagene's meeting with the water-women in *Das Nibelungenlied*, Av. 25, of whom it is said that 'they floated on the waves before him like water-fowl' (*Si swebten sam die vogele vor im ûf der fluot*, *NL* 1536), and this led him to believe what they said was trustworthy. They warn Hagene of the treacherous death he is about to suffer, just as Wagner's Rhine Maidens warn Siegfried (*Ring* 8487–91). Like Hagene in *Das Nibelungenlied*, Wagner's Siegfried reacts with heroic contempt for death.

G. III.1.2
Before he sees the Rhine Maidens, Siegfried muses over how he has become separated from the other huntsmen (*Ring*, 8416–17):

Ein Albe führte mich irr',	*An elf has led me astray,*
daß ich die Fährte verlor.	*so that I lost the trail.*

In *Das Nibelungenlied* (930, *Av.* 16), Hagene suggests that they split up on the hunt.

Götterdämmerung, Act Three, Scene Two

G. III.2.1
The hunting companions stop for a meal in the forest. They bring out drinking horns and leather bags (*Ring*, 8564–99).

Das Nibelungenlied tells of the hunters' meal in the forest, and the thirst that tormented Sîfrit after the hunt (*NL* 963–70, *Av.* 16). In *Þiðreks saga* they kill a wild boar, and start to cut it up (347 (391)). Earlier that morning Hǫgni had made sure the breakfast meal was heavily salted, and served the saltiest bits to Sigurðr, to make him thirstier (345 (390)).

G. III.2.2
Siegfried begins to tell the story of his life (*Ring*, 8600–8682).

None of the sources Wagner appears to have used for this episode include such an account of the hero's life.

G. III.2.3
Hagen gives Siegfried a drug which reverses the effect of the one he was given in Act I (see G. I.2.2) (*Ring*, 8683–87, 8709–14):

Hagen:	
Trink' erst, Held,	*Drink first, hero,*
aus meinem Horn:	*from my horn:*
ich würzte dir holden Trank,	*I've seasoned a sweet-tasting drink*
die Erinnerung hell dir zu wecken,	*to stir your memory afresh*
daß Fernes nicht dir entfalle!	*so that distant things don't escape you!*
. . .	
Siegfried:	
Den Helm löst' ich	*I loosed the glorious*
der herrlichen Maid;	*woman's helmet;*
mein Kuß erweckte sie kühn: –	*emboldened, my kiss awoke her: –*
o wie mich brünstig da umschlang	*oh! how fair Brünnhilde's arm*
der schönen Brünnhilde Arm!	*clasped me in its ardour!*
Gunther:	
Was hör' ich?	*What's that I hear?*

Wagner may not have had any prototype for the drink that restores Siegfried's memory. It is possible, however, that he knew such a phenomenon from *Sǫrla þáttr*, one of the shorter Heroic Sagas. Here (ch. 7) a sorceress (the goddess Freyja in disguise) gives Heðinn a drink which makes him lose his memory and commit an atrocity against his sworn brother Hǫgni. Some time later he meets the sorceress again, she gives him another drink, and he regains his memory (*Fornaldar sögur Norðurlanda* I 375–78). It seems that there was no German translation of *Sǫrla þáttr* that Wagner could have known, but he may have seen the Latin version (which he could certainly have read) in *Sagan af Hiedine og Hogna. Historia duorum regum Hedini et Hugonis*, Uppsala 1697.

As stated in connection with Act I Scene 2 (G. I.2.2), the drink of forgetfulness comes from *Vǫlsunga saga* (ch. 28). Later, when Brynhildr and Gunnarr's wedding is celebrated, the saga says (ch. 29):

> *Ok er lokit er þessi veizlu, minnir Sigurð allra eiða við Brynhildi ok lætr þó vera kyrt.*
>
> *(And when it [the feast] was over, Sigurd remembered all his vows to Brynhild, but he gave no sign.)*

G. III.2.4

Siegfried's words about Brünnhilde have sealed his fate (*Ring*, before 8715):

Zwei Raben fliegen aus einem Busche auf, kreisen über Siegfried, und fliegen dann, dem Rheine zu, davon.

(Two ravens fly up out of a bush, circle over Siegfried and then fly off in the direction of the Rhine.)

These are clearly Óðinn's ravens, which are described in the eddic poem *Grímnismál* 20. The Prose Edda says of them (*SnE* G38):

> *Hrafnar tveir sitja á ǫxlum honum ok segja í eyru honum ǫll tíðindi þau er þeir sjá eða heyra. Þeir heita svá: Huginn ok Muninn. Þá sendir hann í dagan at fljúgja um allan heim ok koma þeir aptr at dǫgurðarmáli. Þar af verðr hann margra tíðinda víss.*
>
> *(Two ravens sit on his shoulders and speak into his ear all the news they see or hear. Their names are Hugin and Munin. He sends them out at dawn to fly over all the world and they return at dinner-time. As a result he gets to find out about many events.)*

G. III.2.5

The flight of the ravens gives Hagen his chance to strike (*Ring*, 8715–17):

Hagen:

Erräth'st du auch	*Can you also guess*
dieser Raben Geraun'?	*what those ravens whispered?*

Siegfried fährt heftig auf und blickt, Hagen den Rücken zukehrend, den Raben nach.

(Siegfried starts up suddenly and, turning his back on Hagen, watches the ravens fly away.)

Hagen:

Rache riethen sie mir!	*To me they counselled vengeance!*

Hagen stößt seinen Speer in Siegfrieds Rücken.

(Hagen thrusts his spear into Siegfried's back.)

The murder of Siegfried in the forest has its main prototypes in *Þiðreks saga* 347 (391) and *Das Nibelungenlied* (916–1001, *Av.* 16). It also appears that Sigurðr is murdered out of doors in the eddic poems

Guðrúnarkviða II (4–8) and *Brot af Sigurðarkviðu* (5–7) and the prose passage at the end of this latter poem (*Frá dauða Sigurðar*), which acknowledges the different versions of the hero's death:

> *Hér er sagt í þessi kviðu frá dauða Sigurðar, ok víkr hér svá til, sem þeir dræpi hann úti. En sumir segja svá, at þeir dræpi hann inni í rekkju sinni sofanda. En þýðverskir menn segja svá, at þeir dræpi hann úti í skógi.*
>
> *(Here it tells in this poem about the death of Sigurd, and here it turns out that they killed him in the open, but some say that they killed him inside in his bed while asleep. But Germans say that they killed him out in the forest.)*

Ravens appear in both *Guðrúnarkviða II* 8 and *Brot af Sigurðarkviðu* 5, the one in the latter as harbinger of bad news. It says:

Soltinn varð Sigurðr	*Dead was Sigurd*
sunnan Rínar,	*south of the Rhine,*
hrafn at meiði	*a raven on a tree*
hátt kallaði.	*called loudly.*

In *Das Nibelungenlied* (*NL* 981, *Av.* 16) the spear is driven into Sîfrit's back as he lies down at a spring to quench his thirst. After this he gets up to fight for a while. In *Þiðreks saga* too he is drinking at a brook, but does not fight once he has been pierced by the spear (347 (391)):

> *Ok þá kemr at Sigurðr sveinn ok slæst þegar niðr at bekkinum sem aðrir þeir. Ok þá stendr upp Hǫgni, er hann hefir drukkit, ok tekr sitt spjót báðum hǫndum ok leggr milli herðar Sigurði svein, svá at stendr í gegnum hans hjarta ok út um brjóstit.*
>
> *(And then Boy Sigurd came up and immediately flung himself down like the others of them. Then Hogni stands up when he has had a drink, and takes his spear in both hands and thrusts it between Boy Sigurd's shoulders so that it sticks through his heart and out through his breast.)*

In the eddic poem *Sigurðarkviða inn skamma* (21–24), the Prose Edda (*SnE* S41) and *Vǫlsunga saga* (ch. 32), Sigurðr is killed in his bed.

G. III.2.6

Siegfried, dying, fully remembers his love (*Ring*, 8722–39):

Brünnhilde –	*Brünnhilde –*
heilige Braut –	*hallowed bride –*
wach' auf! öffne dein Auge! –	*awaken! Unclose your eyes! –*
Wer verschloß dich	*Who locked you*
wieder in Schlaf?	*in sleep once again?*
Wer band dich in Schlummer so bang? – –	*Who bound you in slumber's dread bonds? – –*

Der Wecker kam;	*One came to wake you;*
er küßt dich wach,	*his kiss awakes you*
und aber der Braut	*and once again he breaks*
bricht er die Bande: –	*the bride's bonds: –*
da lacht ihm Brünnhilde's Lust! –	*and Brünnhilde's joy laughs upon him. –*
Ach, dieses Auge,	*Ah! Those eyes –*
ewig nun offen! –	*now open forever! –*
Ach, dieses Athems	*Ah, this breath's*
wonniges Wehen! –	*enchanted sighing!*
Süßes Vergehen –	*Sweet extinction, –*
seliges Grauen – :	*blissful terror – :*
Brünnhild' bietet mir – Gruß!	*Brünnhild' gives me her greeting!*

A comparable declaration of love may be seen in a long exchange in *Vǫlsunga saga*, when Sigurðr, like others, tries to persuade Brynhildr out of her bitterness, but she accuses him of betrayal and hostility to her. Sigurðr replies (ch. 31):

> *'Annat er sannara. Ek unna þér betr en mér, þótt ek yrða fyrir þeim svikum, ok má því nú ekki bregða, því at ávallt er ek gáða míns geðs, þá harmaði mik þat er þú vart ekki mín kona. En af mér bar ek sem ek mátta, þat, er ek var í konungshǫll, ok unða ek því þó at vér várum ǫll saman . . . Gjarna vilda ek at vit stigum á einn beð bæði ok værir þú mín kona . . . Eigi munða ek þitt nafn,' sagði Sigurðr, 'ok eigi kennda ek þik fyrr en þú vart gipt, ok er þetta inn mesti harmr . . . Heldr en þú deyir, vil ek þik eiga, en fyrirláta Guðrúnu' . . . 'Eigi vil ek þik,' sagði Brynhildr, 'ok engan annara.'*
>
> *('The truth is rather different,' replied Sigurd. 'I loved you more than myself — though I met with trickery, and now that can't be changed — for when my wits were unclouded it always grieved me that you weren't my wife. But I bore up as best I could, for I was in a royal hall. And yet I was glad that we were all together . . . I would like us to sleep together,' replied Sigurd, 'and you would be my wife . . . I had no memory of your name,' said Sigurd, 'nor recognised you before you were married — and that is my greatest sorrow . . . . Rather than you should die, I'll marry you and leave Gudrun' . . . 'I don't want you,' said Brynhild, 'nor any other man.')*

G. III.2.7 (*Ring*, 8739)

Auf die stumme Ermahnung Gunthers erheben die Mannen Siegfrieds Leiche und geleiten sie, mit dem Folgenden, in feierlichem Zuge über die Felsenhöhe langsam von dannen.

(At Gunther's silent command, the vassals lift up Siegfried's body and, during the following, carry it away slowly in solemn procession over the cliff top.)

Das Nibelungenlied (999, *Av.* 16) has the following account:

> *Dô die herren sâhen daz der helt was tôt,*
> *si leiten in ûf einen schilt, der was von golde rôt,*
> *und wurden des ze râte, wie daz solde ergân*
> *daz man ez verhæle, daz ez het Hagene getân.*

(When those lords saw that the hero was dead they laid him on a shield that shone red with gold, and they plotted the ways and means of concealing the fact that Hagen had done the deed.)

Þiðreks saga says only (347 (391)):

Nú taka þeir upp lík Sigurðar sveins ok fara með heim til borgar.

(Now they lift up the body of Boy Sigurd and take it back to the castle.)

Götterdämmerung, Act Three, Scene Three

G. III.3.1
Back in the Gibichungs' hall, Gutrune is awaiting her husband's return (*Ring*, 8743–50):

Schlimme Träume	*Troubled dreams*
störten mir den Schlaf! –	*disturbed my sleep! –*
Wild wieherte sein Roß: –	*His horse was neighing wildly: –*
Lachen Brünnhilde's	*Brünnhilde's laughter*
weckte mich auf. – –	*woke me up. – –*
Wer war das Weib,	*Who was the woman*
das ich zum Ufer schreiten sah? –	*I saw going down to the shore? –*
Ich fürchte Brünnhild'! –	*I'm afraid of Brünnhild'! –*

Two eddic poems mention Brynhildr's chilling laughter. One is *Brot af Sigurðarkviðu* (10):

Hló þá Brynhildr	*Then Brynhild laughed*
– bœr allr dunði –	*– the whole dwelling resounded –*
einu sinni	*just once*
af ǫllum hug:	*with all her heart:*
'Lengi skuluð njóta	*'Long shall you enjoy*
landa ok þegna,	*lands and subjects,*
er þér frœknan gram	*now the brave prince*
falla létuð.'	*you've made fall.'*
Þá kvað þat Guðrún,	*Then said Gudrun,*
Gjúka dóttir:	*Gjuki's daughter:*
'Mjǫk mælir þú	*'Very great abominations*
miklar firnar;	*have you spoken;*
gramir hafi Gunnar,	*may fiends take Gunnar,*

gǫtvað Sigurðar!	*murderer of Sigurd!*
Heiptgjarns hugar	*Thought bent on hatefulness*
hefnt skal verða.'	*shall be avenged.'*

In *Sigurðarkviða in skamma* 30 Brynhildr laughs, but says nothing, and is answered by Gunnarr. In *Vǫlsunga saga*, when Brynhildr rejoices over Guðrún's grief, Gunnarr responds (ch. 32):

> *Eigi hlær þú af því at þér sé glatt um hjartarœtr, eða hví hafnar þú þínum lit? Ok mikit forað ertu, ok meiri ván at þú sér feig.*
>
> *(You're not laughing because you feel happy deep down in your heart — else why does your colour leave you? You're a monster and very likely a doomed woman.)*

Þiðreks saga gives a more detailed account of the events of the night (348 (391)):

> *Ok nú stendr drottning Brynhildr uppi á borg ok sér, at Gunnarr konungr ok hans bróðir Hǫgni ok Gernoz ríða til borgar, ok svá, at þar munu þeir fara með Sigurð svein dauðan. Hún gengr ór borginni móti þeim ok mælti, at þeir hafi veitt allra manna heilastir, ok biðr nú fœra Grímhildi.*
>
> *(And now Queen Brynhild is standing up on the castle and sees that King Gunnar and his brother Hogni and Gernoz are riding towards the castle, looking as though they must be bringing the dead Boy Sigurd. She goes out of the castle to meet them and said that they have had the luckiest hunt of all men and tells them to bring their catch to Grimhild.*

G. III.3.2

Entering the hall ahead of Siegfried's body, Hagen mocks Gutrune (*Ring*, 8765–66, 8768–73):

Hagen:

Jagdbeute	*The spoils of the chase*
bringen wir heim.	*we're bringing home.*
. . .	
Auf! Gutrun'!	*Up, Gutrun!*
Begrüße Siegfried!	*Welcome Siegfried!*
Der starke Held,	*The doughty hero*
er kehret heim.	*is coming home.*

Gutrune:

Was geschah, Hagen!	*What's happened? Hagen!*
Nicht hört' ich sein Horn!	*I didn't hear his horn!*

In *Brot af Sigurðarkviðu* 6, Guðrún alone appears to be there to see the cortège arrive:

Úti stóð Guðrún,	*Outside stood Gudrun,*
Gjúka dóttir,	*daughter of Gjuki,*
ok hon þat orða	*and this was the thing*
alls fyrst um kvað:	*she first said:*
'Hvar er nú Sigurðr,	*'Where is Sigurd,*
seggja dróttinn,	*lord of warriors,*
er frændr mínir	*now my kinsmen*
fyrri ríða?'	*are riding in front?'*

G. III.3.3

Hagen maintains the pretence the plotters agreed on (*Ring*, 8779–81):

Gutrune:

Was bringen die?	*What are they bringing?*

Hagen:

Eines wilden Ebers Beute:	*A wild boar's prey:*
Siegfried, deinen todten Mann!	*Siegfried, your dead husband!*

Þiðreks saga reports a similar exchange (ch. 348 (391)):

> *Þá svarar Hǫgni: 'Eigi var hann myrðr. Vér eltum einn villigǫlt, ok sá inn sami villigǫltr veitti honum banasár.' Þá svarar Grímhildr: 'Sá sami villigǫltr hefir þú verit, Hǫgni, ok engi maðr annarra,'—ok nú grætr hún sárliga.*
>
> *(Then Hogni answers: 'He was not murdered. We were chasing a wild boar, and that same boar gave him a death wound.' Then Grimhild answers: 'That same boar was you, Hogni, and no other man.' And now she weeps bitterly.)*

After the plot against Sîfrit's life (*NL* 864, *Av.* 14) Prünhilt largely disappears from the first part of *Das Nibelungenlied*, or rather becomes inactive. She sits, however, on her throne and hears Kriemhilt's laments unmoved (*NL* 1100, *Av.* 18). She is next mentioned in the latter part of the poem, when the emissaries of King Etzel of the Huns visit the Burgundians, long after Sîfrit's death (*NL* 1426, *Av.* 24). In *Þiðreks saga*, her gloating over Sigurðr's death and Grímhildr's grief is rather more pronounced, but after this she more or less disappears from this story too (ch. 348 (391)). All Brünnhilde's actions after this in the *Ring* are drawn principally from the purely Icelandic sources.

G. III.3.4

Gutrune now berates Gunther (*Ring*, 8785–90):

Siegfried! Siegfried erschlagen!	*Siegfried! Siegfried slain!*
Fort, treuloser Bruder!	*Away, faithless brother,*

Du Mörder meines Mannes!	*my husband's murderer!*
O Hilfe! Hilfe!	*Oh help me! Help me!*
Wehe! Wehe!	*Woe! Ah woe!*
Sie haben Siegfried erschlagen!	*They've slaughtered Siegfried!*

Guðrún's grief at the murder of Sigurðr is described in various places in the Poetic Edda, often at length, in complex and moving terms. *Guðrúnarkviða II* includes this stanza (12):

Nótt þótti mér	*The night seemed to me*
niðmyrkr vera,	*to be pitch-black,*
er ek sárla satk	*as I sat sorrowfully*
yfir Sigurði;	*over Sigurd;*
úlfar þóttumz	*wolves seemed to me*
ǫllu betri,	*better than all*
ef þeir léti mik	*if they made me*
lífi týna	*lose my life*
eða brendi mik	*or burned me*
sem birkinn við.	*like birchwood.*

G. III.3.5

Gunther abandons the agreed pretence (*Ring*, 8791–94, 8798–8802):

Gunther:

Nicht klage wider mich!	*Hold me not to blame!*
Dort klage wider Hagen:	*Blame Hagen there:*
er ist der verfluchte Eber,	*he's the accursèd boar*
der diesen Edlen zerfleischt'.	*that rent the noble hero's flesh.*

. . .

Hagen:

Ja denn! Ich hab' ihn erschlagen:	*Yes, then! I slew him:*
ich – Hagen –	*I – Hagen –*
schlug ihn zu todt!	*I struck him dead!*
Meinem Speer war er gespart,	*He was marked out by my spear*
bei dem er Meineid sprach.	*by which he'd falsely sworn.*

In *Das Nibelungenlied* (1001, *Av.* 16) Hagene says immediately after the murder that he himself will bring Sîfrit's body to Kriemhilt, and that he cares nothing for her grief. *Guðrúnarkviða II* makes passing reference to Gunnarr's bad conscience (7):

Hnipnaði Gunnarr,	*Gunnar hung his head,*
sagði mér Hǫgni	*Hogni told me*
frá Sigurðar	*about Sigurd's*
sárum dauða:	*bitter death:*
'Liggr of hǫggvinn	*'He lies cut down*

fyr handan ver
Gothorms bani,
of gefinn úlfum.'

beyond the water,
the slayer of Gothorm,
given to wolves.'

And *Brot af Sigurðarkviðu* says (7):

Einn því Hǫgni
andsvǫr veitti:
'Sundr hǫfum Sigurð
sverði hǫgginn,
gnapir æ grár jór
yfir gram dauðum.'

Alone Hogni
gave answer to this:
'Asunder Sigurd
with sword we've cut,
the grey horse ever droops his head
over the dead prince.'

G. III.3.6

Hagen kills Gunther, having claimed the Ring for himself (*Ring*, 8803–05, 8814):

Heiliges Beute-Recht
hab' ich mir nun errungen:
d'rum fordr' ich hier diesen Ring.
. . .

I've now acquired
the sacred right of conquest:
and so I demand this ring.

Er greift nach Siegfrieds Hand; diese hebt sich drohend empor . . . Alles bleibt in Schauder regungslos gefesselt.

(He reaches towards Siegfried's hand, which raises itself threateningly . . . All remain transfixed with horror.)

In none of the works used for comparison here is an attempt made to steal a ring from Siegfried/Sigurðr's dead body. In *Das Nibelungenlied* (1043–45, *Av.* 17), Sîfrit's wound begins to bleed when Hagene approaches the body; this is a familiar motif, but not found elsewhere in the sources about the Volsungs.

G. III.3.7

Brünnhilde now enters (*Ring*, 8814–23):

Brünnhilde:

Schweigt eures Jammers
jauchzenden Schwall!
Das ihr alle verriethet,
zur Rache schreitet sein Weib.
Kinder hört' ich
greinen nach der Mutter,
da süße Milch sie verschüttet:
doch nicht erklang mir
würdige Klage,
des höchsten Helden werth.

Silence your grief's
exultant clamour!
His wife, whom you all betrayed,
comes in quest of revenge.
I heard children
whimpering for their mother
since they'd spilt some fresh milk:
but no sound I heard
of a worthy lament
befitting the greatest of heroes.

The closest parallel to these lines is found in these stanzas of *Brot af Sigurðarkviðu* (14–15):

Vaknaði Brynhildr,	*Brynhild awoke,*
Buðla dóttir,	*Budli's daughter,*
dís skjǫldunga,	*lady of the Skjoldungs,*
fyr dag litlu:	*a little before day:*
'Hvetið mik eða letið mik	*'Urge me or hinder me*
– harmr er unninn –,	*– the injury is done –,*
sorg at segja	*to tell my sorrow*
eða svá láta!'	*or thus to die!'*
Þǫgðu allir	*All were silent*
við því orði,	*at this speech,*
fár kunni þeim	*few could understand*
fljóða látum,	*this behaviour of women,*
er hon grátandi	*as she, weeping,*
gørðiz at segja,	*began to tell*
þat er hlæjandi	*what, laughing,*
hǫlða beiddi.	*she'd asked the men for.*

G. III.3.8

Gutrune guesses that Brünnhilde was part of the conspiracy (*Ring*, 8824–27):

Brünnhilde! Neid-erbos'te!	*Brünnhilde! Grieved by your grudge!*
Du brachtest uns diese Noth!	*You brought this harm upon us!*
Die du die Männer ihm verhetztest,	*You who goaded the men against him,*
weh', daß du dem Haus genah't!	*alas, that you ever came near this house!*

These few lines of Gutrune's appear to combine elements from more than one source. First, the answer of Gjúki's daughter Gullrǫnd to Brynhildr in the eddic poem *Guðrúnarkviða I* 24:

Þegi þú, þjóðleið,	*Desist, you hated by all,*
þeira orða!	*from these words!*
urðr ǫðlinga	*Ruin of princes*
hefir þú æ verit;	*have you ever been;*
rekr þik alda hverr	*every wave of ill fate*
illrar skepnu,	*drives you along,*
sorg sára	*you bitter grief*
sjau konunga,	*of seven kings,*
ok vinspell	*the greatest destroyer*
vífa mest.	*of women's friends.*

Secondly, Sigurðr's words when he is mortally wounded in the eddic poem *Sigurðarkviða in skamma* 27:

Ek veit gǫrla,	*I know well*
hví gegnir nú:	*what is the reason now:*
ein veldr Brynhildr	*Brynhild alone causes*
ǫllu bǫlvi.	*all the trouble.*

G. III.3.9

Brünnhilde does not deny Gutrune's accusation, yet she has an answer (*Ring*, 8828–34, 8839–41):

Brünnhilde:

Armsel' ge, schweig!	*Wretched woman, peace!*
Sein Eheweib war'st du nie:	*You were never his lawful wife:*
als Buhlerin	*as wanton alone*
bandest du ihn.	*you bound him.*
Sein Mannes-Gemahl bin ich,	*His rightful wife am I,*
der ewige Eide er schwur,	*to whom he swore eternal vows*
eh' Siegfried je dich ersah.	*ere Siegfried ever saw you.*
. . .	

Gutrune:

Wie jäh nun weiß ich's,	*How swiftly I see it now:*
Brünnhild' war die Traute,	*Brünnhild' was his one true love,*
die durch den Trank er vergaß!	*whom the philtre made him forget.*

Here the roles of the women in *Das Nibelungenlied* (847–50, *Av.* 14) and *Þiðreks saga* (343 (388)), where Kriemhilt/Grímhildr accuses Prünhilt/Brynhildr of having been Sîfrit/Sigurðr's mistress, are reversed. In *Vǫlsunga saga*, after the confrontation in the river, and before Sigurðr's death, the two women sit together in their bower, and Brynhildr confides in Guðrún about the vows she exchanged with Sigurðr (ch. 30):

> *Ekki hǫfum vér launmæli haft ok þó hǫfum vit eiða svarit, ok vissu þér þat, at þér véltuð mik, ok þess skal hefna.*
>
> *(What we said was no secret, making vows as we did, and you knew you were playing me false, but I'll be revenged.)*

G. III.3.10

The preparation of Siegfried's pyre begins (*Ring*, 8842–54):

Brünnhilde (to the vassals):

Starke Scheite	*Heavy logs*
schichtet mir dort	*heap up for me here*
am Rande des Rhein's zu Hauf':	*in a pile at the edge of the Rhine:*
hoch und hell	*high and bright*

lod're die Gluth,	*let the flames flare up*
die den edlen Leib	*and consume the noble limbs*
des hehrsten Helden verzehrt! –	*of the most exalted hero! –*
Sein Roß führet daher,	*Lead his stallion hither:*
daß mit mir dem Recken es folge:	*let it follow the warrior with me:*
denn des Helden heiligste	*for my own body yearns*
Ehre zu theilen	*to share in the hero's*
verlangt mein eigener Leib. –	*holiest honour. –*
Vollbringt Brünnhilde's Wort!	*Do as Brünnhilde bids!*

Die jungen Männer errichten, während des Folgenden, vor der Halle, nahe am Rheinufer, einen mächtigen Scheithaufen: Frauen schmücken diesen dann mit Decken, auf welche sie Kräuter und Blumen streuen.

(During the following, the young men raise a huge funeral pyre outside the hall, near to the bank of the Rhine: women cover it with rugs over which they strew herbs and flowers.)

The pyre being covered in rugs and flowers appears to be derived from Brynhildr's words in the eddic poem *Sigurðarkviða in skamma* 66:

Tjaldi þar um þá borg	*Hang there around the pyre*
tjǫldum ok skjǫldum,	*tapestries and shields,*
valarift vel fáð	*foreign cloth well dyed*
ok Vala mengi.	*and many slaves.*

G. III.3.11 (*Ring*, before 8899, 8920 and 8931; 8920–30)

[Brünnhilde] winkt den Mannen, Siegfrieds Leiche auf den Scheithaufen zu tragen; zugleich zieht sie von Siegfrieds Finger den Ring ab und betrachtet ihn sinnend . . . Sie hat den Ring sich angesteckt . . .

([Brünnhilde] signals to the vassals to bear Siegfried's body to the funeral pyre; at the same time she draws the ring from his finger and gazes at it thoughtfully . . . She has placed the ring on her finger . . .)

After seizing a firebrand, Brünnhilde directs Wotan's ravens and Loge to Walhall:

Fliegt heim, ihr Raben!	*Fly home, you ravens!*
Raunt es eurem Herren,	*Whisper to your lord*
was hier am Rhein ihr gehört!	*what you heard here by the Rhine!*
An Brünnhilde's Felsen	*Make your way*
fahrt vorbei:	*past Brünnhilde's rock:*
der dort noch lodert,	*tell Loge, who burns there,*
weiset Loge nach Walhall!	*to haste to Valhalla!*
Denn der Götter Ende	*For the end of the gods*
dämmert nun auf:	*is dawning now:*

so – werf' ich den Brand	*thus do I hurl the torch*
in Walhall's prangende Burg.	*into Valhalla's proud-standing stronghold.*

Sie schleudert den Brand in den Holzstoß, welcher sich schnell hell entzündet. Zwei Raben sind vom Felsen am Ufer aufgeflogen und verschwinden nach dem Hintergrunde.

(She hurls the firebrand on to the pile of wood, which quickly ignites. Two ravens have flown up from the rock on the riverbank and disappear into the background.)

The burning of Walhall, here caused by Loge at Brünnhilde's instigation, is in the Prose Edda evidently part of the giant Surtr's destruction of the whole earth by fire (*SnE* G51):

> *Því næst slyngr Surtr eldi yfir jǫrðina ok brennir allan heim.*
>
> *(After that Surt will fling fire over the earth and burn the whole world.)*

In *Vǫluspá* (49–52) and the Prose Edda (*SnE* G51) Loki is also on the side of the fire-giant Surtr at Ragnarǫk (the doom of the powers).

G. III.3.12

[In May 1856 Wagner sketched a farewell for Brünnhilde which he did not ultimately use. In its versified form it culminates in her splendid words (*Ring*, p. 125; *Wagner's Ring* 1993, 363; cf. the second illustration on p. 102):

Enden sah ich die Welt.	*I saw the world end.*

These echo the words of the seeress towards the end of *Vǫluspá* (57–58) and makes clear that Wagner at that time saw *Götterdämmerung* as Ragnarǫk, the end of the world as well as of the gods.]

G. III.3.13

In the final version of his opera, Wagner was content simply to let Brünnhilde look forward to embracing Siegfried once more (*Ring*, 8931–53):

Brünnhilde:

Grane, mein Ross,	*Grane, my horse*
sei mir gegrüßt!	*take this my greeting!*
Weißt du auch, mein Freund,	*Do you know, my friend,*
wohin ich dich führe?	*where I'm taking you now?*
Im Feuer leuchtend	*Lit by the fire,*
liegt dort dein Herr,	*your lord lies there,*
Siegfried, mein seliger Held.	*Siegfried, my blessed hero.*

Dem Freunde zu folgen,	*You whinny with joy*
wieherst du freudig?	*to follow your friend?*
Lockt dich zu ihm	*Does the laughing fire*
die lachende Lohe ? –	*lure you to him? –*
Fühl' meine Brust auch,	*Feel how the flames*
wie sie entbrennt,	*burn in my breast,*
helles Feuer	*effulgent fires*
das Herz mir erfaßt:	*seize hold of my heart:*
ihn zu umschlingen,	*to clasp him to me*
umschlossen von ihm,	*while held in his arms*
in mächtigster Minne	*and in mightiest love*
vermählt ihm zu sein! –	*to be wedded to him! –*
Heiajaho! Grane!	*Heiayoho! Grane!*
Grüß' deinen Herren!	*Greet your master!*
Siegfried! Siegfried! Sieh'!	*Siegfried! Siegfried! See!*
Selig grüßt dich dein Weib!	*In bliss your wife bids you welcome!*

Sie sprengt das Roß mit einem Satze in den brennenden Scheithaufen.

(With a single bound she urges the horse into the blazing pyre.)

Brünnhilde's actions at the end of the opera, and the funeral pyre she shares with Siegfried, are derived from a number of eddic poems, especially the prose introduction to *Helreið Brynhildar* and *Sigurðarkviða in skamma* 65–70, as well as the Prose Edda (*SnE* S41) and *Vǫlsunga saga*. The funeral pyre is described as follows in *Vǫlsunga saga* ch. 33:

Nú er búit um lík Sigurðar at fornum sið, ok gert mikit bál. Ok er þat er mjǫk í kynt, þá var lagt á ofan lík Sigurðar Fáfnisbana ok sonar hans þrévetrs, er Brynhildr lét drepa, ok Guttorms. Ok er bálit var allt loganda, gekk Brynhildr þar á út . . . Ok eptir þetta deyr Brynhildr ok brann þar með Sigurði, ok lauk svá þeira ævi.

(So Sigurd's body was laid out according to the ancient custom, and a great pyre was built. And when it was properly alight the body of Sigurd Fafnisbane was laid upon it, also the body of his three year old son whom Brynhild had ordered to be slain, and Guttorm's. And when the pyre was blazing, Brynhild went out on to it . . . And after that Brynhild died and was burnt there with Sigurd, and so their days ended.)

In the eddic poem *Sigurðarkviða in skamma*, Brynhildr says to Gunnarr (65):

Biðja mun ek þik	*I shall ask you*
bœnar einnar,	*for one boon,*
sú mun í heimi	*this will in the world*
hinzt bœn vera:	*be my last request:*

láttu svá breiða	*let be built on the plain*
borg á velli,	*a pyre so broad*
at undir oss ǫllum	*that beneath us all*
jafnrúmt sé,	*there be enough space,*
þeim er sultu	*for those who died*
með Sigurði.	*with Sigurd.*

The Icelandic sources, however, all differ from Wagner's version in that the horse Grani does not go with Sigurðr and Brynhildr to the funeral pyre; instead, the famous sword is again laid between them. In *Sigurðarkviða in skamma*, Brynhildr says to Gunnarr (68):

Liggi okkar enn í milli	*Let there lie again between us*
málmr hringvariðr,	*the ring-adorned metal,*
egghvast járn,	*the sharp-edged iron,*
svá endr lagit,	*as once it was laid,*
þá er vit bæði	*when we both*
beð einn stigum	*lay down in one bed,*
ok hétum þá	*and had the name*
hjóna nafni.	*of man and wife.*

The role of the horse, on the other hand, is reminiscent of the funeral pyre of the god Baldr and his wife Nanna, as recounted in the Prose Edda (*SnE* G49):

Þá var borit út á skipit lík Baldrs, ok er þat sá kona hans Nanna Nepsdóttir þá sprakk hon af harmi ok dó. Var hon borin á bálit ok slegit í eldi . . . Hestr Baldrs var leiddr á bálit með ǫllu reiði.

(Then Baldr's body was carried out on to the ship, and when his wife Nanna Nep's daughter saw this she collapsed with grief and died. She was carried on to the pyre and it was set fire to . . . Baldr's horse was led on to the pyre with all its harness.)

G. III.3.14 (*Ring*, before 8954)

Sogleich prasselt der Brand hoch auf, so daß das Feuer den ganzen Raum vor der Halle erfüllt . . . Als der ganze Bühnenraum nur noch von Feuer erfüllt erscheint, verlischt plötzlich der Glutschein, so daß bald bloß ein Dampf-gewölke zurückbleibt, welches sich dem Hintergrunde zu verzieht, und dort am Horizonte sich als finstere Wolkenschicht lagert.

(The flames immediately flare up so that the fire fills the entire space in front of the hall . . . When the whole stage seems to be engulfed in flames, the glow suddenly subsides, so that soon all that remains is a cloud of smoke which drifts away to the back of the stage, settling on the horizon as a layer of dark cloud.)

The eddic poem *Vǫluspá* describes Ragnarǫk (the doom of the gods) thus (57):

Sól tér sortna,	*The sun will go dark,*
sígr fold í mar,	*earth sink in the sea,*
hverfa af himni	*from heaven vanish*
heiðar stjǫrnur;	*bright stars;*
geisar eimi	*steam surges*
við aldrnara,	*with life's warmer [fire],*
leikr hár hiti	*high flame flickers*
við himin sjálfan.	*against the very sky.*

G. III.3.15

The fire dies down, the river overflows its banks, and the Rhine Maidens appear. Hagen dives into the river for the ring, and the Rhine Maidens drag him down into the deep (*Ring*, before 8954).

This incident has no parallel in the early sources.

G. III.3.16 (*Ring*, after 8954)

Helle Flammen scheinen in dem Saale der Götter aufzuschlagen. Als die Götter von den Flammen gänzlich verhüllt sind, fällt der Vorhang.

(Bright flames seem to flare up in the hall of the gods, finally hiding them from sight completely. The curtain falls.)

Wagner wrote six versions of the end of the *Ring* libretto. Finally, he decided to let the music speak for itself: there is a gleam of hope of a new and better world, as the atonement theme is heard from the orchestra.

After the description of Ragnarǫk, *Vǫluspá* says (59):

Sér hon upp koma	*She sees come up*
ǫðru sinni	*a second time,*
jǫrð ór ægi,	*earth from ocean,*
iðjagrœna.	*again green.*

GÖTTERDÄMMERUNG: SURVEY OF MOTIFS

The Ring	Eddic poems	Prose Edda	Vǫlsunga saga	Þiðreks saga	Nibelungenlied	Hürnen Seyfrid
Norns	Norns	Norns				
Betrothal with Alberich's ring	Ring as keepsake	Betrothal with Andvari's ring	Betrothal with Andvari's ring	Ring as keepsake	Ring as keepsake	
Brünnhilde's noble teaching	Sigrdrífa's wise counsel		Brynhildr's wise counsel			
Siegfried and Brünnhilde's vows	Sigurðr and Brynhildr's vows	Sigurðr and Brynhildr's vows	Sigurðr and Brynhildr's vows			
Hagen son of dwarf				Hǫgni of elvish descent		
Siegfried's challenge					Sîfrit's challenge	
Grane a valkyrie horse	Grani of divine descent	Grani of divine descent	Grani of divine descent	Grani of divine descent		
Drink of forgetfulness	Forgetfulness and trickery		Drink of forgetfulness			
Blood-brotherhood	Blood in footprints	oath-brothers	oath-brothers	oath-brothers	brothers-in-law	
Refusal of oath		[*Gísla saga*]				
Siegfried takes Brünnhilde's virginity	No intercourse	Birth of child	Birth of child	Loss of virginity	Unclear	

The Ring	Eddic poems	Prose Edda	Vǫlsunga saga	Þiðreks saga	Nibelungenlied	Hürnen Seyfrid
Sword between	Sword between	Sword between	Sword between			
Recognition of ring		Recognition of ring	Recognition of ring	Recognition of ring	Recognition of ring	
Brünnhilde affirms intercourse with Siegfried			Brynhildr demands Sigurðr confess to intercourse	Guðrún demands Brynhildr confess to intercourse	Kriemhilt demands Brünnhild confess to intercourse	
Brünnhilde's provocation	Brynhildr's defiance		Brynhildr's defiance	Brynhildr's defiance	Prünhilt's defiance	
Siegfried's piercing look			Sigurðr's piercing look			
Plot to kill Siegfried	Plot to kill Sigurðr	Plot to kill Sigurðr	Plot to kill Sigurðr	Plot to kill Sigurðr	Plot to kill Sîfrit	
Siegfried vulnerable in the back				Vulnerable in one spot	Vulnerable in one spot	Vulnerable in one spot
Double wedding	Double wedding				Double wedding	
Siegfried drinks, recovers memory			Sigurðr recovers memory		[Drink restores memory: *Sǫrla þáttr*]	
Two ravens	Óðinn's ravens	Óðinn's ravens				
Murder in wood	Both	Murder in bed	Murder in bed	Murder in wood	Murder in wood	Murder in wood
Brünnhilde lets herself burn with Siegfried	Brünnhilde lets herself burn with Sigurðr	Brünnhilde lets herself burn with Sigurðr	Brünnhilde lets herself burn with Sigurðr			

CORRESPONDENCE OF NAMES IN THE *RING*

The Ring	Eddic poems	Prose Edda	Vǫlsunga saga	Þiðreks saga	Nibelungenlied	Hürnen Seyfrid
Alberich	Andvari	Andvari	Andvari	Álfrekr	Albrîch	Eugel, Eugleyne
Alvater	Alfǫðr	Alfǫðr				
Brünnhilde	Brynhildr	Brynhildr	Brynhildr	Brynhildr	Prünhilt	
Donner	Þórr	Þórr				
Erda		Jǫrð				
Fafner	Fáfnir	Fáfnir	Fáfnir	Reginn		
Fasolt				Fasold		
Freia	Freyja	Freyja				
Fricka	Frigg	Frigg				
Froh	Freyr	Freyr				
Gibichungen	Gjúkungar	Gjúkungar	Gjúkungar	Niflungar	Burgonden	Gybich's sons
Grane	Grani	Grani	Grani	Grani		
Grimhild	Grímhildr	Grímhildr	Grímhildr			
Gutrune	Guðrún	Guðrún	Guðrún	Grímhildr	Kriemhilt	Krimhilt
Gunther	Gunnarr	Gunnarr	Gunnarr	Gunnarr	Gunther	Günther
Hagen	Hǫgni	Hǫgni	Hǫgni	Hǫgni	Hagene	Hagen
Heervater	Herfǫðr					
Hunding	Hundingr	Hundingr	Hundingr			
Loge	Loki	Loki, Loge				

The Ring	Eddic poems	Prose Edda	Vǫlsunga saga	Þiðreks saga	Nibelungenlied	Hürnen Seyfrid
Mime	Mímir/Reginn	Mímir/Reginn	Reginn	Mímir		
Nibelheim	Niflheimr	Niflheimr		Niflungaland	Nibelunge lant	
Nibelungen	Niflungar	Niflungar	Niflungar		Nibelunge	Nybling
Notung	Gramr	Gramr	Gramr	Gramr	Balmunc	
Rhein	Rín	Rín	Rín	Rín	Rîn	Reyn
Siegfried	Sigurðr	Sigurðr	Sigurðr	Sigurðr, Sigfreðr	Sîfrit, Sîvrit	Seyfrid
Sieglinde	Sigrlinn		Signý		Sigelint	Siglinge
Siegmund	Sigmundr	Sigmundr	Sigmundr	Sigmundr	Sigemunt	Sigmund
Siegvater	Sigfǫðr	Sigfǫðr				
Wala	Vala/vǫlva					
Walhall	Valhǫll	Valhǫll				
Walvater	Valfǫðr	Valfǫðr				
Wanderer	Gangráðr	Gangleri				
Wotan	Óðinn	Óðinn	Óðinn			

Of the 55 proper names in the *Ring* (7 of these only in early versions), 31 have correspondences in eddic poems, 29 in the Prose Edda, 18 in *Vǫlsunga saga*, 15 in *Þiðreks saga*, 13 in *Das Nibelungenlied*, and 10 in *Das Lied vom Hürnen Seyfrid*. The remainder (mainly valkyries and Rhine Maidens) were either invented by Wagner himself, or adapted from early German poems and legends or Jakob Grimm's *Deutsche Mythologie*. All names are modified to conform to German linguistic patterns.

SUMMARY

The Aims of the Ring

Richard Wagner's intention was never to set to music other people's verse — neither the Eddas nor *Das Nibelungenlied*. He wrote his own librettos. The fact remains, however, that he sought the bulk of his ideas for the stories, dialogue and scene-setting of *Der Ring des Nibelungen* in eddic poems, the Prose Edda and *Vǫlsunga saga*, as well as in some episodes of *Þiðreks saga* and *Das Nibelungenlied*. It is to be hoped that the above account has made this clear.

Wagner brought together myths of gods and legends of heroes. In the mid-nineteenth century this was a novel idea; he may have found a prototype in the myth of the dwarf Andvari and his gold in the Prose Edda. Here the curse on the ring is a sort of *leitmotiv* for the destruction of all gods, men, dwarves and monsters who gain possession of the ring or covet the gold hidden in the Rhine. This way of combining stories of gods and heroes also occurs in *Vǫlsunga saga* and in some eddic poems.

Using all these different elements, Wagner created an entirely independent work of art in four parts, adapting characters and events to the rules of his own creation. The various Old Icelandic poems and stories are often inconsistent in their treatment of the same events. From these primary sources Wagner constructed his own myth, picking, choosing and adapting to his own taste so as to create a logical course of events. His construction is undeniably very ingenious, and it is worth reiterating that borrowed motifs comprise only a part of the whole work.

Wagner's mythical world depicted in *Der Ring des Nibelungen* has become more real to most nations of the world than the original fragmentary Norse-Icelandic myths, which have never been widely read. The *Ring* has thus had a deep influence on perceptions of Norse mythology.

Wagner's story closely parallels the structure of the eddic poem *Vǫluspá*: an idyllic life of gods, a curse on the gold, betrayal and oath-breaking, the downfall of the gods, the end of the world, and an indistinct hope of salvation. *Vǫluspá* can be seen as a backcloth to Wagner's whole myth, though there are few exact borrowings. But the influence of this poem can be perceived throughout the *Ring*.

Wagner's fundamental message is, in short, a warning against the curse of covetousness and hunger for power; those who fall victim to the curse misuse the pure resources of nature (the gold) to gain power over others (the ring), cutting themselves off from love in return. Alberich, Wotan, Fafner, Mime and Hagen all give way to this temptation. This leads to betrayal and yet more betrayal by gods, men, giants and dwarves, culminating in wholesale devastation. The virtuous, ignorant human, brought into the world to save it from destruction, also falls victim to treachery.

For well over a century, efforts have been made all over the world to explain and interpret Wagner's myth. Tens of thousands of books and essays have been written about Wagner, and several hundred more are added each year. Much of this focuses on the *Ring*, because of both the length of the cycle, and the variety of ways in which it can be interpreted. All this debate is enough to make the head spin.

Because of commonly-held prejudices sometimes held by those unfamiliar with the *Ring*, it should be stated that the opera-cycle is not a glorification of warriors and heroes. In all four operas battles and vengeance play only a minor role, whether by comparison with the average ninteenth-century opera, with the action films of today, or even with real life. Examples of bloodshed may be counted on one's fingers.

In *Das Rheingold* the giant Fafner slays his brother, the giant Fasolt, over the gold. In *Die Walküre* the goddess Fricke has Hunding kill Sigmund for adultery. *Siegfried* slays the dragon, who is a symbol of how gold can change people into monsters. He then slays Mime for his treachery. The only real murders are carried out in the final parts of *Götterdämmerung*, when Brünnhilde demands the death of Siegfried in revenge for his deceit and her own dishonour. Hagen murders both Siegfried and Gunther in order to gain the power of the ring. There are no 'heroic' battles in the *Ring*.

Main Sources of Inspiration

Wagner composed his myth in an organised way. Though his operas are generally regarded as long, and the *Ring* itself takes altogether about 15 hours in performance, he had to compress a lot of material into its framework. Let us recall here what Wagner's sources appear to have been for the individual ideas in each of the operas.

Das Rheingold

The episode of the Rhine Maidens is Wagner's own invention.

Most of the other motifs may be traced back to the Prose Edda: gods, goddesses, giants, the citadel-builder, Iðunn's apples, Loki's journey, a black elf, the dwarf's gold, Andvari's ring and the curse upon it, Fáfnir, a magical helmet, the rainbow bridge Bifrǫst, Valhǫll. The seeress Erda, however, is mainly traceable to the eddic poems *Vǫluspá* and *Baldrs draumar*.

Die Walküre

The motifs of this opera are mainly drawn from the first eleven chapters of *Vǫlsunga saga*: the tree growing in the middle of the hall, Óðinn's sword in its trunk, the sword that only Sigmundr can draw out, the life of father and son in the woods, love between twins, Óðinn shattering a sword, and a Valkyrie put to sleep with flames around her rock. Various characters from *Vǫlsunga saga* are omitted, however.

Wisdom as the bed-price of the goddess Erda is mainly based on the account of Óðinn's visit to Gunnlǫð in the Prose Edda (*SnE* G58), while Brynhildr's warning of death is from *Hákonarmál* in *Heimskringla (Hákonar saga góða* ch. 31). The ride of the valkyries is mentioned in *Vǫluspá*, and in fact the whole concept of valkyries is found only in Icelandic literature.

Siegfried

The events in the smithy are a mixture of elements of the stories of the boyhood of Sigurðr in *Reginsmál*, the Prose Edda, *Vǫlsunga saga* and *Þiðreks saga*, while there are also traces of *Das Lied vom Hürnen Seyfrid* and the Grimms' folk-tale (no. 4) of the boy who went out into the world to learn fear. Sieglinde's difficult childbearing or long gestation parallels the long pregnancy in *Vǫlsunga saga*.

The contest of wisdom between Wotan and Mime resembles a similar contest between Óðinn and a giant in the eddic poem *Vafþrúðnismál*, while the slaying of the dragon and Mime, and understanding the speech of birds, have parallels in the eddic poem *Fáfnismál* and in *Vǫlsunga saga*.

The awakening of the seeress is reminiscent of the eddic poem *Baldrs draumar* and various other awakenings in the Eddas, while the confrontation between Wotan and Siegfried bears some resemblance to the eddic poem *Fjǫlsvinnsmál*.

Siegfried's passing through the fire and the awakening of the valkyrie on the mountain have their closest parallels in the eddic poem *Sigrdrífumál* and *Vǫlsunga saga*, though they are also reminiscent of the Sleeping Beauty story.

The dialogues between Alberich and Wotan are entirely Wagner's invention.

Götterdämmerung

The initial scene with the Norns is derived from the Prose Edda and the eddic poem *Helgakviða Hundingsbana I.*

The farewell of Siegfried as he leaves Brünnhilde is reminiscent of *Sigrdrífumál, Vǫlsunga saga* and *Þiðreks saga.*

The drink of forgetfulness is entirely from *Vǫlsunga saga*, while Siegfried's second plunge through the flames to Brünnhilde is from the same saga, and also appears in the Poetic and Prose Eddas.

The relationship with Gunther, the quarrel between the women, accusations of treachery against Brünnhilde, and the killing of Siegfried are common to all the sources used here for comparison. But the hunting expedition and the details of the murder in the forest occur only in *Þiðreks saga* and *Das Nibelungenlied.*

Siegfried's dialogue with the Rhine Maidens and the role of Alberich are Wagner's own invention, but may be inspired by an episode in *Das Nibelungenlied.*

Brünnhilde and Siegfried's funeral pyre is derived from the eddic poem *Sigurðarkviða in skamma*, the Prose Edda and *Vǫlsunga saga.*

Wagner's Points of Emphasis

Some examples may be mentioned where Wagner emphasises different points from those prominent in the original sources.

Alberich becomes Wotan's principal adversary; there is no real prototype for this role, either in the Albrîch of *Das Nibelungenlied* or in the Andvari of Icelandic texts. The curse on the ring is certainly derived from Andvari's curse, and in *Das Nibelungenlied* Albrîch is said to guard a hoard of gold, but otherwise these characters play only minor roles in the original sources. On the other hand, the roles of gods other than Wotan and Fricka are much less important in Wagner's work than the corresponding figures in the Poetic and Prose Eddas.

Siegfried's long-standing and bluntly-expressed antipathy for his foster-father, the blacksmith, has little parallel in the purely Icelandic versions of the story, but it appears clearly in *Þiðreks saga* as soon as the young Sigurðr grows into a youth. Nor do they get along well in *Das Lied vom Hürnen Seyfrid*, but there the smith is only the boy's master, and not his foster-father. There is no such smith in *Das Nibelungenlied*.

More symbolic significance is attached to the ring itself by Wagner than in any of his sources. Even so, the curse on the ring resembles, more than anything else, what is told of the dwarf Andvari in the Prose Edda, though there it does not lead to the end of the world as in Wagner's version.

It should be emphasised yet again that as the work developed, Wagner became increasingly independent. He gradually thinned out some of the detail and developed his own ideas. Yet a remarkable number of borrowed features remain in the completed opera-cycle, as has been indicated here. Of these, about four-fifths can be said to be derived solely from Old Icelandic texts, one-sixth are common to all the sources, and about one-twentieth may be attributed entirely to German texts.

Conclusion

One could maintain, of course, that all this process of comparison is irrelevant, that only Wagner's actual librettos, his own creation and the development of his ideas, have any significance. But as long as people all over the world feel the need to trace Wagner's original sources for the *Ring*, in book after book, and in the programme for every production — generally without much knowledge of the subject — it is a worthwhile task to demonstrate which sources proved most useful to him. (A recent example of ignorance of this topic is in the programme of a production of *Das Rheingold* at the Royal Theatre in Stockholm in 1997: Gunilla Petersén, 'Richard Wagner och Nibelungernas ring. *Rhenguldet*', 12–15.)

It should be stated here that the focus of this book has been solely on exploring, by comparison with original sources, where Wagner sought inspiration in Old Icelandic and other medieval literature. Some readers may feel that the writer has been over-bold in his assertions, while others may believe he should have gone further. A conscious decision was made not to discuss Wagner's philosophy or possible influences from his personal life on his work. These topics have already been addressed extensively by hundreds of other writers, and their works can easily be consulted if the reader does not feel able to form his or her own opinion. The principle here has been to stick to tangible examples, although some are certainly a little hard to grasp.

EPILOGUE

The Reception of Wagner's Works in Iceland

Though Wagner took so much of his material for his operas from Icelandic literature, neither this fact nor the operas themselves have been well known in Iceland until recently. There are scattered mentions, mostly positive, of Wagner and his operas in Icelandic books and periodicals from 1876 onwards, and some of his music was performed in Iceland by the Icelandic Symphony Orchestra from 1950 onwards; recordings by the Icelandic singer Pétur Jónsson, who had performed in Wagner's operas in Germany, had been heard on the radio during the previous decades and helped to make Wagner's music better known in Iceland. In the second half of the century some Icelanders went to see performances in Bayreuth, and programmes about Wagner began to be broadcast on radio and television. Many Icelanders had the opportunity to see films of all Wagner's operas in the 1980s and 1990s.

A milestone was reached when it was decided to perform a shortened version of the *Ring*-cycle in the National Theatre during the Arts Festival in Reykjavik in 1994, the fiftieth anniversary of Icelandic independence. This was produced under the auspices of Richard Wagner's grandson Wolfgang Wagner and first performed on 27 May, 1994, with Icelandic singers in all roles except those of Wotan, Brünnhilde and Siegfried, and in the view of most who saw it, it was a great success. Since then Wagner's operas can be said to have achieved some popularity among Icelanders, and links with Bayreuth have been maintained. In 1995 a Richard Wagner Society was founded in Iceland and is flourishing today, maintaining links with the International Association of Wagner Societies.

BOOKS REFERRED TO

Arndt, Ernst Moritz, *Geist der Zeit,* Teil 3, 1814.

Arthúr Björgvin Bollason, *Ljóshærða villidýrið,*1990.

Árni Björnsson, 'Prerequisites for Saga Writing', *Approaches to Vínland*, ed. Andrew Wawn and Þórunn Sigurðardóttir, 2001, 52–59.

AWF = Richard Wagner, *The Art-Work of the Future and other Works*, trans. William Ashton Ellis (reprinted from *Richard Wagner's Prose Works* I, 1895), 1993.

Beethoven, Ludwig van, *Sämtliche Briefe und Aufzeichnungen*, 1907.

Bonstetten, Christian Victor von, *Der Mensch im Süden und im Norden oder über den Einfluß des Clima's*, 1825.

Bouhour, Charles, *Les entretiens d'Ariste et d'Eugene*, 1671.

Böldl, Klaus, '"Götterdämmerung". Eddufræði í Þýskalandi á 18. og 19. öld og ahrif þeirra á Richard Wagner', *Skírnir* 1996, 357–88.

Böldl, Klaus, *Der Mythos der Edda. Nordische Mythologie zwischen europäischer Aufklärung und nationaler Romantik*, 2000.

Communication to my friends, A, see *Eine Mitteilung an meine Freunde.*

Dokumente = Dokumente zur Entstehungsgeschichte des Bühnenfestspiels Der Ring des Nibelungen, ed. Werner Breig and Hartmut Fladt, 1976 (Richard Wagner, *Sämtliche Werke* 29 I).

Eddic poems see Poetic Edda.

Egils saga Skalla-Grímssonar, ed. Sigurður Nordal, 1933 (Íslenzk fornrit II). Trans. Christine Fell, 1975.

Espiard de la Borde, F. I., *L'Esprit des Nations*, 1752.

Ettmüller, Ludwig, *Vaulu-Spá. Das älteste Denkmal germanisch-nordischer Sprache, nebst einigen Gedanken über Nordens Wissen und Glauben und nordische Dichtkunst*, 1830.

Ettmüller, Ludwig, *Die Lieder der Edda von den Nibelungen. Stabreimende Verdeutschung nebst Erläuterungen,* 1837.

Faulkes, Anthony, ed., *Two Versions of Snorra Edda from the 17th Century* I–II, 1977–79.

Fornaldar sögur Norðurlanda I–IV, ed. Guðni Jónsson, 1950.

Fouqué, Friedrich Baron de la Motte, *Sigurd der Schlangentödter. Ein Heldenspiel in sechs Abentheuren*, 1808.

Fouqué, Friedrich Baron de la Motte, *Held des Nordens,* 1810.

Gísla saga Súrssonar, ed. Björn K. Þórólfsson, 1943 (Íslenzk fornrit VI). Translated by George Johnston as *The Saga of Gisli* in *Three Icelandic Outlaw Sagas*, 2001.

Golther, Wolfgang, *Sagengeschichtliche Grundlagen der Ringdichtung Richards Wagners*, 1902.

Gregor-Dellin, Martin, *Richard Wagner, sein Leben, sein Werk, sein Jahrhundert*, 1995.

Grimm, Jakob, *Deutsche Mythologie*, 1835; third ed. 1854.

Grimm, Wilhelm, *Altdänische Heldenlieder, Balladen und Marchen*, 1811.

Grimm, Wilhelm, *Deutsche Heldensage*, 1829.

GSD = Richard Wagner, *Gesammelte Schriften und Dichtungen* I–X, 1871–83; 2nd ed. 1887–88; 3rd ed. 1897; 4th ed. 1907; 5th ed., 12 vols, 1911.

Guðrún Þórðardóttir, 'Svanameyjar í Völundarkviðu', *Mímir* 1998, 72–78.

Hagen, Friedrich Heinrich von der, *Die Edda-Lieder von den Nibelungen zum erstenmal verdeutscht und erklärt*, 1814.

Haymes, Edward R., and Susan T. Samples, *Heroic Legends of the North*, 1996.

Heiberg, J. L, 'Théories antiques sur l'influence morale du climat', *Scientia* XXVII, 1920, 453–64.

Heimskringla I–III, ed. Bjarni Aðalbjarnarson, 1941–51 (Íslenzk fornrit XXVI–XXVIII). Trans. E. Monsen and A. H. Smith, 1932; Samuel Laing (Everyman's Library), 1961, 1964.

Huber, Herbert. *Richard Wagner. Der Ring des Nibelungen, nach seinem mythologischen, theologischen und philosophischen Gehalt Vers für Vers erklärt*, 1988.

Huntington, Ellsworth, *Civilization and Climate*, 1915.

Jóhannes Jónasson, '"Vituð ér enn . . ."', *Lesbók Morgunblaðsins* 19. des. 1998, 19–21.

Keyser, Rudolf, *Nordmændenes Videnskabelighed og Litteratur i Middelalderen*, 1866.

Kleffel, Johann Christoph, *Abhandlungen von den Verehrungen der alten Nordischen Völcker gegen ihre Könige*, 1749.

Koch, Ernst. *Richard Wagner's Bühnenfestspiel Der Ring des Nibelungen in seinem Verhaltnis zur alten Sage wie zur modernen Nibelungendichtung betrachtet*, [1875].

Kühnel, Jürgen, *Richard Wagners 'Ring des Nibelungen'*, 1991.

Lachmann, Karl, *Zu den Nibelungen und zur Klage*, 1836.

Lied vom Hürnen Seyfrid, Das, ed. Wolfgang Golther, 1911.

Lohenstein, Daniel Caspar von, *Großmüthiger Feldherr Arminius oder Herrman*, 1689.

MacPherson, James, *Fragments of Ancient Poetry collected in the Highlands of Scotland and translated from the Gaelic or Erse Language*, 1760.

Magee, Elizabeth, *Richard Wagner and the Nibelungs*, 1990.

Magnus, Johannes, *Historia de omnibus Gothorum Sveonumque regibus*, 1554.

Majer, Johann Christian, *Germaniens Urverfassung*, 1798.

Maurer, Konrad, *Ueber die Ausdrücke: altnordische, altnorwegische & isländische Sprache*, 1867.

Maurer, Konrad, *Über die norwegische Auffassung der nordischen Literaturgeschichte*, 1869.

Mein Leben = Richard Wagner, *Mein Leben* I–II, 1986. Trans. by Andrew Gray as *My Life*, 1983.

Meynert, Johann Fridrich, *Staffel der Kultur auf welcher die Deutschen im fünften Jahrhunderte stunden. Aus Vergleichung der deutschen und englischen Sprache gefunden*, 1797.

Mitteilung an meine Freunde, Eine (1851): extract in German in *Dokumente* 46–54; full German text in *Drei Operndichtungen nebst einer Mitteilung an meine Freunde*, 1851; translation in *AWF* 267–392.

Mone, Franz Joseph, *Untersuchungen zur Geschichte der teutschen Heldensage*, 1836.

My life see *Mein Leben.*

Nibelungen-Mythus, Der, in *GSD*, 2nd ed., 1887–88, II 156–66; English version in *Pilgrimage to Beethoven and other Essays by Richard Wagner*, trans. William Ashton Ellis, 1994, 299–312 (reprinted from *Richard Wagner's Prose Works* VII, 1898). The original version, *Die Nibelungensaga (Mythus)*, 1884, in Strobel 26–33. See also *SSD* II 155–66.

NL = *Das Nibelungenlied*, ed. Karl Bartsch, 1948. Trans. A. T. Hatto, 1965.

Percy, Thomas, *Reliques of Ancient English Poetry*, 1765.

Poetic Edda = *Edda. Die Lieder des Codex Regius nebst verwandten Denkmälern*, ed. Gustav Neckel, 4th edn rev. Hans Kuhn, 1962; *Norrœn Fornkvæði*, ed. S. Bugge, 1867 (repr. 1965).

Ring = Huber 1988.

Sabor, Rudolph, *Richard Wagner. Der Ring des Nibelungen*, 1997.

Schiller, Friedrich, *Sämtliche Werke* I, 1958.

Schulze, Hagen, *Kleine deutsche Geschichte*, 1996.

Schütze, Gottfried, *Drei kleine Schutzschriften für die Alten Deutschen*, 1746.

von See, Klaus, *Völkisches Denken in Deutschland zwischen Französischer Revolution und Erstem Weltkrieg*, 1975.

Simrock, Karl, trans., *Die Edda, die ältere und jungere, nebst den mythischen Erzählungen der Skalda*, 1851.

SnE = Snorri Sturluson, *Edda*. Part 1, *Prologue and Gylfaginning*, 1988; Part 2, *Skáldskaparmál*, 1998. Ed. Anthony Faulkes; Snorri Sturluson, *Edda*. Trans. Anthony Faulkes, 1987, reprinted 1998. All cited by chapter number (*SnE* G = *Gylfaginning*, *SnE* S = *Skáldskaparmál*; note that the first few chapters of *Skáldskaparmál* are conventionally numbered as a continuation of *Gylfaginning*).

SSD = Richard Wagner, *Sämtliche Schriften und Dichtungen* I–XII. 6th ed., 1913.

Strobel, Otto (ed.), Richard Wagner. *Skizzen und Entwürfe zur Ring-Dichtung*, 1930.

Sørensen, Villy, 'Griechische und nordische Mythologie als Inspirationsquellen Richard Wagners', *Programmheft* V *der Bayreuther Festspiele*, 1989, 1–24.

Vischer, Friedrich Theod., 'Vorschlag zu einer Oper', *Kritische Gänge* II, 1844, 397–436.

Vǫlsunga Saga. The Saga of the Volsungs, ed. and trans. R. G. Finch, 1965.

Wagner's Ring of the Nibelung. A Companion, ed. Stewart Spencer and Barry Millington, 1993. Paperback reprint 2000.

Walch, Johann Georg, ed., *Philosophisches Lexicon*, 1726.

Westernhagen, Curt von, *Richard Wagners Dresdener Bibliothek 1842–1849*, 1966.

Wiessner, Hermann, *Der Stabreimvers in Richard Wagners 'Ring des Nibelungen'*, 1924 (Germanische Studien 30).

Wille, Eliza, *Fünfzehn Briefe Richard Wagners mit Erinnerungen und Erläuterungen*, 1935.

Zschackwitz, Joh. Ehrenfried, *Erläuterte Teutsche Alterthümer*, 1743.

Þiðreks saga, ed. Guðni Jónsson, 1951; ed. C. R. Unger, 1853; ed. H. Bertelsen, 1905–11.

Þorsteinn Gylfason, 'Richard Wagner as a Poet', in *Wagner's Ring and its Icelandic Sources*, 1995, 77–86.

LIST OF ILLUSTRATIONS

INDEX OF NAMES

Personal names of real people are indexed, except for Richard Wagner. Titles of medieval Icelandic and German works of literature are also included. The Icelandic letters Þ, æ, Q, ö come at the end of the alphabet, but ð is treated as d.